BUSINESS BASICS
An Outline of Business
Theory and Practice

ABOUT THE AUTHOR

1. Professor Emeritus, Graduate School of Management, University of California, Los Angeles, and Impartial Labor-Management Arbitrator. Formerly: Professor of Business Administration, UCLA; Managing Editor, *California Management Review*; U.S. State Department Adviser to Spain and Professor of Industrial Organization Escuela de Organización Industrial, Madrid, Spain; Professor of Management, U.S. Army University, Shrivenham, England; Visiting Lecturer, Universities of Amsterdam and Rotterdam, The Netherlands; North Dakota State Director of Distributive Education and Professor of Marketing and Management, University of North Dakota; Instructor in Economics, Brooklyn College; Industrial Engineer, Armour & Company, New York Metropolitan Area.

2. Publications: *The Development of Labor Relations Law* (American Council on Public Affairs, Washington D. C., 1941); *Employer-Employee Relations* (Golden State Publishers, Los Angeles, 1944 and 1946); *Industrial Economy and Labor Control* (Golden State Publishers, Los Angeles, 1945); coauthor, *The Management of Personnel and Labor Relations* (McGraw-Hill, New York, 1950); *Business Organization* (Littlefield, Adams & Co., Totowa, N. J., 1952); coauthor, *Industrial Relations and the Government* (McGraw-Hill, New York, 1954); *Introduction to Business Enterprise* (John Wiley & Sons, New York, 1960); coauthor, 2d ed. (1970); correspondence courses for University of California and U.S. Armed Forces Institute; and numerous articles in journals and magazines.

BUSINESS BASICS

An Outline of Business Theory and Practice

WAYNE L. McNAUGHTON, Ph.D.

Professor Emeritus, Graduate School of Management
University of California, Los Angeles

1981

LITTLEFIELD, ADAMS & CO.
Totowa, New Jersey

Library of Congress Cataloging in Publication Data

McNaughton, Wayne Leslie, 1902–
  Business Basics

  (A Littlefield, Adams Quality Paperback No. 317)
  Includes bibliographies and index.
  1. Business. I. Title.
HF5351.M22   658.4   75–33928
ISBN 0–8226–0317–9

Printed in the United States of America

PREFACE

The purpose of this volume is to provide the reader with a well-rounded grasp of the business setting. The whats and whys of business are described, with less emphasis being placed on the hows. For the pre-business student or for the general reader, this book provides a background and a foundation—a starting point. It provides enlightenment as to why business exists and where it came from; it gives the reader a bird's-eye view of the macro-organization, the world of business, and a close-up view of the micro-organization, the individual firm.

From this point the student of business can do advanced work in one or more of the major divisions of business management and then, perhaps, specialize in one of them. Many skills, essential to the effective functioning of business organizations, are acquired in trade and technical schools as well as in certain college and university courses. Techniques and procedures usually differ from company to company and are learned as part of the company's employee training program and through on-the-job experience.

Business concerns range in size and diversity from those consisting of one individual to gigantic organizations employing thousands of persons. They all have one chief purpose: to create and supply goods and services. With the exception of a relatively few governmental and monopolistic situations, all compete in local, national, and international markets with other business concerns. With the same exceptions, they strive for profits out of which operating expenses are paid, including wages and salaries. If net profits consistently accrue, the firm stays in business and expands. On the other hand, if costs consistently exceed income the firm goes out of business or is taken over by another company or by more capable managers.

Some material from the author's previous book, BUSINESS ORGANIZATION, has been used with permission.

The author is grateful to his wife, Mariel, for her encouragement and assistance.

Wayne L. McNaughton
Kelseyville, California
October, 1975

CONTENTS

BUSINESS BASICS
An Outline of Business
Theory and Practice

PART I
THE WORLD OF BUSINESS

Part I is concerned with the broader aspects of business. Chapter 1 deals with descriptions, general definitions, and a very brief historical background. Chapter 2 provides a link between the body of theory known as economics and business organization. Chapter 3 describes the legal organizational forms into which business concerns are grouped.

CHAPTER 1

THE NATURE AND ORIGINS OF BUSINESS

Business exists for the purpose of supplying ultimate consumers with goods and services. Primitive societies satisfied their wants directly and simply. Each family provided its own food, clothing, and shelter. Under such conditions of self-sufficiency there was no mechanism for systematically producing, financing, storing, transporting, and selling goods, and business did not exist. But as self-sufficiency disappears and as systems of exchanging goods and services appear, the term *business* becomes applicable.

THE CONSUMER

Before considering the nature of business it is necessary to examine the nature of the consumer, the being who gives business its reason for existence.

The Industrial or Commercial Consumer. There are close to twelve and one-half million business concerns in the United States. These organizations buy and sell a bewildering variety of goods and services. Some buy goods and services and sell their products to other business concerns, which are known as industrial or commercial consumers. *Industrial consumers* buy steel and other kinds of raw materials and hire skilled and unskilled employees. They produce such things as punch presses, cranes, trucks, and countless other items used to produce goods for ultimate consumers. *Commercial consumers* buy office equipment, equipment and supplies for dentists and physicians, buses, and other items used in performing services for ultimate consumers.

The Ultimate Consumer. The *ultimate consumer* uses goods and services for personal satisfaction. In the last analysis, the vast, complex organization of business exists for the sole benefit of this individual.

The Nature of Human Wants. Practically all the wants of ultimate consumers are satisfied through business organizations. Under our free-enterprise, capitalistic system, anyone may (with some restrictions) enter any business he chooses. He is motivated in part by the hope of making reasonable profits or a good salary or wage. The consumer usually must first work to produce income which, in turn, is spent to satisfy part or all of his wants. Since human wants are insatiable and the means by which they are satisfied are limited by nature it is necessary for most persons to work for a living.

Some wants, based upon human biological needs, are common to all consumers; others vary from person to person. The basic needs for food, clothing, and shelter, although common to all, may be satisfied in a great variety of ways. The wants of individuals tend, also, to change with increasing age and with altered circumstances. Over the years, the wants of the nation's consumers have greatly increased.

Although wants are classified as necessities or luxuries, the goods and services used to satisfy these wants vary widely from person to person and from decade to decade. An automobile was a luxury for everyone in the first decade of the present century. Today many deem it a necessity. And so it goes with washing machines, telephones, radios, television sets, and so on. As a rule, an individual considers more and more goods and services to be necessities as his income increases. Very likely the person has never lived whose wants were all completely satisfied. But desires vary in intensity from person to person, and the difficulty and inconvenience, if not the impossibility, of working hard enough to satisfy *every* want is obvious.

As one's income increases, his wants tend to multiply; but as his income decreases his wants tend to persist. Want satisfaction is limited by income; however, wants can be satisfied in advance of income by the use of various forms of consumer credit. The term *standard of living* is used to denote in a general way the aggregate wants of a person, a family, or the inhabitants of a geographical area. It connotes reasonable aspirations. *Level of living*, less frequently used, indicates the degree of actual want satisfaction.

Investigations conducted over the years point to the existence of four generalizations, which have come to be called the *laws of consumption*. They indicate that as income increases:

1. The percentage spent for food decreases.
2. The percentage spent for clothing remains nearly constant.
3. The percentage spent for housing remains nearly constant.
4. The percentage spent for all other items increases.

Consumer Income. In 1973, per capita personal income in the United States ranged from $5,938 in Connecticut and $5,933 in Alaska to $3,566 in Mississippi and $3,853 in New Mexico.

Consumer Choice. Consumers must choose between the desirability of having more wants satisfied and the inconvenience of doing more work, between the desirability of having more wants satisfied now and the risk of going into debt, between the desirability of having larger savings accounts and the undesirability of postponing the satisfaction of many wants, between satisfying some wants and not satisfying other wants, and between one good or service and another designed to satisfy a particular want.

The subjective measure of want-satisfying power of a good or service is known as its *utility*. When consumers compare entertainment with food, clothing with education, or a high-priced car with a home, they think in terms of *relative utility*. The utility of a meal is high to a person who is hungry. After he has eaten, the utility of another meal is considerably lower. The utility of one car is high, that of a second car is much lower. We see in this tendency a principle called *diminishing utility*.

Although the consumer does compare relative utilities, and although the principle of diminishing utility does operate in spreading consumers' choices over a wide range of goods and services, the process of choice and selection often shows little evidence of much rational forethought. This is evidenced by the relative success salespeople and advertising have in influencing choices. Utilities have a way of changing in value with the immediacy or remoteness of the want-satisfying good. The utility of a demonstration car being driven by a potential consumer may be greater than that of a college education; the utility of a television set demonstrated in the home may be greater than that of a deep-freeze unit seen in the pages of a magazine.

Influencing Consumer Choices. The choices of individuals can be influenced within fairly broad limits. Many business concerns have made fortunes for their owners by determining areas within which consumer choices could easily be changed, by supplying goods or services in these areas, and by advertising effectively. Horse-drawn buggies, for example, cannot successfully be sold in large quantities, no matter how diligent the sales promotion; neither can automobiles of extremely advanced design. But conventional cars which embody some new feature at the same or a modest increase in price can be sold in enormous quantities. Specifically, how in practice are consumers' choices influenced?

BY PRODUCT DIFFERENTIATION. Consumers are influenced to purchase one vendor's product instead of the same type of product sold by another vendor by making it different in some respect and then by drawing attention to that difference. This method of influencing consumer choice is often effective even though the difference cannot be detected by the consumer. Sales promotion has merely to claim that the product contains "Xtyb, the miracle ingredient," which may be an inert filler, then appeal to the consumer to ask for the product by name. Of course, genuine improvements are constantly being made, patented, and publicized. If the attention of the consuming public is properly drawn to such innovations, choices are almost certain to be influenced.

Selection from among identical products, as well as choice of one product from among many different products, can be influenced by devices that closely resemble product differentiation. Liberal exchange privileges, better credit terms, more willing sales service, pleasanter personal contacts and environment, delivery service, prompter service, better repair facilities, and the like, have a way of influencing consumers.

BY THE USE OF BRANDS AND TRADEMARKS. Product differentiation would mean little unless the goods were distinctively named. Brands and trademarks are chosen for their memory-retention value, after which they are advertised. Although branded goods may be higher in price and lower in quality than unbranded goods, consumers tend to select the better-known brands.

BY ADVERTISING. Skillful brand selection is of little value if the brand is not effectively advertised. The combined forces of product differentiation, branding, and advertising tend to place companies in a semimonopolistic position with regard to the markets of their products.

BY OFFERING BARGAINS. American consumers have been conditioned to a fixed-price, one-price, or asked-price policy. Sellers usually have a "take it or leave it" attitude. Price tags are displayed and consumers pay the prices indicated. There is little active bargaining; consumers rarely offer vendors less than the prices displayed or asked. This, coupled with the difficulty the consumer finds in judging the quality of goods, sets the stage for a powerful type of sales appeal—the price concession. Illustrative of this device is the dealer who quickly sold out a slow 5-cent item by marking it 15 cents and advertising "only 10 cents while they last." The public tends to associate quality with price but, at the same time, resists price increases. Thus, the store that prices a product at 53 cents, marked down from $1.00, generally sells more than another store that sells the same item, under another name, for 49 cents.

A similar type of appeal is the use of *loss leaders*. These usually are branded items whose qualities and prices are well known to the public. By cutting prices on these items, sometimes below cost, customers are attracted to the store, where they also tend to buy other products at their regular prices or, perhaps, at inflated prices. Federal law and some state laws prohibit selling below cost plus a reasonable profit as being a form of unfair competition.

Another type of price appeal is that of charging, say, $4.98 instead of $5.00. Smart buyers think $5.00 when they see $4.98 on the price tag, but the less wary are influenced to buy.

A practice that often creates ill will, but one which continues to be used by many retailers, is to advertise products at very low prices, then rely on personal salesmanship to switch the attention of those enticed into the store to higher-priced merchandise.

A similar practice is to advertise incomplete prices, then add to such prices the cost of extras, delivery, taxes, service, and so on. Automobile dealers formerly followed the practice of advertising their products at f.o.b. factory prices. They now are required by law to show on each car its complete price including delivery cost, cost of extras, and tax.

BY FINANCING THE CONSUMER. If the vendor can make it easy for a customer to possess a high-priced article by accepting a small down payment, the customer will of necessity be limited in his ability to buy other goods and services. Consumer financing permits the user to possess the article sooner. The vendor retains the title and reserves the right to repossess the article if the payments are defaulted. A small "carrying charge" usually is added to the total price, a charge which often is excessive in terms of rate per dollar per annum on the unpaid balance. Federal law now requires this actual annual percent rate to be disclosed to the prospective purchaser. Installment financing helps the consumer to save for expensive items for which he might otherwise not voluntarily save.

The Consumer Movement. In the decade from 1925 to 1935 widespread interest in consumers' problems took root and rapidly grew. There seems to have been a latent suspicion in the minds of consumers that all was not well with the producer-consumer relationship, for when a book appeared on the market expounding the necessity of "getting your money's worth," there was a tremendous response. Other books appeared; agencies were developed for testing consumer goods (two reliable private organizations were Consumers' Research and Consumers Union, organized in 1929 and 1936, respectively, as nonprofit corporations); consumer groups were formed; self-sufficiency was advocated and practiced to some degree; consumer-retail councils were formed; attempts were made to put a department into the federal government that would actively protect the interests of consumers; hearings were begun on a new federal pure foods, drugs, and cosmetics statute; the Good Housekeeping Institute was established; Sears Roebuck & Co. began placing "Infotags" on their merchandise; the substitution of grade labeling in place of branding was widely advocated; department stores set up consumer testing departments; and many other similar activities were enthusiastically carried on. Although these activities did have a salutary effect upon the unscrupulous business concerns, they did not bring about the extreme reforms they tried to accomplish.

In more recent years interest in consumer protection has revived. Ralph Nader, a private champion of the consumer, has uncovered and publicized many examples of dangerous automobile construction, mislabeling, and fraudulent advertising. At the same time, trade associations have become more alert and governmental agencies have taken more definitive action toward protecting consumers.

THE NATURE OF BUSINESS

The word *business* is used in a number of senses. In a loose and general sense it means what a person does for a living. In response to the question, "What line of business are you in?" one may receive such answers as the following: "Music, I play in an orchestra"; "Meat packing, I manage the shipping department"; "Groceries, I own a store"; "Dentistry"; "Photography"; "Engineering"; or even "Government, I'm a clerk in the Recorder's office."

Business Defined. In a more restricted and narrower sense business is *the exchange of goods, money, or services for mutual benefit.* Business transactions are being performed in each of the illustrations given. A *businessman*, or a person in business for himself, is one who personally exchanges goods and services for money, or is directly responsible for such exchange. In some service areas, those performing business transactions are known as *professionals* (described at a later point).

Those who work for large business organizations are *officers* (president, vice-president, treasurer, secretary), *department heads* (production, receiving, shipping), *professionals* (engineers, accountants, nurses), and *employees* (laborers, clerks, typists).

Classification of Business Concerns. Businesses can be classified into *extractive, manufacturing* or *industrial, commercial,* and *personal service.*

EXTRACTIVE BUSINESS. Extractive businesses are those which exploit the natural resources of land and water. Agriculture, lumbering, hunting, fishing, and mining are the chief examples.

MANUFACTURING BUSINESS. Businesses that change the form of materials are manufacturing concerns. They may change raw materials (ore into iron, iron into steel, beets into sugar, petroleum into gasoline, steers into sides of beef) or semifinished goods (wheels and other parts into automobiles, stamped gears and other shapes into clocks). There are three types of manufacturing. *Synthetic* manufacturing puts several parts together to make one finished product (automobiles). *Analytic* manufacturing starts with one raw material from which are made many different products (petroleum). *Conditional* manufacturing includes processes that are neither synthetic nor analytic. Examples include aging and drying (tobacco, liquor, cheese, salt).

Some writers consider construction to be manufacturing (synthetic); others feel that this business possesses enough characteristics of its own to constitute a separate class. Certainly the highway builder, the constructor of houses, and the river and harbor dredger seldom, if ever, call themselves manufacturers. But rarely, for that matter, do we refer to the gasoline refiner, the meat packer, or the ore refiner as a manufacturer. The term popularly is applied only to synthetic industries. In practice many industries combine all three forms of manufacturing. In such concerns the predominating process determines the classification. We speak of meat packing as an example of analytical manufacturing, yet a number of raw materials are put together to make sausage, and this product must age for varying periods of time.

COMMERCIAL BUSINESS. *Commerce* includes the various marketing functions of buying, selling, collecting, grading, storing, transporting, communicating, and insuring. When transfers of title are involved, certain activities such as financing, finding sources of or outlets for goods, and providing information are included.

PERSONAL SERVICE. An increasing proportion of the population is engaged in service businesses such as barber shops and beauty parlors, theaters, motels and hotels, and restaurants. Although teachers, physicians, dentists, lawyers, and business consultants properly belong in this category, it has become customary to refer to them as *professional* persons. Arguments used for placing them in a class by themselves are: they sell their skill and services on a personal basis; some of them do a certain amount of charity work; their training is intellectual in nature, requiring knowledge as a supplement to, or in place of, manual skill; their money income does not constitute the chief measure of their success; they pursue their calling for others and not so much for their own self-interest; and they observe a code of ethics which presumably puts them on a higher plane and in a class apart from other breadwinners. Professional persons certainly merit a separate classification, but with equal certainty they constitute an important part of the business life of the community.

HISTORY OF BUSINESS

When man's prehistoric ancestors first traded their surplus possessions for the excess items of others, business came into being.

Early Times. Discoveries during recent years have led archaeologists to believe that trade between far removed peoples was more extensive and was practiced in earlier centuries than hitherto was believed possible. The cities of Mesopotamia traded widely from India to Egypt. The inscriptions on clay tablets remind one of modern accounting procedures. Local and foreign trade occupied the time of thousands of merchants, and courts enforced contracts just as they do today.

The Mesopotamians traded bronze articles for furs and slaves as far away as Scandinavia. As the centuries passed, trade around the Mediterranean flourished, and during the Roman era merchants carried cloth, coral, and pearls to the Azores and Canaries and east to remote Tibet and China, where they obtained white furs, pepper, green tea, and silk. For many years the Phoenician merchants maintained a monopoly on trade west of Gibraltar by spreading tales to frighten sailors, most of whom, as a result, refused to sail out into the Atlantic.

The Middle Ages. Much exchange of goods took place at fairs throughout Europe during the Middle Ages. From the twelfth through the seventeenth century a powerful business organization called the Hanseatic League existed in northeastern Europe. At one time it included ninety cities and controlled much of the business and commerce of the continent. Business concerns comprising the organization minimized competition within and presented a united front against competitors without. Prices and wages were closely regulated as they were in England under Queen Elizabeth I and later. This close control of government over business is known as *mercantilism*.

The Industrial Revolution. About the middle of the eighteenth century power-driven machines, gathered together in factories, began replacing the manual skills of laborers who produced goods in their homes. The changes resulting from the transition from the *domestic* system of producing goods to the *factory* system are known as the *industrial revolution*.

During the same period a new government-business relationship developed in England. No longer was it popular for the government to regulate business. Adam Smith's *The Wealth of Nations*, published in 1776, was widely read. In this book Smith advocated noninterference by the government in business affairs. He believed that the best interests of the country would be served if each individual were allowed freedom to pursue his own best interests. This system came to be known as *laissez faire*.

Business Organization in the United States. England's attitude toward her colonies in the eighteenth century held that they should serve as sources of raw materials and as markets for her manufacturers. As a result of this policy, the American colonies were far behind industrially when the Revolutionary War broke out. Because of this and because of chronic shortages of laborers, who were constantly enticed westward by frontier opportunities, American businessmen were under exceptionally strong pressures to develop mechanical devices to produce goods. The expansion of business was helped materially by such inventions as the cotton gin, the telegraph, and the steamboat. Transportation was aided by the construction of the Erie Canal and railroads to the West. Express companies helped in the distribution of goods, and a widespread banking system aided financially.

After the Civil War, the United States began to experience some of the disadvantages of laissez faire. In a society that included many relatively powerful individuals or business concerns, the best interests of the country were not always served by allowing individuals to pursue their own best interests free from regulation by government. Because of abuses by combinations in restraint of trade, such laws as the Interstate Commerce Act of 1887, the Sherman Act of 1890, and the Clayton Act of 1914 were enacted. Trusts, holding companies, and bigness have not been outlawed; monopolistic price agreements, unfair competition, and restraint of trade have.

Although labor has been relatively scarce until recent years, individual employees have nearly always been at a disadvantage when dealing with employers. Hence, employees have organized so as to present a united front. At first the government frowned on this activity; later it was tolerated, then approved and encouraged.

UNITED STATES BUSINESS

Business depends on four so-called *factors of production.* They are: (1) natural resources, (2) labor, (3) capital, and (4) entrepreneurship, or initiative in establishing and operating business concerns.

American business operates under a *capitalistic* economic system. Individuals, or companies whose stock is owned by individuals, own the capital used to establish and operate business organizations. Since there is a minimum of interference by government in the exercise of judgment by the owners of capital, the American system is also called *free enterprise.*

American business also is characterized by *rapid change, intricate organization,* the importance of *personal service,* and, as stated above, the presence of a moderate amount of *government control.*

The Business Unit. There are millions of small business units in America. Nevertheless, the world thinks of the United States as a country of giant corporations. In insurance, transportation, manufacturing, public utilities, banking, and many other lines of business, a relatively few concerns own most of the assets or account for most of the business in their fields. Although there has been a certain amount of suspicion leveled at big business, there is a disposition to tolerate or even encourage bigness when it is in the public interest and if it is properly regulated. When regulation has not proved satisfactory, the public has frequently turned to government ownership.

Separation of Ownership and Management. Whereas a concentration of assets typifies American business, their *ownership is widely scattered*. Large corporations are owned by hundreds or thousands of small shareholders whose interests lie primarily in the profit possibilities of their stockholdings. These owners readily turn control of their properties over to professional managers who tend to perpetuate themselves in their positions.

Structure of Industry. Concentration and integration are found in American business. *Concentration* is the horizontal combination of two or more business units at the same level of production or distribution. Examples are chain stores or branch banks. *Integration*, on the other hand, is the vertical combination of two or more successive units, such as wholesaling and retailing, manufacturing and wholesaling, or mining and refining.

Roundaboutness of Business. Modern business is characterized by *roundaboutness*. Before a person can engage in business he must spend money. Assume that a man has invented a new type of can opener and desires to manufacture it himself. Among the many things he must do are to arrange for a plant, buy machinery and equipment, make drawings, make dies, buy tools, register and pay the fees required by governmental authorities, determine the best markets and make sales contacts, investigate credit ratings, advertise the new product, buy materials and supplies, hire the right kinds of employees, pay transportation costs, begin operations and distribute the product, meet a weekly payroll and pay other running expenses—all before the money starts coming in from his first sales. A substantial amount of capital must continuously be invested and risked in the hope that the products of the concern will eventually be sold for enough to cover the expenditures and bring a profit.

The Functions of Business. In the production of goods and services many functions must be performed by the businessman. He should understand the workings of the economic system; he must deal with the government in one way or another; he must choose the legal form of ownership; he must learn and apply certain skills such as accounting and statistics; he must seek out and use all kinds of business information; he must organize his business for control and learn to manage it; he must finance his business and engage in various types of promotional activities; if he manufactures a product, he must apply a whole host of special skills including production methods, plant location and site selection procedures, plant layout techniques, and the creation and managing of materials and production control systems; he must understand labor organization, personnel management, and collective bargaining; he must master the marketing procedures and possibilities, including wholesaling, retailing, purchasing, selling, advertising, transporting, storage, and the like; he should understand the possibilities in foreign trade; he must establish price policies; and he must assume business risks and learn how to minimize and shift them. These constitute, in general terms, the functions of business and the subject matter of this volume.

QUESTIONS FOR DISCUSSION

1. According to the textbook business exists for consumers. Are you a consumer? Is General Motors a consumer? Can consumers also be producers? Explain your answers.
2. What is the difference between standard of living and level of living?
3. Explain the principle of diminishing utility.
4. How are loss-leaders used? Is this practice legal?
5. Give an example of a "consumer protection" activity.
6. Give examples of synthetic, analytic, and conditional manufacturing.
7. Why were sailors afraid to venture into the Atlantic during the Middle Ages?
8. What was the attitude of England toward her colonies with respect to business in the eighteenth century?
9. Distinguish between concentration and integration of business concerns.
10. What do we mean, in general, by the functions of business?

SELECTED REFERENCES

Anderson, Ronald A., *Government and Business*, 3rd ed., South-Western Publishing Co., Cincinnati, 1966.

Beard, Miriam, *History of Business, Vol. I. From Babylon to the Monopolists*, U. of Michigan Press, Ann Arbor, 1962.

————, *History of Business, Vol. II. From the Monopolists to the Organization Man*, U. of Michigan Press, Ann Arbor, 1963.

————, *A History of the Business Man*, Macmillan Co., New York, 1938.

Cameron, Ian, *Lodestone and Evening Star, The Epic Voyages of Discovery*, E. P. Dutton & Co., New York, 1966.

Dillard, Dudley, *Economic Development of the North Atlantic Community*, Prentice-Hall, Englewood Cliffs, N. J., 1967.

Kriz, Joseph A., and Curt Duggan, *Your Dynamic World of Business*, McGraw-Hill, New York, 1973.

Krooss, Herman E., *American Business History*, Prentice-Hall, Englewood Cliffs, N. J., 1972.

Mai, Ludwig H., Men and Ideas in Economics: A Dictionary of World Economists Past and Present, Littlefield Adams & Co., Totowa, N.J., 1975.

Nemmers, Erwin E., *Dictionary of Economics and Business*, 3rd ed., Littlefield, Adams & Co., Totowa, N. J., 1974.

CHAPTER 2

BUSINESS AND ECONOMICS

Economics is chiefly concerned with production and income. It makes the basic judgment that an economy is improved with more goods and not with less goods, and that progress results from expanding production and rising levels of living. It is concerned with income security, and it assumes that instability of income is not desirable. It assumes, too, that proper distribution of income is desirable, that most of the income should not be commanded by a relatively small number of people, and that everyone shall receive enough to live decently. Economics assumes, further, that any increase in the variety of goods contributes to progress. Economic well-being not only depends upon an income which can be exchanged for a variety of goods, but that income must be earned under good conditions of work and it must be adequate to provide for leisure.

Economics deals with the production of economic goods, although it does not explain the techniques of production or how to make a living. It pictures the interactions of production, income, exchange, and other business activities, and points the way toward a better system.

Economics as a Social Science. Economics employs scientific method in collecting and evaluating data, in discovering significant relationships, in testing hypotheses, and in formulating principles or laws. The data with which the economist works are subject to relatively wide variations, and the results attained are not as precise as are those attained by the chemist or physicist. Nevertheless, economics is as much a science as these are, for the determinants of a science are the methods and procedures which are used, and not the exactness of its results.

Economics, it must be emphasized, is concerned with a developing, changing cosmos. The material with which the economist works is not the same today as it was yesterday. A law or principle which was true under mercantilism (close governmental regulation) may not be true under a laissez-faire economy (little government regulation). Consequently, the economist must state his premises very carefully. He cannot say, for instance, that a lowered price always results in greater demand, but he says "under these specific conditions" a lowered price will increase demand.

The economist investigates many specific subjects within this general area of how people make their livings. He develops tools of analysis which aid in discovering significant facts. It is not the purpose of this chapter to present a condensed account of economic theory or to catalog the various subjects which the discipline encompasses. It is enough to delimit the general area within which the economist operates, indicate something concerning his methods, and present some of the most important subjects with which he is concerned. In addition, this chapter will sketch briefly some of the characteristics of the free-enterprise and planned economies together with a few basic concepts and materials with which economists work.

Economists deal specifically with production and income. They examine, describe, and criticize the framework of the economic system. They consider such matters as resources, organization for production, the legal and managerial structure of business enterprises and what determines their sizes, and the complicated systems of finance. A whole area of activity is concerned with money: its nature and functions, how it affects banking and how banks affect it, its changing value, and how it is used in balancing international trade. One of the most vital areas concerns that of business cycles: what their causes are and how they can be controlled. Then there are the areas of supply and demand and how their interaction determines market prices, costs of producing and marketing goods, monopoly and competition, variations in productivity and income, the effects of unions upon wages, the nature of interest, international trade, and the effects of governmental policies upon all these areas.

Some Basic Concepts of Economics. Before economists can begin, they must define precisely the terms they use. A few examples of such definitions follow:

1. *Goods* are things wanted by human beings, and to the degree they are wanted they possess *utility*. If they are limited, scarce, and not free, and if they are transferable, they are *economic goods*. When one gets the most out of such goods, he is said to be *economizing*; he is being frugal.

2. The term *value* is applied to measure relative degrees of desirability. If one good is said to be twice as valuable as another, one unit of the first will exchange for two units of the second. Values customarily are expressed in terms of money, and money values are termed *prices*. The value of a good is determined by the price it will bring in the market.

3. The economist says that *production* takes place when economic goods are made available or when utility has been added to economic goods.

4. The term *distribution* can be confusing, for it is used in two senses. The economist uses it in a static sense, that is, how all goods are shared among the population at a given time. The businessman uses the term in a dynamic sense. To him it is the process of moving goods through the channels of trade.

5. By *income* is meant the command over goods. Income and production are two sides of the same thing, for one's production of goods provides command over other goods. In a pecuniary society we express income in terms of money. Goods received directly (without the use of money) in return for other goods or services constitute *payment in kind*.

The American Economic System. Our economic system grew out of *division of labor* or *specialization*. The system has the effect of forcing people to cooperate in producing needed goods and services. As mentioned in the previous chapter, the "American way" is known as *free enterprise* or *private enterprise*. Under a free or private economy, private individuals voluntarily undertake to produce. There may be considerable governmental regulation, but the emphasis is on freedom of the individual to choose his occupation. This system, also, admits the right of individuals to own property and to exclude others from its use, the right to make independent decisions in the management of such property, the right to quit business, the right to make contracts and to associate with others, the right to have contracts enforced, and the right to compete.

Also as previously mentioned, the person who has command over sufficient capital, and who believes he can produce something (goods or services) which he can sell at a profit, becomes an *entrepreneur* if he goes into business. The entrepreneur, who may act alone, with partners, or within the corporate form of organization, assumes the risks of loss of capital through competition, unexpected changes in prices, legal curbs, fire, theft, etc.

Although all progressive ideas need not be embodied in the form of capital equipment, there is a definite connection between progress and *capital*. As capital increases, our standards of living rise. There is close correlation between the national well-being of the various countries and the value per worker of their capital equipment.

Capital goods are classified as fixed and circulating. Fixed or *durable capital* is represented by such items as buildings, factory machinery and equipment, trucks, cleared land, farm livestock (cows, sheep, horses) and machinery, graded rights of way, rails and rolling stock, dams and generating equipment, and so on. Essentially, fixed capital lasts over a period of time during which it is used to produce other goods. But, as capital goods do not last forever, their cost must be prorated to the goods they produce.

Circulating capital goods are represented by stocks of supplies, raw materials, semifinished goods, and finished goods. Although the value of such goods owned by a businessman may not vary from year to year, the individual items are continuously being used up and replaced. Such goods, whether they are partly finished machines, oil, canned goods on a grocer's shelves, or raw materials such as pig iron and cotton, require the investment of capital.

When savings from net income are added to existing wealth, *net investment* results. The term *gross investment* refers to the process of using savings to replace worn-out capital goods.

Capital, in whatever form, results when society produces

more than it consumes and puts the difference into capital goods, or invests the difference in some other productive manner. The formation of capital results from saving and investing.

Under the capitalistic system of free enterprise the entrepreneur does not risk his capital in a business which is not expected to pay *profits*. He satisfies himself that the possibilities of adequate profits are strong enough to outweigh the probabilities of loss. Profits in some businesses are low, but they are secured consistently and losses are few and small. In other businesses profits are high but for one reason or another losses often are heavy and the risk of doing business is great. So the economist attributes the continued existence of private business to the receipt of profits. Such profits need not be received over short periods of time; but if a businessman continues operations in the face of consistently recurring losses, he generally is motivated by the *expectation of profits*. Successive losses over long periods of time tend to weaken this motive.

The Planned Economy. Every well-managed organization functions on the basis of plans. *Managerial control* is, in part, the correcting of deviations in practice from *planned performance*. Planning may begin with a statement of long-range objectives. Under this type of planning, executive control involves guiding the organization toward those objectives, and in thus guiding the concern, it becomes necessary to curb the liberty of those members of the organization whose personal inclinations would lead away from the stated goals. Americans willingly give up segments of their liberty if the goals are democratically determined and if the control exercised by management actually leads in directions determined by qualified majorities. A common mistake made by managers of business concerns (and of political units) is to arrogate the function of setting goals and establishing policies, ignoring and excluding all others from the process. The process of setting goals and policies is subjective in nature. Inherently it can never be anything else. Admittedly, some individuals are more adept at planning than are others, but after the plans are drawn, a period of discussion should be provided, the length of which is determined by the importance of the action. A vote should be taken. Trivial rules are often imposed and emergency measures adopted without the consent of the governed, but such acts should always be subject to review by the electorate.

A planned business operates more smoothly than an unplanned business; so should a planned economy operate more smoothly than an unplanned economy. The problem in America seems to have been how to have a planned economy and how not to have one at the same time. The heart of the matter can be expressed in two questions: (1) to what extent should individuals give up their liberties for the sake of over-all efficiency? and (2) how can one insure that the ultimate power is retained by the people?

Under a laissez-faire economy, one in which there is a minimum of government interference, business concerns tend to minimize waste and loss by combining for the purpose of planning. Without such planning, business concerns tend to build duplicate facilities, engage in needless and wasteful sales promotion, and force one another out of business through cutthroat competition and in other ways. The combinations which have been formed to deal with such wastes have not always been in the public interest for, although they have served to eliminate the waste of competition, they frequently have resulted in monopolies which have raised prices and reduced service.

The public has asked governmental protection against such practices, and it has been given in two forms: the regulation of monopolies and the breaking up of monopolies into smaller, competing units. Planning is permitted under the first type, the benefits being passed along to the public in the form of lower prices. (Most public utilities fall in this category.) Planning is made difficult in the second type, for the competing units usually are forbidden to have interlocking directorates, to circulate price information, to divide sales territories, or to cooperate in other ways.

Business concerns have found it impossible to deal with business cycles without government assistance, and considerable planning has been attempted for the purpose of preventing periodic booms and depressions.

Nongovernment Planning. Industry-wide planning began with "gentlemen's agreements," trade associations, open-price associations, and the like. The chief emphasis was placed on price controls and output limitations. Such forms of planning were not effective because of the activities of those who cut prices in violation of the agreements. It was difficult to punish such offenders. Consequently there developed a strong trend toward merging into one corporation as many of the competing units in one industry as possible.

The Sherman Antitrust Act of 1890 was designed to break up such associations, trusts, and corporations which proved to be monopolistic in character. The Clayton Act of 1914 provided further controls and attempted to provide certain exemptions from control.

During World War II a group of prominent businessmen formed a Committee for Economic Development which set out to plan for the postwar period. By obtaining information from a great many business enterprises concerning their postwar plans and needs, the committee was enabled to amass and publish valuable material.

Near the end of the war there were numerous planning boards in existence, but their effectiveness was limited by their inability to apply controls. Economic planning necessarily limits certain rights, and those whose liberties are curtailed by the plans do not willingly conform. Consequently plans are of little use unless they are enforced, and the logical place for such control lies in the government.

Government Planning. In 1933 the National Industrial Recovery Act and the Agricultural Adjustment Act provided the nation with its first large-scale economic planning. Although both statutes were declared unconstitutional by the Supreme Court, the trend toward government planning had been established.

The National Resources Committee was formed in 1935 for the purpose of coordinating government planning, and many established departments and commissions extended their duties into the realm of planning.

Because of the necessity for mobilizing all the nation's productive resources under conditions of total war, economic planning was given considerable impetus during World War II. Price fixing and rationing were undertaken by the Office of Price

Administration; the Selective Service organization and the War Manpower Commission planned for the utilization of armed services and civilian personnel; and the War Production Board planned in the field of production. In addition to these the government set up and enforced during the war many other planning activities.

As a result of Vietnam war expenditures and other lavish governmental spending, it became necessary for the government to deal with price inflation. Another area requiring widespread governmental planning and control is that of pollution. For many years industrial wastes, insecticides, and sewage have been dumped into our rivers, lakes, and coastal waters; wastes, trash, and junk have been allowed to accumulate throughout the land; and smoke and noxious fumes have poured into the air. In recent years the public has begun to rebel against these conditions. Many bills brought before state legislatures were defeated by pressure groups objecting to the high costs of remedial programs. Other bills have passed setting up bodies and appropriating funds for studying the situation. Controls have been imposed on many of the worst offenders. The subject of government planning is further discussed in Chapter 26.

What Economic Planning Seeks to Accomplish. Economic planning has as its aims:

1. The reduction of wasteful competition.
2. The reduction of unemployment.
3. The reduction of duplication of productive facilities.
4. The elimination of extremes in the business cycle.
5. The prevention of waste, particularly of natural resources.

Objections to Economic Planning. If allowed to continue, it is claimed that economic planning would result in:

1. The destruction of capitalism.
2. The destruction of individualism and the encouragement of regimentation.
3. An inept bureaucratic substitute for self-interest in the management of business concerns.

QUESTIONS FOR DISCUSSION

1. What, in general, is economics concerned with?
2. What are economic goods?

3. Distinguish between value and price.
4. What are two senses in which the term distribution is used?
5. Distinguish between money income and real income.
6. What is an entrepreneur?
7. Give an example of nongovernment industry-wide planning.
8. Give an example of government planning that affects business.
9. What does economic planning seek to accomplish?
10. What are some objections to economic planning?

SELECTED REFERENCES

Bach, George Leland, *Economics: An Introduction to Analysis and Policy*, 8th ed., Prentice-Hall, Englewood Cliffs, N. J., 1974.

Canterbery, E. Ray, *The Making of Economics*, Wadsworth Publishing Co., Belmont, Cal., 1975.

Goldman, Marshall I., *Ecology and Economics*, Prentice-Hall, Englewood Cliffs, N. J., 1972.

Maher, J. E., *What Is Economics?* John Wiley & Sons, New York, 1969.

Samuelson, Paul A., *Economics: An Introductory Analysis*, 9th ed., McGraw-Hill, New York, 1973.

Thompson, Arthur A., *The Economics of the Firm: Theory and Practice*, Prentice-Hall, Englewood Cliffs, N. J., 1973.

CHAPTER 3
FORMS OF BUSINESS OWNERSHIP

Most business concerns in the United States are single proprietorships, general partnerships, or corporations. Occasionally, however, we run across six other forms of business ownership. They are limited partnerships, syndicates, joint-stock companies, Massachusetts trusts, unincorporated associations, and cooperatives. Most business concerns are organized in the manner best befitting the circumstances. Assume, for instance, that a man or woman starts a clothing store. The most natural form of organization would be the single proprietorship. If, over the years, profits were plowed back into the firm and many branch stores were set up, the organization still could be the same, a proprietorship. On the other hand, the company could easily be changed to a partnership if others were to join in the ownership, or to a corporation should limited liability be desired. Conversely, a corporation can be dissolved and changed to a partnership or a proprietorship if one or more persons desire to assume ownership. The required legal formalities are simple.

Which Form Should Be Used? Questions which influence the form of business organization a concern should take are not numerous. Naturally, the question of *capital* is always one that must be considered. A well-known small corporation, with a good credit rating, probably could sell its stock or borrow money without trouble. A new, unknown corporation of the same size would have more trouble in this respect than a partnership, since creditors could take only the assets of a corporation (not those of the shareholder owners), whereas they could levy on the assets of a partnership (or proprietorship) plus the personal assets of the owners.

Another question involves *responsibility toward fellow owners*. Since the acts of each partner bind all the other partners, it may be that the owners would rather incorporate. Officers of a corporation are responsible only to the organization, and not to each other.

Questions of *taxation* and *government control* are important. A well-known chain store changed its form of organization from corporation to partnership, with a substantial saving in taxes. New corporations are often under very close control by state authorities whereas new partnerships and proprietorships are not.

If *continuing life* is desired for the organization, it should be incorporated. A proprietorship dies with its owner. A partnership must be reorganized as a new concern when a partner withdraws or another joins.

These factors and possibly others must be considered carefully when a new business is organized. However, as has been pointed out, if conditions change and it becomes desirable to alter the legal form of the organization, this can be done with relative ease.

The Individual Proprietorship. The *individual proprietorship*, also called *sole proprietorship* and *single proprietorship*, is owned and usually managed by one person. Small stores and shops usually can be assumed to be proprietorships. There are close to nine and three-quarters million such concerns in the United States. They carry such names as Bob's Coffee Shop, Mary's Dress Shop, Crossroads Grocery, Smith's Hardware, Rossville Machine Shop, or Main Street Radio & TV Shop. As a rule, they are managed by the owner, who may hire a few or many employees, and they are financed out of the owner's savings and borrowings. So as to fix legal and financial responsibility many states require registration of all fictitious names of non-incorporated concerns doing business therein.

Although most single proprietorships are small, some are very large. It is not possible to identify a proprietorship from its name, except that if the name identifies the company as a corporation we know it is not a single proprietorship.

ADVANTAGES. The first advantage in organizing as a proprietorship is *convenience*. There is no need to explain to anyone why the business was started, why it was located where it was, or why it was terminated. An occupational permit usually is required by local authorities, and periodic inspections are made if food is handled. In common with other businessmen, the proprietor must comply with all local, state, and federal laws concerning zoning restrictions, pollution regulations, employee safety and health, tax reports, union relations, and so on.

The proprietorship pays comparatively *low taxes*. Local permit fees are low and the owner is not required to submit an income tax report separate from his own.

The proprietorship is subject to *little government regulation*. There are no reports to government agencies, the owner can move to another state, or he can do business in other states with few if any restrictions. However, he must, as previously noted, register his business name if it is fictitious.

Another advantage in this form is *low organization cost*. There should be little or no expense involving brokers, investigators, promoters, and attorneys.

Normally, the proprietorship enjoys a relatively *high credit rating* because, as previously mentioned, his personal assets constitute legal security for the debts of the business.

There is a *freedom of action* in this form not found in the others. There is no need to consult with others or be blamed for wrong decisions and delay in taking action.

Although responsibilities are greater, *profits are maximized*. The single proprietor takes pleasure in being his own boss and pocketing all the profits. If there is a loss, he knows he is solely responsible.

Another advantage of the proprietorship is *privacy*. Secrets such as formulas, processes, agreements with customers and suppliers, wages, profits, and so on, can more easily be kept. Also, the income tax reports of individuals are not made public as are those of corporations.

DISADVANTAGES. Although small proprietorships enjoy better credit ratings than small corporations, as size increases proprietorships have more difficulty in raising capital. Some individuals, of course, have very large fortunes that can be invested in a single proprietorship, but the vast majority of such organizations acquire additional needed capital by taking in partners or selling stock, thus changing the legal form.

The single proprietorship suffers from *lack of breadth and experience* found in other types of organization. Although there is satisfaction in being one's own boss, there are advantages in working with a group of individuals having varying capabilities and backgrounds.

The proprietorship is *not permanent*. When the owner retires the business either dies, is sold to another proprietor, or is taken over by some other concern.

Previously mentioned is the disadvantage of *unlimited liability* of the owner for the debts of the business.

Many proprietorships find difficulty in getting and keeping employees. The best employees usually go where there are opportunities for advancement or they tend to leave to start their own businesses. There frequently is a lack of glamor and a feeling of insecurity in working for a one-man business.

The General Partnership. Most of the states have adopted a Uniform Partnership Act, which defines this form of business organization as "an association of two or more persons to carry on as co-owners a business for a profit." General partnerships are commonly found in the real estate, insurance, finance, retail, and wholesale areas of business. This form is also found in the services, construction, and manufacturing, but to lesser degrees elsewhere. There are nearly one million such organizations in the United States.

The *articles of copartnership*, drawn up by individuals who wish to associate themselves together in this form of organization, provide the guide to their relationships. Duties of the partners, salaries to be paid, and division of gains and losses are indicated. Senior and junior partners are found in many concerns, particularly law firms. It is common for two individuals to start a law firm, naming it for themselves, say Aaron and Brown. Later, Clark and Dell join the firm as *junior partners*. Usually the name of the firm remains the same and the two founders are known as *senior partners*. As the years pass, it may be that many more junior partners are added. Then Clark may be promoted to the rank of senior partner and frequently the firm name is changed to include his name. Legally, when partners are added or dropped, a new firm comes into being and the existing one is dissolved, although business may continue as usual at the same place and under the same name. If the name Aaron, Brown, and Clark becomes well known, it is common to retain the name Aaron, even after his death.

The public should know that each general partner is liable for all the debts of the firm, and within the scope of the business any act of one serves to bind the others.

Partnerships frequently are formed so as to complement the technical abilities and financial situations of individuals.

ADVANTAGES. Some states require partnerships to file their articles of copartnership. No other formalities are required; hence an advantage of this form is *ease of formation*. Generally, the partnership is formed when it starts doing business.

It is believed by many that *greater specialization* is an advantage of this form. Certainly, in some types of business, a partnership comprising several types of skill can serve the public better. In many law firms it is common for each partner to specialize in some aspect of the law such as divorce, patent, criminal, labor relations, real estate, and so on.

The question of *motivation* may in some organizations be an advantage of the partnership. It is true that the single proprietor is highly motivated since he gets all the profits or must take all the losses. On the other hand, each partner gets his full share of the profits and must take his share of the losses. In addition, however, there is the incentive of desiring to get and keep the good will of each of the other partners.

In common with proprietorships, partnerships have *less government regulation* than do corporations. Other advantages include: *best employees tend to stay, capital is more easily obtained*, and *credit rating is relatively higher*.

DISADVANTAGES. From the standpoint of management, the *divided authority* found in the general partnership usually is a disadvantage. Another is the *danger of disagreements* on important matters. These two handicaps make this form of ownership organization *less flexible* than other forms.

Perhaps the gravest disadvantage of the general partnership

form is the *unlimited liability* each partner must assume by law for all the debts of the company. Should one or more partners prove to be dishonest or incompetent, the personal resources of the other partners would be jeopardized. If one partner is, for some reason, forced to make good the net loss of his bankrupt concern, he can sue for and recover the just shares of the other partners.

The *limited life* of the general partnership constitutes a disadvantage of this form. Legally, a partnership must end each time there is a change of any kind, such as death, withdrawal, expulsion or admission of a partner, and when a partner is declared insane or bankrupt. The greater the number of partners, the greater is the firm's legal instability. For this reason, *long-term loans are difficult to obtain.*

It often is difficult to withdraw from a partnership. The person who desires to withdraw may be unable to persuade the remaining partners to buy him out at what he thinks is a fair price, or, if a replacement can be found who has enough money to buy out the disaffected partner, it may well be that he will not be accepted into the firm because of his limited personal resources, negative personality, lack of skill or training, or for any number of other reasons.

The Limited Partnership. Most of the states have recognized the serious disadvantages of general partnerships and have by statute provided for the organization of *limited partnerships.* If one or more of the partners agree to full financial responsibility, the liability of the other partners may be limited to their investment in the firm. Such arrangements must be included in the articles of partnership (or copartnership as it usually is called), a copy to be filed at the court house. Although limited partners may not participate in management, they can be hired by the firm to engage in nonmanagerial employment. In case of bankruptcy of the company, a limited partner might be held fully liable, in spite of the articles of partnership, if it can be shown that in fact he did participate in management.

Some states provide for the formation of *mining partnerships.* These firms need not dissolve on the withdrawal of a partner. Shares of ownership are issued to the partners, which can be sold and bought without the consent of the other partners, and profits are distributed on a per share basis. Although personal liability is limited with respect to bankruptcy and other contingencies, the personal assets of the owners of shares in mining partnerships can be levied on for operating expenses, if necessary.

A few states permit the formation of *limited partnership associations* which are not recognized outside the state of organization. These limit the liability of all partners to the amounts they have invested. Each such partnership must register with the state.

If a partner does not participate in management and, at the same time, he is known to the public as a member of the firm, he is a *silent partner*. On the other hand, a partner who is not known by the public to be a member of the firm but who is active in its management is a *secret partner*.

A partner who does not participate in the management of his firm and who is not known to the public as a member of the concern is a *dormant*, or *sleeping*, *partner*. If it becomes known that secret and dormant partners are connected with the firm, they become general partners in the eyes of the law.

ADVANTAGES. The chief advantage of the limited partnership is that it enables a person with money, or some other special asset, to join a partnership and help it without incurring unlimited liability as a result. The limited partner finds an investment medium that does not carry undue risk and the firm *more easily acquires capital or other benefits*.

DISADVANTAGES. In addition to the disadvantages found in the general partnership, the limited partnership often involves *additional registration formalities, doubtful validity outside the state* in some cases, and *uncertainty as to limited partners' status*. Although the common law respecting general partnerships is fairly well established, there is some uncertainty and inconsistency in the law as it pertains to limited partnerships. In one case, for instance, a limited partner thought his personal property would not be used to satisfy the debts of the firm, but when the company went bankrupt a judge ruled him to be a general partner inasmuch as he had been seen leaving the concern's place of business and hence was presumed to be engaged in its management. Although the limited partnership association provides limited liability for all its partners, a disadvantage is that it usually is *taxed as a corporation.*

The Syndicate or Joint Venture. A *joint venture* is a form of partnership for a temporary purpose. In England in American colonial days, and later in America, it was common for groups of individuals of limited means to pool their resources for the purpose of sending a shipload of locally manufactured goods to foreign countries to be traded for their produce. When the ship returned and the cargo was sold, the profits were distributed to the members of the group on the basis of their investments, and the organization was dissolved. Had the ship gone down, the individuals would have lost not only the original investments but their share of the expenses as well.

Such joint ventures are still used to some extent. A group of women hold a rummage sale, a group of businessmen build and sell an office building or a residential development, or a group of construction corporations build a dam.

It is customary for large stock or bond issues to be sold by groups of brokers. Joint ventures in the area of finance are called *syndicates*, or *underwriting syndicates*. As a rule a syndicate continues in active operation for handling further issues of securities and does not necessarily dissolve after the first venture is concluded. Neither does it dissolve if one partner sells his share to another person or company. Usually, the joint venture or syndicate is managed by the person or company that takes the initiative in organizing it.

The Joint-Stock Company. The *joint-stock company* is a transitional form between the partnership and the corporation. When business concerns or individuals form such a company, they usually draw up *articles of association* which set forth the outlines of its organization and operation. Share certificates evidence part ownership, and these can be exchanged with no restrictions. Holders of share certificates vote for directors who manage the business. As in the partnership, each certificate holder is potentially liable for all the debts of the organization. There are not many joint-stock companies in the United States today, although the form was very popular from the fifteenth to the eighteenth centuries.

ADVANTAGES. This form is *easy to organize* and has a *higher credit rating* than comparable corporations. *Flexibility of ownership* and *long life* result from transferability of shares and the fact that withdrawal of one of the owners does not terminate it. There is *no joint responsibility for management* among the shareholder owners, and it is *not closely regulated by the state*.

DISADVANTAGES. An important disadvantage of the joint-stock company is that all owners have *unlimited liability* for the debts of the concern. This, together with the fact that in many states this form of business is *taxed as a corporation*, makes the joint-stock company unacceptable to most persons in business.

The Business Trust (Massachusetts Trust). When the state of Massachusetts prohibited corporations from holding real estate, a common-law trust form of ownership organization came into being. This form, made up of trustees who are the legal owners, and trust certificate holders who are the beneficiaries, is variously called a *business trust*, a *Massachusetts trust*, or a *common-law trust*. It is formed when the *beneficiaries* (original owners or investors) turn over their shares of ownership or money to the *trustees* in exchange for *trust certificates*. The trustees then manage the business in the interest of the beneficiaries, who receive periodic reports, and dividends if profits are made.

Although a trust may superficially resemble a corporation, it is actually very different. The beneficiaries or shareholders of a trust do not have the right to meet and elect officers. The trustees sometimes are a self-perpetuating body, though usually their power ceases after a stated term of years or at the death or incapacity of the last remaining trustee. An incompetent or dishonest board of trustees usually cannot be removed from office except by court action.

Beneficiaries are not liable for the debts of the concern except to the extent of their individual investments. On the other hand, each trustee carries unlimited liability. The act of one trustee does not bind the others unless ratified by them. The trust has no legal existence of its own, so that lawsuits must be brought against the trustees and not against the company.

The word *trust* is used in two senses, and confusion often results. In the 1880s business in the United States was dominated by a few companies. These companies reduced competition and raised prices to the detriment of the public. Since these monopolistic groups were organized into trusts, the word *monopoly* soon became associated in the public mind with *trust*. When the Sherman Act of 1890 was passed outlawing organizations in restraint of trade, it was popularly called the Antitrust Act. It should be kept in mind that the Sherman Act outlawed monopolies and not the trust form of organization. The business trust should not be confused with the term *trust* as used synonymously with *monopoly*.

ADVANTAGES. The business trust has several advantages. *Liability of shareholders is limited, shares are transferable, government regulation is not close*, it is *flexible in operation,* and it can be *expanded or contracted easily.*

DISADVANTAGES. The disadvantages include *too much centralization of power* in the trustees, *unfamiliarity of the investing public* in this form, *limited life* making the sale of its securities difficult, and *heavy taxation* which in some states is as onerous as corporation taxation.

The Unincorporated Association. The *unincorporated association* is made up of a number of individuals with some common interest. It usually is informal in nature, though many are subject to strictly drawn agreements. Among the more informal types are neighborhood property-owners' associations. These may meet frequently to discuss local problems (garbage disposal, water, police and fire protection, vandalism, taxes, building restrictions, and so on) and to petition county or city officers.

Other, more formal, types include trade associations, professional associations, fraternities, credit associations, clearing houses, and stock and commodity exchanges.

Most associations assess dues on their members, elect officers to transact the organization's business, and hold local, regional, and national meetings or conventions. Members of these associations can, as with partnerships, be held accountable for the liabilities of the organization.

The Corporation. A corporation is treated by the law as though it were a person. Originally, in England, corporations were chartered by the king. Later, in the United States, a special act of the legislature was required, but in the early part of the nineteenth century general incorporation laws were enacted by most of the states under which the secretary of state in each state was given the power and duty to issue charters. Today there are approximately one and three-quarters million business corporations in the United States.

In 1819 Chief Justice John Marshall defined a corporation as "an artificial being, invisible, intangible, and existing only in the contemplation of the law. Being a mere creature of the law, it possesses only those properties which the charter of its creation confers upon it, either expressly or as incidental to its very existence. These are such as are supposed best calculated to effect the object for which it was created. Among the most important are immortality, and, if the expression may be allowed, individuality, properties by which a perpetual succession of many persons are considered as the same, and may act as a single individual. They enable a corporation to manage its own affairs, and to hold property without the perplexing intricacies, the hazardous and endless necessity, of perpetual conveyances for the purpose of transmitting it from hand to hand. It is chiefly for the purpose of clothing bodies of men in succession with these qualities and capacities that corporations were invented, and are in use. By these means, a perpetual succession of individuals are capable of acting for the promotion of a particular object, like one immortal being."

When a corporation is formed, the founders and original owners turn their money over to the treasurer of the new organization and receive shares of *common stock*. The holders of such stock have the right to one vote per share at the annual stockholders' meetings. Dividends also are paid on a per share basis. When more capital is needed, the corporation may issue more stock, which usually is sold through financial syndicates. When additional stock is issued it serves to weaken the voting rights of existing stockholders. Hence, *preferred stock*, carrying no voting rights, often is issued. Such stock can be preferred as to dividends and precedence of repayment in case of bankruptcy or dissolution. Often fixed dividends are stated for preferred stock, to be paid prior to distribution of regular dividends to common stockholders. Both types of stock can be sold and bought freely.

At the annual stockholders' meetings directors are elected to represent the owners in the management of the company. Votes may be cast in person or by proxy. The directors appoint a president, vice-president, secretary, and treasurer. The shareholders enjoy liability limited to investment and they are not expected or allowed to assume managerial duties. In some states shareholders must pay the difference between the cost of the stock and its stated par value (if such value is greater) in the event of bankruptcy of the firm.

Although a corporation must be chartered by one state it can, with permission from other states, do business in those states as well. A corporation doing business in a state in which it was chartered is known there as a *domestic corporation*. A corporation doing business outside the state in which it was chartered is known in those other states as a *foreign corporation*. A corporation chartered by a foreign country but doing business in the United States is considered to be an *alien corporation*.

The terms *private, close*, and *closed* are applied to corporations whose stock is closely held by a few individuals, relatives, trust funds, or foundations, and is not publicly traded. The Ford Motor Company was such a company until 1956, when members of the family began selling their stock to the general public, whereupon the newspapers proclaimed that the company had "gone public." This was an unfortunate use of words, because *public corporations* are set up by public authority for public purposes. Actually, a corporation whose stock is in the hands of members of the general public is an *open corporation*. Public corporations are increasingly becoming known as *governmental corporations*.

Quasi-public, or *quasi-governmental, corporations* are set up by private individuals for public purposes, usually with governmental help. Toll roads and bridges often are financed through the sale of state-guaranteed bonds.

Nonprofit corporations do not distribute gains or dividends to their owners. Examples are social, religious, charitable, recreational, and educational organizations. Often such corporations do not issue stock and, therefore, are called *nonstock corporations*. *Stock corporations* may or may not be organized for profit.

Perpetual corporations have no termination date in their charters. *Limited-term corporations* must renew their charters periodically as they expire.

The first task in organizing a corporation is to select the state. Each state has its own incorporation requirements, and for the purposes of the company it is necessary to become familiar with the laws of several states and make the most favorable selection. If the company expects to do business nationally, it is well to select the state of incorporation carefully. On the other hand, if the company expects to do business only in California where the laws are fairly strict, there is no advantage in incorporating in a state with less strict laws, since foreign and alien corporations obtaining permits to do business in California must comply with California incorporation requirements.

The secretary of state of the state selected will send incorporation blanks and information on request. It must be noted that it is necessary to comply exactly with the requirements of the law. Although an attorney is not required for the incorporation procedure, legal help at this point can be useful. Many states maintain even closer surveillance over the issuing of stock than over incorporation procedures. In most cases, fees paid to the state depend on the amount of stock authorized.

ADVANTAGES. The outstanding advantage of the corporate form of organization is *limited liability*, which attracts the investor who would not care to risk more than the cost of his shares of stock. As a result, corporations find it *relatively easy to secure capital*.

From many standpoints, potentially *perpetual life* is an advantage.

Lawsuits need not be brought against the managers as individuals, since the corporation is a *legal entity*.

Ownership is easily transferred by the simple process of buying and selling stock. Corporations keep records of their shareholders for the purpose of issuing dividend checks. They usually pay a financial institution to act as *registrar* and *transfer agent*.

The former guarantees that the shares have been properly issued and the latter keeps the stock transfers straight.

Although *flexibility* is not an outstanding characteristic of corporations, they can nevertheless be changed in some respects without excessive resistance. On request to the state and by paying the required fees, the number of authorized shares of stock can be raised. Many states issue charters with such broad terms that the corporation can engage in practically any type of business, as its directors may from time to time decide. On the other hand, those states that issue more restrictive charters usually react favorably to requests for modifications.

DISADVANTAGES. State authorities *closely regulate* corporations. *Periodic reports* are required also by federal bureaus. These reports and other requirements result in considerable extra expense.

Matters concerning corporations usually are made public, which results in *little privacy* in many important areas of the business. Competitors often can use to their advantage financial facts that have been made public concerning certain corporations.

Corporations are *more heavily taxed* than other forms of organization. They pay approximately 50% income taxes. When their profits are distributed to the stockholders, these individuals then must pay income taxes on these amounts (less $100).

Among the various states, partnership law is fairly uniform and well established. *Corporation law is not uniform.* Corporations, also, are relatively *difficult and expensive to organize.*

Since the owners of corporations enjoy limited liability, the *credit rating of corporations is low* compared with other forms of organization of the same size and condition.

The *impersonal nature* of corporations is a disadvantage. The managers of other forms of business tend to take more personal interest in their customers.

The Cooperative. The cooperative association is owned by the members, and each owner periodically receives dividends based on the extent to which he has patronized the organization. Although most cooperatives are incorporated under special state laws, they are unlike noncooperative corporations in other respects, chief of which is that votes are based on one per member instead of one per share of stock held.

Small co-ops elect managers directly, but the larger organizations elect boards of directors who in turn appoint managers and formulate policies.

Co-ops are divided into producers' and consumers' organizations. *Producers' cooperatives*, as the name indicates, are made up of those who produce and who are interested in disposing of their products. They pledge themselves to sell exclusively through the co-op, which often results in monopolistic situations that are specifically exempted from the federal antitrust laws. Often cooperative efforts among producers in a given area will result in the creation of valuable trademarks, more efficient marketing procedures, and higher prices. Receipts less expenses are paid to members on the basis of patronage.

Although the marketing aspects of producers' cooperatives have been fairly successful in the United States, particularly in farming, actual producing activities have not. There is practically no collective farming or manufacturing, but such activities as purchasing supplies, threshing, ginning, spraying, conditioning, and packing have been done extensively on a cooperative basis.

Consumers' cooperatives are made up of individuals who buy goods and services. *General stores* sell at market prices and rebate profits to the cooperative owners on the basis of patronage. The familiar college co-op sells books and supplies to students and outsiders at market prices, but instead of rebating surplus funds to individual students, it is customary to use the money for assisting athletic programs and other student-body activities.

Financial associations include mutual companies, credit unions, and savings and loan companies.

Mutual companies, in turn, include life insurance companies and savings banks. When an individual buys a policy from a *mutual life insurance company* he becomes a part owner. Theoretically, he is entitled to vote for members of the board of directors of his company. He enjoys limited liability and does not pay income taxes on dividends inasmuch as the government labels such payments as partial refunds of premiums already paid by the member-owners.

Individuals who deposit money in *mutual savings banks* also thereby become members of such companies. These banks can borrow from the federal home loan bank system and their deposits are insured just as in differently organized banks.

Credit unions are formed within companies, lodges, and other groups of individuals with common interests. To become a member, an individual must purchase at least one share, although there is no limit. The value of a share is placed anywhere from ten dollars down. From these funds loans are made to members who apply and qualify. Directors and officers are elected at annual membership meetings. The officers appoint committees, among which usually is a credit committee.

Credit unions are found throughout the world. They are very popular in India and Japan, although about half of all such organizations (approximtely 22,064) are found in the United States.

Savings and loan associations can be organized either as mutually owned or privately owned corporations. Close to nine-tenths of all such institutions are, however, mutuals. Mutual companies are chartered by states; savings and loan associations may be chartered either by a state or by the federal government.

Savings and loan associations are organized to accept funds from depositors and to lend these funds to borrowers for the purpose of financing the construction of homes.

There are approximately 2,000 housing cooperatives in the United States, many of which are apartment units, a type that has become increasingly popular in recent years.

ADVANTAGES. As a rule, cooperatives are organized among farmers and wage earners. It has for many years been the policy of the federal and state governments to assist these groups. One way to do this has been to encourage the formation of cooperatives. Members of such organizations have been *exempted from certain restrictive legislation* and have been *accorded more favorable tax treatment*.

DISADVANTAGES. Unfortunately, many cooperatives are *poorly managed* due to the fact that officers are expected to serve without pay and to economize in other ways. Producers are *not free* to sell in markets of their own choice and at their own prices. Stores often *cannot sell sufficient volume* to keep costs low. Savings to members often are not sufficient to overcome such drawbacks as poor location of the store, lack of services and variety of merchandise, lack of advertising, and the innate proclivity of most members to shop in several stores and buy reasonably priced items wherever they are found. "Free riders" often take advantage of the favorable prices and conditions obtained by the cooperative when they resign or refuse to join, thus avoiding their just share of expenses, then compete to their own advantage against the organization.

QUESTIONS FOR DISCUSSION

1. What factors should the promoters of a new business organization consider when they are deciding the legal form it should take?
2. What are the characteristics of the general partnership?
3. What is a limited partnership and what are its advantages?
4. Have you ever engaged in a joint venture? If so, describe it. If not, give a few examples of this form of business organization.
5. In what two senses is the term business trust used?
6. What are the distinguishing characteristics of the corporate form of business organization?
7. What are the advantages and disadvantages of the corporate form of organization?
8. What are the distinguishing characteristics of the cooperative form of business organization?
9. How are credit unions formed and operated?
10. What are some advantages and disadvantages of the cooperative form of business organization?

SELECTED REFERENCES

Anderson, O. J., *Outline of Business Law*, Littlefield, Adams & Co., Totowa, N. J., 1964.

Anderson, R. A., and W. A. Kumpf, *Business Law*, 9th ed., South-Western Publishing Co., Cincinnati, 1973.

Bonneville, Joseph H., and Lloyd E. Dewey, *Organizing and Financing Business*, 6th ed., Prentice-Hall, Englewood Cliffs, N. J., 1959, Chap. V.

Broom, H. N., and J. G. Longenecker, *Small Business Management*, 4th ed., South-Western Publishing Co., Cincinnati, 1975.

Corley, R. N., and R. L. Black, Jr., *The Legal Environment of Business*, 3rd ed., McGraw-Hill, New York, 1973, Chap. 7.

Curran, W. S., *Principles of Financial Management*, McGraw-Hill, New York, 1970, Chap. 2.

Donaldson, E. F., and J. K. Pfahl, *Corporate Finance*, 3rd ed., Ronald Press Co., New York, 1969, Part I.

Husband, W. H., and J. C. Dockeray, *Modern Corporate Finance*, 7th ed., Richard D. Irwin, Homewood, Ill., 1972, Chaps. 3 and 4.

Lusk, H. F., *et al.*, *Business Law*, 3rd ed., Richard D. Irwin, Inc., Homewood, Ill., 1974, Part VI.

Niswonger, C. R., and P. E. Fess, *Accounting Principles*, 11th ed., South-Western Publishing Co., Cincinnati, 1973.

Voorhis, Horace J., *American Cooperatives*, Harper, New York, 1961.

PART II
FINANCIAL ORGANIZATION

Part II is concerned with the founding of business organizations, the combination of existing concerns into larger enterprises, how businesses obtain long-term and short-term financing, and the institutions that facilitate the various financing processes.

CHAPTER 4

BUSINESS PROMOTION
AND COMBINATION

Every new business is the result of an idea. The product or service may be novel, an old product or service may be used in a new way, or the idea may only be a new location for a well-known type of business. As long as the entrepreneur establishes the concern for himself alone, or for himself and a few associates, he is not called a promoter, even though he may have to perform the functions of promotion. But if he starts a new enterprise for many participants, whether or not he stays in the concern after it is launched, he is a promoter.

BUSINESS PROMOTION

Perhaps the first duty of the promoter is to investigate the idea. He asks if it is sound, if the service or product will be needed, and if the expected profit will warrant the risk. Patent positions are investigated; marketing investigations are made; schedules of required equipment are drawn up; tentative layouts are made; building locations and sites are checked; estimates are obtained for building costs, machinery and equipment, supplies and materials, labor, and overhead items; profit expectations are calculated and break-even charts are constructed; and needed capital is estimated.

If the idea seems to be feasible, the promoter then begins a series of activities, the results of which will determine whether or not the project is possible. Can the money be raised? Can the necessary labor be obtained? Are there legal restrictions? These and many other questions must be answered before the actual work of forming the concern begins. If the promoter can count on a few investors for all the necessary capital, it will not be necessary to seek the help of investment bankers; but if stock issues must be floated, the amount of needed capital may have to be increased. Not only must needed capital include money to pay commissions[1] to investment bankers and to buy such things as buildings, machinery, equipment, materials, and supplies; but funds must be available to finance sales, pay labor, meet overhead expenses, and (in most cases) absorb losses until the project gets under way.

If after studying the alternative choices of ownership organization, the promoter decides to incorporate, he must select a state. Some states have high incorporation fees and low taxes; some have low incorporation fees and high taxes; some have restrictive requirements for incorporators; and so on. If the state in which business is to be done has rigid entry requirements for foreign corporations, there may be no advantage in incorporating in a state with easier requirements.

If the promoter desires to stay in the organization in a managerial capacity, he must set up a capital structure which will prevent a combination of investors from squeezing him out. He may provide an issue of preferred stocks and possibly of bonds, neither of which carry voting power but both of which have compensating advantages to investors. He may then take his own pay for promoting the enterprise in the form of common (voting) stock, and any cash investment he makes may be made in the same type of securities. If he and his friends retain control of a considerable fraction of the voting stock, and if the rest of such stock is scattered among many investors, his control will be secure.

Promoters often do not care to remain in the businesses they start. Such individuals take their pay either in the form of stock, a cash fee, or both.

---

1. Somewhere from 20 percent of the aggregate par value of the issue down to 10 percent and even lower for large amounts of stock issued by particularly sound concerns.

BUSINESS COMBINATION

The function of promotion is involved not only when a new business is started, but it is called on to expand existing businesses and to effect various forms of combinations.

Why Businesses Combine. The twentieth century has seen the formation of many very large business concerns. Most of them have come into being through the combination of two or more existing concerns. Such combinations would not have taken place had there not resulted enhanced possibilities for profits. These possibilities come about in a number of ways.

REDUCTION OF COMPETITION. To the extent that existing competition is wasteful, the combination of competing units is advantageous. Such combination often involves the reduction of duplicate facilities with consequent lowering of costs. Larger concerns, too, can replace many mediocre managers with a few really well-qualified individuals, who are able to produce at higher profits with the same prices.

DESIRE TO DOMINATE THE INDUSTRY. It seems clear that many business combinations have resulted from a desire on the part of certain individuals to dominate or monopolize an entire industry. Without the antitrust laws this tendency would be carried even further.

ACTIVITIES OF PROMOTERS. Certain combinations have been brought about by promoters and investment bankers as a means of enhancing their own financial positions. Although the act of bringing about a consolidation involves enormous difficulties, the results often are exceedingly lucrative.

Combination Types. Combination takes place in three general ways: vertically, horizontally, and in complementary patterns. It is possible for a combination to take place in one of these ways, or in two or three of them at once.

VERTICAL COMBINATION, OR INTEGRATION. Called integration in the United States and rationalization in Europe, vertical combination takes place when a number of concerns in one industry but at different levels of production and distribution unite under one management. A completely integrated concern would control the production of its raw materials and supplies; their transportation; processing, assembling, and transporting the finished goods to the concern's own warehouses; and finally their retailing to the consuming public.

The process of integration can start at either end, or at any point in between the production of the raw materials and the final retailing of the finished product. It is common, however, for manufacturers to reach back for control over sources of their raw materials and to reach forward for control over the distribution of their products. Often large retailers, such as department stores, attempt to assure themselves of reliable sources of merchandise or supplies by gaining control of manufacturing concerns.

HORIZONTAL COMBINATION, OR CONCENTRATION. Horizontal combination results when two or more concerns within an industry at the same level of production and distribution unite under one management. Chain stores constitute the best-known example of this form of combination. Widespread concentration has taken place among manufacturers: steel corporations have joined hands to produce new supercorporations, meat-packing companies have bought up smaller meat packers throughout the United States and in many foreign countries and continue to operate them as branch plants, and petroleum refining companies have followed somewhat the same pattern. In many cases of such concentration, units located in uneconomical areas have been dismantled.

COMPLEMENTARY, OR CIRCULAR, COMBINATION. There have been many examples of manufacturers who acquired concerns producing complementary products to round out their lines. This form of combination, the complementary or circular type, takes advantage of certain potential economies which can best be explained by illustrations. Ten manufacturers, with ten separate food products, have ten separate sales forces calling on the same retailers. All ten products require delivery in refrigerated trucks and storage in special display fixtures. A promoter might be able to convince the owners of these businesses that they should combine, simply on the basis of the elimination of duplicate facilities.

The complementary aspects of products are not restricted to the sales end. New concerns are brought into the orbit of a combination because they are useful in bringing about manufacturing economies. This type of combination is commonly found in the chemical industries, in pharmaceuticals, and in meat packing. An interesting example of the combination of both types of influence is the meat-packing concern which acquired a sandpaper manufacturing company to aid in the economical utilization of one of their by-products, glue. One of the important products of the new concern was emery boards (fingernail files). Glue and sandpaper continued to be sold to the furniture trade and in other markets, while their emery boards and toilet soap (another product developed to effect manufacturing economies) were sold in still a different market. To utilize more efficiently the salesmen's efforts in this latter market, the meat packer acquired control of a well-known concern manufacturing perfumes and toilet preparations.

Ways by Which Combinations Are Formed. Combinations are formed in a number of ways. Some provide more formal procedures than others and each is designed to accomplish a specific purpose.

THE CONSOLIDATION. A consolidation, or amalgamation, brings together into one newly-formed corporation two or more business units that formerly were independent. The new concern does not merely buy up a controlling interest in each of the units, it actually buys their assets, and the absorbed companies go out of existence. If they were corporations their charters are returned to the state.

THE MERGER. A merger results when one of a group of business units buys out the others.

THE HOLDING COMPANY. A holding company controls one or more other companies through the ownership of their stock. When the stock of the controlled company is widely diffused, a strong minority holding often is sufficient for purposes of control. Holding companies may be corporations, joint-stock companies, Massachusetts trusts, or partnerships.

A *pure holding company* is one which does not operate a business. It merely holds a controlling interest in one or more operating or other pure holding companies. An operating company may own a controlling interest in one or more other companies. Such a company is an *operating and holding company*. A *consolidated holding company* is formed for the sole purpose of taking over the stocks of a group of existing companies. *Intermediate holding companies* or *subholding companies* are holding companies which in turn are controlled by other holding companies.

CONSOLIDATION BY LEASE. A consolidation mechanism frequently used by railroad companies is the lease. Many of the properties of well-known railroad systems were rounded out through the long-term leasing of extension and feeder lines.

THE TRADE ASSOCIATION. A nonprofit organization of concerns in the same industry is known as a trade association. The purpose of this type of organization is to promote the interests of its members, who generally are competitors and who retain control of their individual businesses. It attempts to get agreements among its members on prices, sales terms and customs, quality standards, new markets, new products, and so on.

THE GENTLEMEN'S AGREEMENT. So-called gentlemen's agreements form the basis for restrictive arrangements among manufacturers. Such agreements have, in the past, most frequently encompassed such matters as exclusive territories for each of the manufacturers so as to reduce competition, and various types of price structures.

As the name indicates, gentlemen's agreements require no enforcement. If they are violated, no penalties are assessed. They are oral in nature and each participant pledges on his honor to carry out their provisions.

THE POOL. A pool is like a gentlemen's agreement, except that the freedom of action of the participating companies is governed by a written contract which usually carries penalties for violation. *Simplex pools* are set up for one purpose only; *duplex pools* are established to deal with more than one. Pools are formed to deal with price matters, with a division of profits, with a division of markets, with production quotas, and with patents.

THE CARTEL. Cartels began in Germany for much the same purposes for which pools were used in the United States. There is little, if any, difference between the two when employed on the national level. The term "cartel," however, is commonly understood to be an international pool. International cartels have controlled world production, prices, and distribution of dyes, sugar, tin, magnesium, optical lenses, diamonds, and other products.

THE COOPERATIVE. Some business firms have combined under the principles of cooperation. Perhaps the best-known example of this form of cooperation is the voluntary grocery retailing chain. Independent grocers buy exclusively from a cooperative wholesale house, which rebates surplus funds on the basis of patronage. Such organizations provide merchandising, layout, advertising, and other services to member grocers.

There are various forms of marketing, consumers', financial, credit, service, and production cooperatives.

THE TRUST. One of the most publicized of all the devices for consolidating business units is the trust. First used in 1879, it effectually combined a number of oil companies into the Standard Oil Trust. Several large trusts were subsequently formed in various industries, and soon the word "trust" became associated in the minds of the public with any large combination of businesses.

Trusts (as a combination device) operate somewhat as follows. The stocks of the participating companies are transferred to a group of trustees. As new corporations are formed in the industry, stocks are issued to stockholders who then transfer them to the trustees. The powers granted to trustees often are enormous. Trustees can vote all the stock in their possession, elect themselves to the boards of directors of the participating corporations, declare dividends or not as they choose, buy the bonds of the controlled companies, buy new companies, abolish member companies, and regulate output, markets, prices, and policies of all the companies under their direction. Each shareholder receives trust certificates in exchange for his stock certificates. Trust certificates are transferable, and now carry voting rights. Although the trust agreement usually specifies the length of life of the trust, the certificate holders sometimes have the right to terminate the arrangement sooner.

THE COMMUNITY OF INTEREST. Effective combination of an informal nature often results from interlocking directorates or other forms of common interest. When the courts ordered the monopolies to be broken up, some such arrangement as the following often was made:

Five trustees are ordered to dissolve the trust into the original ten corporations.

Since it normally would be impossible to establish the *status quo ante* the formation of the trust (if it had been in existence many years), it usually would be necessary to give each trust-certificate holder his proportionate share in *each* of the ten original companies.

Inasmuch as each of the five trustees was known to the certificate holders as being an experienced manager of their properties, it stood to reason that one or more of the five trustees would be elected to the board of directors of each of the ten corporations.

Thus, although ten competing corporations have been formed, each now has on its board one to five spokesmen for each of the other nine corporations.

Communities of interest have come about through the activities of members of wealthy families who buy controlling interests in the same group of corporations. Banking interests have followed the same procedure.

It is not necessary that interlocking directorates be formed before a community of interest can develop. Three newspapers, for instance, each unable to use the entire output of a paper mill, but each desirous of ensuring a stable source of newsprint, might buy into the same mill. Each might own 20 percent of the voting stock, thus being unable when acting alone to control the policies of the mill. But, acting together, they could dictate production quotas, prices, and so on, in conformity with their common desires.

CONGLOMERATE COMBINATIONS. Recent years have seen the rise of the conglomerate combination. Companies have acquired other promising companies in a wide variety of industries. These conglomerates have been formed partly as a result of Justice Department activity in breaking up combinations of competing business concerns. If the management wishes to expand its activities it does so for various reasons other than to reduce competition illegally.

Conglomerates frequently take place as a result of a newspaper *tender offer*. If one company offers to pay a stated price for shares of stock in another company, it may be that the first company will acquire a controlling interest in the second company. This process, if followed for a variety of other companies, may result in a consolidation or amalgamation, a series of mergers, or a holding company.

Examples. Examples of these forms are as follows:

In 1967 the Hayes Industries Company and the Albion Malleable Iron Company consolidated to form the Hayes-Albion Corporation. They manufacture automotive parts (47%), castings (33%), textiles (10%), and miscellaneous products (10%).

In 1968 the Bunker Ramo Corporation merged the Amphenol Corporation into its organization. The Bunker Ramo Corporation manufactures electronic goods (52%), computer information systems (18%), knitted fabrics (20%), and government systems (10%).

One of the most interesting examples of a conglomerate is the Greyhound Corporation, a bus company which in recent years has become a holding company with approximately 120 subsidiaries. Its sales in 1973 were scattered among the following categories: bus operations (17.0%), food processing and pharmaceutical products (72.5%), computer and industrial leasing (1.6%), miscellaneous service operations (3.7%), food service (3.6%), and cattle feeding (1.6%). Among many other activities, this bus company produces Armour Star meat products.

An equally interesting and better known conglomerate is International Telephone and Telegraph Company. Its sales in 1973 were split among the following areas: telecommunication equipment (24%), industrial products (20%), automotive and consumer products (13%), natural resources (5%), defense and space programs (4%), food processing and services (11%), consumer services (7%), business and financial services (5%), telecommunication operations (2%), and operations being divested (9%). Somewhat incongruously, this telephone and telegraph company produces Hostess brand cakes.

QUESTIONS FOR DISCUSSION

1. What is involved when a new business concern is promoted?
2. Why do business concerns combine?

3. Business combination takes place in three general ways. Describe them.
4. Differentiate between consolidations and mergers.
5. What is a pure holding company?
6. Distinguish cartels from pools.
7. In what ways does a community of interest serve to create a business combination?
8. What is a conglomerate combination?
9. How are tender offers used in connection with business combinations?
10. Why would anyone wish to participate in the formation of a conglomerate?

SELECTED REFERENCES

Baumback, Clifford M., Kenneth Lawyer, and Pearce C. Kelley, *How to Organize and Operate a Small Business*, 5th ed., Prentice-Hall, Englewood Cliffs, N. J., 1973.

Bonneville, Joseph H., and Lloyd E. Dewey, *Organizing and Financing Business*, 6th ed., Prentice-Hall, Englewood Cliffs, N. J., 1959, Chap. V.

Cherry, Richard T., *Introduction to Business Finance*, Wadsworth Publishing Co., Belmont, Cal., 1973, Part 5.

Corley, R. N., and R. L. Black, Jr., *The Legal Environment of Business*, 3rd ed., McGraw-Hill, New York, 1973, Chap. 7.

Haney, Lewis H., *Business Organization and Combination*, Macmillan Co., New York, 1934.

Newman, William H., and James P. Logan, *Strategy, Policy, and Central Management*, 6th ed., South-Western Publishing Co., Cincinnati, 1971, Chaps. 15 and 24.

Vance, Stanley C., *Managers in the Conglomerate Era*, John Wiley & Sons, New York, 1971.

CHAPTER 5
LONG-TERM FINANCE

Some businesses operate with capital furnished by the owners. Other concerns borrow on a long-range basis. Of course it is possible, and a fairly common practice, for the owners to furnish some capital and to borrow the rest. Also, it is considered sound practice to retain all or part of the company's profits to be added to capital. This is known as plowing profits back into the business.

When a person invests in a corporation he receives in return certain legal instruments known in general as *securities*. Usually investments are made through such financial institutions as investment banks, brokerage houses, and stock exchanges.

Financing Unincorporated Companies. The best and safest way for unincorporated concerns to obtain long-term capital is *from the owners*. Often wealthy persons are willing to become *silent partners*. They make substantial investments but do not wish to assume all the responsibilities of a full partnership.

Depending on the personal means of the owners, all or part of the *profits can be plowed back* into the business, as previously mentioned. This is a safe and conservative practice to follow.

Managers of firms desiring to expand rapidly often *mortgage their assets* to raise needed capital. This can be a dangerous practice, particularly for new concerns. The interest on mortgage loans is payable on a regular and fixed basis and must be met whether profits are being made or not. If a promising business with too many such fixed obligations has a year or two of business losses it could easily fail before having a fighting chance of survival.

It is possible for companies with high credit ratings to borrow substantial funds on *intermediate-term notes*, maturing in anywhere from one to five years. Often it is possible for such firms to pay off maturing notes by obtaining new loans of a similar type, thus in effect converting intermediate loans to long-term purposes. The dangers are obvious, however. The existence of the company is dependent on the ability of the officers to renew the notes or obtain new ones, and interest rates are subject to relatively frequent adjustment.

Financing Incorporated Companies. When a company incorporates it obtains long-term funds through the sale of *stock*. Those who hold stock become *part owners* of the company. The company can also raise long-term capital by selling *bonds*. Those who buy the firm's bonds are its *creditors*.

STOCKS

An investor can buy either common or preferred stock. When a firm is first incorporated it usually issues common stock. This gives the purchaser proportionate ownership and the right to cast one vote per share at stockholders' meetings. Later, when the company needs more capital, it could issue more stock and sell it on the market. But this might be unfair to the original stockholders by diluting their interests in the company. Therefore, it is frequently the practice to issue preferred stock, which carries no vote. Such stock usually includes some sort of built-in advantage to induce investors to buy it. Often priorities as to dividend payments, voting rights, and payment on dissolution of the company are distinguished by issuing Class A Preferred, Class B Preferred, Class A Common, Class B Common, and so on. Preferred stock always carries prior claims over common stock but there is no general rule that always gives "A" stock priority over "B."

When a state issues a charter to a corporation the maximum amounts of common and preferred stock are specified. Such limits define what is known as *authorized stock*. Before any stock is issued, *subscribed stock* (or promises to buy) can be sold. Such promises usually must be accompanied with a partial payment. In some states (California is one), new domestic corporations cannot issue stock directly but must place it in escrow until release is approved. In place of stock the share-holders receive *escrow certificates*.

Those who promote or found a corporation often are given *promoters' stock* in return for their contributions. Such stock usually carries certain restrictions as to date of sale by the promoters to others, withholding of dividends, and so on.

Those shares of a company's stock owned by itself are known as *treasury stock*. Usually it has been repurchased on the market. If acquired otherwise it may be *donated stock* or it may be *unissued stock*.

Stock issued by subsidiary or leased companies often is backed by the parent concern. Such securities are known as *guaranteed stock*.

If a stated value is printed on the stock certificate this is known as *par value*. This really has little meaning except for the tax paid when issued, because the stock rarely exchanges hands at this price. Actually, many corporations omit this figure entirely and issue *no par value stock*. The price at which a share of stock exchanges is its *market value*. This, of course, can change from minute to minute as successive transactions are made on the various stock exchanges. It is influenced by many factors which carry different weights in the minds of investors and speculators. Earning power of the company is important, yet a stock can drop week after week in the face of increased earnings. Dividends are important, too, as is the ratio of price to earnings. Stability of the industry, quality of the company's management, prevailing interest rates, changes in domestic and foreign competition, new technical developments, purchases and sales in large quantities by investment institutions, pertinent news of significant political or union developments, and even rumors of significant changes all have their effects on market prices.

The *book value* of a share of stock is found by subtracting liabilities of the concern from the assessed valuation of its assets and dividing by the number of outstanding shares. If the company should go out of business, sell all its assets, and pay off its debts, then the remaining cash divided by the number of out-standing shares would give the *real value* of each share.

COMMON STOCK

Possession of a share of *common stock*, evidenced by a *certificate*, indicates part ownership in a corporation. When a corporation is formed, common stock is the first security issued. Other types may be issued later, but they all must be paid off on dissolution of the corporation before residual cash is distributed to the stockholders.

Cost of Capital. When a business concern is formed, capital funds are contributed by the owners. Buildings, machinery, equipment, raw materials, and supplies may be purchased as the company gets under way. It may be that the company buys certain of these items on credit. The value of everything owned less what is owed to others is called *net worth*, or *equity*.

Assume that the company's equity is $500,000 and it is making a net profit of $50,000 a year, which is 10%. Assume, also, that the management believes it would be advantageous to expand. It is possible to raise more capital in a variety of ways. However, it is decided to borrow money by selling 7% bonds to the public, using the buildings and machinery as security. When money can be borrowed at a rate lower than the expected rate of return on these funds, the process is known as *trading on the equity*. This is good business practice and is widely followed. However, it becomes dangerous when profits fall and may result in the bondholders taking over the business should profits drop below the interest rates. This usually takes place if a company is unable to pay the interest.

If the rate of profits does not fall, trading on the equity can be of benefit to the owners of the business. For instance, if $200,000 worth of 7% bonds are sold, the company's yearly interest expense becomes $14,000. But with 10% profit on $700,000, the yearly income becomes $70,000, with net profit now becoming $56,000 ($70,000–$14,000), instead of $50,000 as it was formerly.

A similar term is used in this connection. Those in business who trade on the equity are said to get more *leverage* out of their capital.

Rights of Common Shareholders. A person who buys stock in a corporation may be interested only in selling it later at a profit. However, if he wishes, he can attend annual stock-holders' meetings where he has the right to participate in the selection of directors and vote on all other matters on the agenda. He has the right to obtain information from the officers concerning the financial condition of the company. Usually, also, he has prior rights in buying new issues of stock. If he does not wish to attend stockholders' meetings he has the right to designate a proxy to vote as he (the stockholder) desires. If his proxy is solicited, he has the right to know the issues and how the proxy vote will be cast.

PREFERRED STOCK

Preferred stocks possess characteristics that lie between common stocks and bonds. Interest on bonds must be paid before dividends on preferred stocks are paid; but dividends on preferred stock must be paid before common stock dividends are paid. On dissolution of a corporation, bond principal and accumulated interest must be paid first, then obligations to preferred shareholders must be satisfied. The common shareholders divide what is left.

Dividends. Priority as to dividends can be noncumulative or cumulative. *Noncumulative preferred stock* is restricted to the dividend period (customarily three months). No dividends can be paid to common stockholders until preferred stockholders have been paid, usually a fixed amount stated on the certificate. It is possible under this type of preferred stock for a corporation's management to defeat the purpose of priority. If dividends are passed on both types of stock in the first period, enough money might be saved to pay both in the second period. Thus, instead of the preferred stock yielding, say, 6% the first period and 6% the second period, while the common stock yields 0% each of the two periods, by passing all dividends the first period, the preferred yields 0% and in the second period yields 6%, while the common also yields 0% the first period and 6% the second period.

Holders of *cumulative preferred stock* must be paid all current and past due dividends before common shareholders receive dividends. The directors can pass the dividends on both preferred and common stock indefinitely, but before the common can receive anything all current and past preferred dividends must be declared and paid. So, using the illustration in the preceding paragraph, if a corporation passed all dividends the first period and desired to pay the common shareholders the second period, it would be necessary to pay cumulative preferred stock 12% first, then if any money was available in reserve, dividends could be declared for the common shareholders.

Participating Features. Most preferred stocks carry a fixed rate at which dividends are to be declared, after which the common can receive any amount declared by the directors. Some preferred stocks, however, provide that any excess available to the common, above that paid to the preferred, is to be shared between the two.

Redeemability. Most preferred stocks are redeemable at the option of management. Redeemability introduces financial flexibility and is advantageous to common shareholders in that if prior claims are reduced ultimate residual values are enhanced. Usually preferred shareholders receive a premium over par if their stock is called in. As a rule they get $5 extra if their stock's par value is $100.

Convertibility. Some preferred stock carries a convertibility provision that gives the holder the right to exchange it for common stock. Normally, if the exchange must be made on a 1-to-1 basis, holders would hesitate to make the trade, since preferred stock has a prior claim on assets and dividends. However, if the common begins rising in value faster than the preferred, the speculative value of the common may outweigh the built-in advantages of the preferred. Occasionally preferred shareholders are forced to convert by the device of offering to exchange on a 1-to-1 basis for a limited time, after which 1 1/4 shares of preferred must be offered for one share of common, then, later, 1 1/2 shares of preferred must be offered, and so on.

Voting Rights. Some preferred stocks carry voting rights, but most do not. Some provide that preferred stockholders can elect a minority group of directors; other issues give the right only if dividends on preferred stock have been defaulted over a certain number of years.

BONDS

Bondholders do not own shares of the company as stockholders do; they are creditors of the company. They have loaned money which will be repaid on a given date. The interest rate is specified as well as the manner of payment.

How Bonds Are Issued. Generally two trustees are appointed by the corporation as representatives of those who purchase the bonds. Frequently one representative is an individual and the other a trust company. The trustees prepare an *indenture* which spells out all the details concerning the new issue. Since each issue is designed to meet a given set of circumstances, no two issues necessarily have the same specifications. Normally, bonds are sold in denominations of $1,000, $5,000, $10,000, and so on. A few are issued in denominations of under $1,000. Those priced at $100 and less are known as *baby bonds*. A purchaser of a bond will not obtain full information concerning its exact nature from the printed matter on its face; to get this he must read a copy of the indenture.

Payment of Interest on Bonds. *Coupon bonds* are issued with coupons printed on them. As the coupons mature the holder clips them off and presents them to his banker or broker, who sends them in for the payment of interest due to date. *Registered bonds* are sold to named persons to whom interest checks are mailed when due. Occasionally the two types of bonds are combined.

Retirement of Bonds. It is customary to retire bonds either by building up a reserve or by paying them off systematically. The first type is called *sinking fund bonds* and the second type is called *serial bonds*. Often companies with the first type will buy in their outstanding bonds with the sinking fund as it accumulates, although it is customary to place the money periodically with a trustee who redeems the bonds when they mature. Serial bonds are issued with varying maturity dates.

Callable bonds give the right to the corporation to pay the holder the face value of the bond plus a small premium if at any time it is desired to pay it off.

Secured Bonds. When a corporation obtains funds from the sale of bonds it may or may not post security for the loan. A common form of secured bond is the *mortgage bond*, of which there are many varieties. A mortgage bond simply means a loan secured by some form of tangible property which can be taken over by the bondholders should the corporation fail to pay interest or principal.

It is possible to use the same property as security for more than one bond issue. The holders of *first mortgage bonds* can obtain satisfaction before the holders of *second mortgage bonds* do. In other words, if the corporation defaults and the security is sold, the first mortgage bonds are paid off first and if any money is left over it is paid to the holders of the second mortgage bonds. Although the holders of the second mortgage bonds may not be paid from the sale of the security, they still have a claim for reimbursement along with other creditors if the defunct corporation has funds from other sources.

A form of specific mortgage bond is the *equipment bond*, secured by such things as punch presses, trucks, railroad cars, and so on. A plate with notice of the fact that it is security for a loan often is riveted to the equipment.

Collateral trust bonds have as their security such items as miscellaneous stocks and bonds, rights, leases, and patents. Such bonds may restrict the security to the original items or they may permit substitution of other items.

Income bonds carry no specific security. They are backed by the general credit of the company, and interest need not be paid unless the company makes a profit. There is a form known as *cumulative income bonds* which provide that interest not paid in bad years must be made up in good years.

Debenture bonds carry no specific security. They are simply promises to pay principal and interest. As a rule they are issued with the understanding that either no other bonds will be issued or, if they are, the debenture holders will have priority. Sometimes the consent of the debenture holders must be granted before other bond issues can be arranged.

It is not unusual for a company to issue *convertible bonds* which can, at the option of the holders, be exchanged at specified rates for other securities of the company.

A form of security issued by receivers of a company being reorganized after bankruptcy is the *receivers' certificate*. Such securities must be authorized by a court and they usually are paid off in cash after a relatively short period of time.

QUESTIONS FOR DISCUSSION

1. What is preferred stock and why is it issued?
2. With respect to stock values, what is the meaning of each of the following: par, no par, market, book, and real?
3. What security is issued to a part owner of a corporation?
4. If you were a corporation treasurer how might you use bonds to "trade on the equity"?
5. What rights do common shareholders have?
6. Distinguish between cumulative and noncumulative preferred stock.
7. If you own a convertible preferred stock and wish to dispose of it what might you do besides sell it?
8. If a stockholder is a part owner of a corporation, what is a bondholder?
9. Distinguish between sinking fund bonds and serial bonds.
10. Define debenture bonds.

SELECTED REFERENCES

Bogen, Jules I., and S. S. Shipman, eds., *Financial Handbook*, 4th ed., Ronald Press Co., New York, 1968, Sections 13 and 14.

Cherry, Richard T., *Introduction to Business Finance*, Wadsworth Publishing Co., Belmont, Cal., 1973, Part 2.

Dauten, Carl A., and Merle Welshans, *Principles of Finance*, 4th ed., South-Western Publishing Co., Cincinnati, 1975.

Serraino, William J., *et al.*, *Frontiers of Financial Management*, South-Western Publishing Co., Cincinnati, 1971. Part V.

CHAPTER 6

SHORT-TERM FINANCE

A company cannot start without capital. We know from the two previous chapters how a new company raises its initial capital. Part of this money is used to purchase land, buildings, and equipment. The value or money represented by such purchases is known as *fixed capital*. The items themselves are *fixed assets*. Part of the initial funds is, however, used for materials, labor, and other on-going expenses. These expenses are recovered in a relatively short period of time through the sale of goods and services. The total of such items is known as *current* or *circulating capital*. The items themselves are *current assets*.

After a business is under way it will have various suppliers, employees, banks, and so on, to whom it owes money on a short-range basis. These debts are known as *current liabilities*. On the other hand, the concern's customers will owe it money, payable within a short time. These accounts receivable are part of the firm's *current assets*. Current assets less current liabilities is the company's *working capital*. Most of a firm's working capital is obtained from long-term sources. Normally, the working capital is adequate for purchasing needed materials and paying expenses while awaiting receipts from sales. If, however, an emergency arises or if there is a pronounced seasonal cycle, the firm will require additional working capital for short periods of time. Recourse to long-term sources results in excess cash being on hand throughout much of the year. This is poor business practice since it results in lower income per dollar invested. The answer is to seek additional short-term financing only for the periods additional working capital is required.

Need for Short-Term Financing. There are countless situations calling for short-term financing. Perhaps the sales force brings in an extra large order. The firm could handle it by adding a temporary night shift at the plant. But more money would be needed to pay for the extra labor, materials, and supplies. If the order could be filled in six weeks and if payment is expected in six more weeks, a 90-day bank loan secured a week or so after work on the order commences should take care of the situation. The loan in this case is *self-liquidating* in that payment by the customer will satisfy the loan when it comes due.

Short-term loans are resorted to when emergencies occur, such as fires, floods, accidents, and so on.

In some industries unusual expenses arise periodically. In agriculture, harvest expenses come when the crop is ripe. In manufacturing, the seasons cause cycles in demand for clothing, sports equipment, toys, fuel, and so on. In services, demand often varies throughout the year. Good examples are the varying need for income-tax assistance and the excessive demand on department stores before Christmas.

Forms of Short-Term Instruments. One form of short-term instrument is the *promissory note*. Such an instrument can be tendered for a loan from many sources, but the most common source is the commercial bank. Bank loans are obtained either on an unsecured or a secured basis. One of the most important factors in obtaining an *unsecured loan* is a record of prompt repayment of previous loans. The loan officer satisfies himself as to the capacity of the borrower, and he is interested in the purpose of the loan. As a rule he asks for a copy of the company's balance sheet and profit and loss statement. The amount of money customarily kept in the company's checking account is determined and frequently the borrower is asked to keep a *compensating balance* of 10 to 20 percent of the amount of the loan.

Banks charge lower interest rates on *secured loans*. For this reason although many business concerns could borrow on an unsecured basis they elect to deposit some form of collateral. It may be possible for a concern to use as security their *warehouse receipts* on excess stored materials or products, *securities*, or *negotiable bills of lading*.

If securities are pledged the bank officer checks their value and sets a loan limit of 50 to 90 percent. If the value of the securities drops, additional collateral or part payment of the loan will be requested. These measures failing, the bank will sell the collateral.

The promissory note includes date, time of loan and due date, amount of loan, place of repayment, rate of interest, and other stipulations, sometimes including a promise to pay the attorney's fees if they must be incurred to recover on a defaulted loan. If a *cosigner* is required he bears *contingent liability* and must pay if the signer defaults.

Commercial paper consists of promissory notes signed by well-known business concerns. Such paper is handled by note brokers or commercial-paper houses which find investors for it.

The *draft* differs from the promissory note in point of origin. Whereas the note is executed by the debtor and delivered to the creditor, the draft is prepared by the creditor and delivered to the debtor. A draft is a written order to pay to a specific person, or to the bearer, a certain sum of money. A *sight draft* is payable on presentation. A *time draft* is payable on a stated date.

A draft which is used in foreign trade is known as a *bill of exchange*.

A *trade acceptance* is a draft, across the face of which the debtor has written the word "accepted," together with the date of acceptance, the place of payment, and his signature. A trade acceptance is a promise to pay and as such it can be negotiated to others.

Open-book accounts are the simplest forms of credit instruments. They merely are notations of the amount owed on the books of account of the creditor and the debtor. The debtor uses his credit power to purchase goods on time, the deferred time of payment ranging from 30 to 90 days, or more. As a rule, the purchaser must "secure a line of credit," or "establish satisfactory credit relations" before he can charge his purchases. This is done in a variety of ways. Some wholesalers merely set an arbitrary limit such as $1,000 for 30 days. If the new customer pays promptly, the amount of credit allowed is increased. The length of the credit period is set by custom in each industry, though individual businesses often establish credit policies independently. A safer way to extend credit to a customer is to require a bank reference and two or three business references with whom the customer has established credit relations. Information concerning new customers often can be found from one of the mercantile services, as for example, Dun and Bradstreet, Inc., or from a credit association. Open-book credit usually carries no rate of interest, except that which often is charged on overdue accounts. Nevertheless, if the concern which extends credit also allows a cash discount, the customer who elects to take time instead of the cash discount actually pays interest. This can be shown by the following example. A sale amounting to $100.00 is made on terms of 2 percent/10, net/30 days. If the bill is paid within 10 days of the date of the invoice, 2 percent may be deducted. For an additional 20 days' credit (the bill must be paid 30 days from date of invoice) the customer must pay $2 "interest" on what otherwise would have been a $98 bill. The rate of interest is found by the formula

$$\$2 = 98 \times \frac{20}{365} \times \text{rate of interest}$$

It amounts to about 37 percent!

Businessmen may finance their accounts receivable through finance companies which specialize in this type of work. At the option of the concern which sells the accounts, the customers may or may not be notified. If the customers are notified, they merely settle with the finance company when the account is due. The finance company buys only the accounts it considers to be good. Interest is charged for the aggregate of these accounts, which is advanced to the company. If the company does not wish to have its customers notified, a representative of the finance company must visit the company each day to receive the payments due the finance company as they come in the mail or otherwise.

Consumer Financing. Commercial banks finance consumers just as they finance businessmen, and open-book credit is used by consumers just as it is used by business concerns. There are however, a few special instruments used for consumers (individuals). A few institutions other than commercial banks deal in this specialized form of financing.

It is customary for banks to require collateral on all loans to individuals. Exceptions are made to this rule for relatively small amounts ($500 or less) or when borrowers obtain cosigners for their notes. Banks often lend money to individuals on a monthly repayment basis, over periods of time up to 18 months. Loans on mortgages are made for longer periods by commercial banks and building and loan associations.

Individuals often find it advantageous to borrow from *small loan companies, finance companies, pawnbrokers,* and *credit unions.* These are special forms of banks which cater to the requirements of individuals, who generally must provide such security as income from salaries and wages, jewelry and other things of value, and chattel mortgages on household furniture or automobiles. Inasmuch as the risks inherent in such loans often are relatively great and the costs of making investigations are high, the interest rates are considerably above those paid at commercial banks for secured loans. Interest rates charged by credit unions are, however, not by any means excessive.

It is unlawful under the federal Truth in Lending Act of 1967 to give misleading information concerning interest rates. The effective annual interest rate must be disclosed and full information must be given concerning service charges, installments, and other pertinent matters.

QUESTIONS FOR DISCUSSION

1. What are some types of things that constitute current assets or circulating capital?
2. How is a firm's working capital calculated?
3. What is a self-liquidating loan?
4. If short-term loans cost more than long-term financing, why not sell more stock or bonds for temporary or seasonal needs and keep the money in the bank against the time of need?
5. Describe a promissory note in detail.
6. What can a firm use as collateral for a short-term bank loan?
7. What is commercial paper?
8. When does a draft become a trade acceptance?
9. A grocer buys from a wholesaler under terms of 2%/10, net/30 days. If he turns down the 2% deduction, what percent interest is he paying for the twenty extra days?
10. What does the federal Truth in Lending Act of 1967 provide with respect to interest information?

SELECTED REFERENCES

Bogen, Jules I., and S. S. Shipman, eds., *Financial Handbook*, 4th ed., Ronald Press Co., New York, 1968, Section 16.

Cherry, Richard T., *Introduction to Business Finance*, Wadsworth Publishing Co., Belmont, Cal., 1973, Part 2.

Dauten, Carl A., and Merle Welshans, *Principles of Finance*, 4th ed., South-Western Publishing Co., Cincinnati, 1975.

Lindholm, Richard W., *Money and Banking*, Littlefield, Adams & Co., Totowa, N. J., 1969.

Serraino, William J., *et al.*, *Frontiers of Financial Management*, South-Western Publishing Co., Cincinnati, 1971, Part VI.

CHAPTER 7

FACILITATIVE SERVICES

Several types of institutions are available to assist business concerns and individuals in satisfying their financial needs. These are commercial banks, savings banks, savings and loan associations, insurance companies, business finance companies, investment banks, commercial-paper houses, trust companies, government institutions, credit unions, loan companies, brokerage companies, stock exchanges, and commodity exchanges.

Commercial Banks. Commercial banks safeguard money and other valuable items. Money is safeguarded by the use of vaults and checks. The business concern or individual first opens a *checking account* at the bank of his choice. Money and checks (which represent money) are then deposited to the account and subsequently money can be withdrawn and checks can be written as needed. No interest is paid on a checking account, but if the balance falls too low a fee may be charged.

A *check* is an order on the bank (legally known as the *drawee*) signed by the depositor (the *drawer*) to pay to the depositor or a third party (the *payee*) a specified sum. The payee can take the check to the depositor's bank or his own bank and obtain cash for it or he can deposit it to his own account. First, however, he must *endorse* it by signing his name on the back of the check.

If a check is given to a company or person having an account in the same bank, and if the check is deposited by the payee, payment is made by the bank's bookkeepers by debiting one account and crediting the other. If two local banks are involved, payment is made through a *clearing house*. Balances are settled among the banks by the use of Federal Reserve drafts. As cash accumulates or is depleted, armored trucks are used to make transfers. When checks drawn on distant banks are deposited, collections are made through Federal Reserve banks.

Bank depositors are protected, further, by the use of safety paper. If a check falls into the hands of a person who attempts to raise the amount by means of erasures or the use of chemicals, the tinted check paper is erased or bleached also, and the alteration becomes plainly visible.

When a person requests cash for a check, the bank teller makes sure that the drawer's and payee's signatures are authentic. Depositors' signatures are on file at the bank and endorsements can be compared with signatures on drivers' licenses or other identification cards. In spite of precautions losses do, of course, occur. Checks often are raised and signatures forged without detection, and other persons' lost I.D. cards are found or stolen and wrongfully used.

Certified checks are guaranteed by the drawer's bank. *Cashiers' checks* are drawn by a bank officer on his own bank. Anyone can purchase such a check for a small fee. *Traveler's checks* are issued by many banks and travel agencies. They are issued in various denominations and must be signed twice by the holder: once at the time of purchase and again when cashed. *Credit cards*, also, are issued by many banks and travel companies as well as by oil companies, department stores, and others. To obtain such a card one must first establish credit with the issuing company. A maximum credit amount is established and a plastic card is furnished. Hotel, gasoline and oil, transportation, and many other types of bills can be charged on presentation of the card. Balances must be settled monthly or arrangements can be made to pay installments and interest on the unpaid amounts. Again, cards can be lost or stolen. On notification of such loss to the issuing company, amounts subsequently dishonestly charged need not be paid by the customer. Unfortunately, extensive fraudulent use can take place prior to notification of loss. Federal law and some state laws now limit the liability of holders of lost or stolen credit cards to fifty dollars.

Vaults safeguard the bank's cash, records, notes, securities, etc. They also contain *safe-deposit boxes* where customers may place their valuables for safekeeping.

Savings Banks. Most commercial banks have savings departments. However, there are some banks that restrict their activities to accepting deposits and lending money. Excess funds over personal loans and cash reserves are invested in real estate mortgages, government bonds, and certain industrial stocks and bonds. The bank's gross profit is income from investments and loans minus interest paid to depositors.

Most savings banks are *stock companies*, that is, they are incorporated and are owned by the stockholders. A lesser number are *mutual savings banks*, owned by the depositors.

Savings and Loan Associations. *Savings and loan associations*, or *building and loan associations* as they are called in some parts of the country, accept deposits and lend money to persons who wish to build homes. Loans may also be made to those constructing business buildings and apartment houses. First mortgages or first trust deeds are required as security for the loans. Federally chartered savings and loan associations must use the word "federal" in their titles and must insure their depositors up to $40,000 with the Federal Savings and Loan Insurance Corporation. State chartered associations may carry such insurance, also.

Insurance Companies. Business concerns and individuals can protect themselves from a great variety of hazards through the services of *insurance companies*. *Policies* are issued by such companies, describing in detail the hazards covered and the payments to be made should loss occur. In return, payments called *premiums* are made periodically by the insured. Accumulations of cash are invested in a variety of ways, including personal loans and mortgages on real property.

Business Finance Companies. Business concerns operating in high risk areas often find it difficult to obtain bank credit. However, *business finance companies* accept such risks and make loans where banks do not. To cover costs of increased losses they charge higher rates of interest. *Factors* receive goods from producers on consignment and sell them to customers. They also perform important finance functions by purchasing the accounts receivable[1] of operating companies. Factors usually

---

1. Most accountants, particularly those working for large companies, believe that the term "accounts receivable" is too inclusive. Although it

specialize in one type of industry and often assist in financing every stage, of production from raw materials, through processing, to the finished products.

Investment Banks. *Investment banks* buy and sell securities. A business concern seeking long-term financing can obtain assistance through these institutions which, if conditions are right, will purchase and dispose of an entire issue of stocks or bonds. This process is known as *underwriting*. If the amount of money involved is excessive, the underwriter will organize a *purchasing syndicate* comprising a number of other investment banks who will share the burden of buying the issue. On the other hand, the underwriter may purchase the entire issue, but form a *selling syndicate* for the purpose of selling the securities to the public. Profits accrue when the securities are sold for more than they cost.

Investment banks that restrict their business to mortgages instead of stocks and bonds are known as *mortgage companies*. Such concerns must keep in touch with institutions and individuals with money to invest and with those who will need to borrow money. The two are brought together and the details of preparing mortgages and collecting payments are handled by the mortgage companies. They charge the borrower a fee which usually is a percentage of the amounts involved.

Commercial-Paper Houses. *Commercial-paper houses* buy and sell short-term unsecured promissory notes issued by business concerns they consider to be safe. Most purchasers of such *commercial paper* are banks which must keep their surplus funds in liquid condition. Purchasers must make their own credit investigations, as commercial-paper houses do not guarantee the notes they handle. As a rule, purchasers have a week or so to return notes they consider unsafe.

Trust Companies. Most commercial banks are also *trust companies*. The trust function involves control of property by a person or institution on behalf of another. The person or institution assuming this relationship acts in a *fiduciary capacity*. A

---

is widely used, there is a tendency toward qualifying it thus: purchases accounts receivable, accounts receivable merchandise, land, buildings, cattle, etc. Some accountants advocate the substitution of an entirely different term such as customers' accounts or trade debtors.

wealthy person frequently puts money in trust for members of his family. Such a person is known as a *trustor*. The manager of the fund is the *trustee* and the members of the family are *beneficiaries*.

There are two general types of trusts: personal and corporate. *Personal trusts*, or *individual trusts* as they sometimes are called, are divided into *court trusts*, where the trustee is accountable to a court, and *private trusts*, which are set up voluntarily between a trustor and a trustee. If a person sets up a trust in his will, it is a *testamentary trust*, but if the trust is set up by a person prior to his death, it is a *living trust*.

Corporate trusts act in a wide variety of ways. If, for instance, a company desired to sell bonds for needed long-term capital, they would approach an investment company which would arrange with a trust company to safeguard the interests of the purchasers of the bonds when issued. The trust company performs, also, a registry service, both for bonds and for stocks, keeping up-to-date lists of holders.

It is common practice for individuals as well as companies to place real estate and other types of property *in escrow* while arrangements are being made to transfer title to it. Bills of sale, deeds, insurance policies, and so on, are turned over to a trustee by the seller while the buyer gives the trustee cash, notes, mortgages, and whatever else is required. These are held until all arrangements for the exchange of property have been completed, after which the trustee gives the cash, etc., to the seller and evidences of title to the buyer.

Government Institutions. The role of government in regulating and assisting business is considered in Chapter 26. Two examples of *government facilitative agencies* are described briefly at this point.

The *Federal Reserve System* was set up in 1913 to facilitate the expansion and contraction of currency (including credit), to provide a source from which banks could borrow, and to make government supervision of banks more effective. The country was divided into twelve Federal Reserve districts and a Federal Reserve bank was located in each. A Board of Governors of seven persons is appointed by the President of the United States to head up the system. The Board can take action independently. Each Federal Reserve bank is managed by a board of nine directors who are elected by the banks in the district. National banks must belong to the system; state banks may.

The Federal Reserve banks perform banking services for their member banks, i.e., they receive deposits, lend them money, and clear checks for them. They also perform services for the federal government, such as issuing paper money and buying and selling government bonds.

The *Securities and Exchange Commission*'s services to business concerns and to the public pertain chiefly to its regulatory activities. The commission was set up in 1934 and was a direct outgrowth of the state "blue-sky" laws, the first of which was enacted in 1911 in Kansas, to prevent dishonest security salesmen from "selling stock in patches of blue sky," as one legislator put it. The SEC attempts to prevent the issuance and trading of fraudulent securities.

Credit Unions. Groups of persons in labor unions, business companies, churches, and so on, frequently organize *credit unions*, which operate somewhat as small banks and which are regulated under state and federal law. Members buy shares on which dividends are paid. Surplus funds are, in turn, loaned to members who wish to borrow, on approval of a loan committee. The interest rate on loans varies, but usually it is not less than 1% per month on the unpaid balance. Some states, however, impose ceiling rates as low as 10% on personal loans.

Loan Companies. Some *loan companies* assist dealers in expensive items, such as automobiles and electrical appliances, in moving their products into the hands of consumers. This usually is done by buying customers' installment contracts and by collecting payments. Other loan companies make loans directly to individuals. They make character loans with no security, or they may take wage or salary assignments or chattel mortgages as security. They may, also, require borrowers' promissory notes to be cosigned.

Brokerage Companies. As stated previously, *brokers* bring buyers and sellers together and assist them in transferring title to property. They do not themselves take title to the property, but obtain their remuneration by charging the buyer or seller, or both, a fee.

At this point, we are interested in stock, bond, and commodity brokerage companies. These companies serve business concerns in a variety of ways. They have representatives on the floors of the major *stock exchanges* who are in a position to buy or sell *listed stocks*, that is, stocks cleared by each exchange for trading. The bonds of companies with listed stocks are also traded on the exchanges. Brokerage houses are in a position, as well, to buy and sell unlisted stocks, in the *over-the-counter market*, for their customers.

Many brokerage houses also have representatives on the floors of the various *commodity exchanges* and can buy and sell contracts for future delivery of such commodities as grain, cocoa, cotton, potatoes, and so on.

Stock brokerage concerns are in a position to lend money to customers who wish to buy securities. These customers open *margin accounts*, margin being the percent of each purchase the customer must furnish. This percent, which is set by the Federal Reserve Board, varies widely over time depending on business conditions. The interest charged by brokerage concerns on unpaid balances also varies widely. At this writing, the margin that must be furnished by customers is 50% and the rate of interest on money borrowed is about 8 3/4%.

Fees per share charged by stock brokers are less for *round lots* (one hundred shares or multiples thereof) than for *odd lots* (less than one hundred shares).

Individuals who exchange their money for stocks do so in the expectation of receiving financial benefits. Those who buy and hold for relatively long periods of time are *investors*. Although they may hope to sell eventually for more than they paid, their primary aim usually is to receive dividends. *Speculators* buy and sell stocks over relatively short time periods in the expectation of making money from price changes. If they buy first for the purpose of selling at a higher price, they are known in Wall Street parlance as *bulls*. If they borrow stocks they do not own (through their brokers) and sell them in the expectation that the market will go down and they can buy them back later at a lower price, they are *bears*. If they make no effort to evaluate the stocks they buy and sell but make their choices at random, they are considered by some to be *gamblers*. Of course these terms and procedures apply as well to other media such as bonds, commodities, real estate, and so on.

When a growing company issues additional stock, present stockholders are given *rights* to buy additional stock at prices below the market. Stockholders may exercise the rights by buying the stock or they may sell the rights through their brokers. As a rule, rights expire after a few weeks or months. If the company desires to extend the life of its rights to five, ten, or twenty years, or indefinitely, their terms, such as number to be exchanged, exchange price, and time limit, are set forth on a certificate called a *warrant*. Sometimes warrants are offered, also, as an inducement to purchase a new issue of bonds. Warrants are leveraged securities in that they tend to rise in value faster than the stock for which they may be exchanged. They usually also fall faster when the stock goes down. Warrants are traded on the American Stock Exchange, over the counter, and to a lesser degree elsewhere.

Puts and *calls*, also called *options*, are traded on the Chicago Board Options Exchange and two other exchanges. A put is an option to sell and a call is an option to buy 100 shares of a given stock at a predetermined price within a definite period of time.

Brokerage firms have research departments that study markets and give their clients the results. They have *board rooms* where up-to-the-minute stock and commodity prices are shown, teletyped news and quotations are received, and records are kept.

Security Exchanges. The largest of the *security exchanges* is the New York Stock Exchange. The American Stock Exchange is also located in New York. There are other similar exchanges located in the larger cities around the country. All of them are organized markets where buyers and sellers of stocks and bonds operate.

Only members can trade on the floor of an exchange. Most members are partners or officers of brokerage companies. Orders to buy or sell are received by teletypewriter from branch brokerage offices and are relayed to the proper member. This person goes to the *trading post* where the given stock, bond, or warrant is traded and there he contacts the specialist who handles it and the exchange is concluded according to instructions of the clients concerned. The essentials of the trade go out to all brokerage officers via the *ticker system* and are displayed to the investing and speculating public. This information is shown on financial pages of newspapers that evening and the following morning. A few such ticker tape and newspaper quotations with explanations are shown as follows:

On the ticker tape, stocks are identified by letters. It shows each transaction immediately after it is concluded.

X 2s 36-3/8 means that 200 shares of United States Steel Corporation stock were exchanged at 36-3/8 dollars per share.

DD 184 means that 100 shares of du Pont changed hands at 184 dollars. No figure in front of the quotation indicates 100 shares.

FIR 1100s 21-1/2 means that 1,100 shares of Firestone Tire & Rubber changed hands at $21.50 per share. The number of shares is shown in full when it is 1,000 or more.

Newspapers show daily or weekly summaries of all transactions.

52-3/8 25-1/2 Dome Petrl 36 449 45 42 44-1/2 +2-3/8 means that during the present calendar year to date Dome Petroleum stock sold at prices from a high of 52-3/8 dollars per share to 25-1/2 dollars; that the present price-earnings ratio is 36; that 449,000 shares were sold during the day (or week if it is a weekly summary); that the highest price for the day was $45, the lowest was $42, and the last (or closing) price was $44.50; and that this closing price was 2-3/8 dollars higher than the closing price yesterday (or a week ago for weekly summaries).

Some newspapers quote bond transactions. Bonds are sold as a rule in thousand-dollar denominations and are quoted in hundreds. For instance,

Ford 8-1/8 90 7.8 24 104 103-7/8 104 +3/8 means that Ford 8-1/8% bonds maturing in 1990, now paying holders 7.8% based on present market price, sold 24 one-thousand-dollar units on the day (or week) in question, with a trading range of $1,040.00 high to $1,038.75 low, and closing at $1,040.00, up $3.75 per bond from the previous report.

Commodity Exchanges. Each *commodity exchange* deals in

one or more specific commodities. The Chicago Board of Trade, and others, handle grain contracts; the New York Cotton Exchange handles cotton, wool, and frozen orange juice; the New York Cocoa Exchange handles cocoa; and so on. Standard quality specifications are established on which trading is based and actual departures from these standards, as determined by official inspectors, result in price modifications.

There are two types of commodity markets: spot and futures. Those who buy in *spot markets* pay cash and receive the product. Those who buy in *futures markets* deposit with the broker about 10% of the value of the product and receive a contract calling for delivery of the product at a specified future time. No interest is charged on the balance. Only about 1% to 2% of all commodity speculators anticipate taking delivery. The others buy contracts in the hope that prices will rise in the near future and with the expectation of selling the contracts for a profit before the date of delivery. Those who buy are in a *long position*. Those who reverse the procedure are in a *short position*.

A speculator who believes that the prices of a commodity will fall may sell it short. This simply means that he sells through his broker an agreement to furnish a given quantity of the commodity at a given future date. The seller's broker's representative on the floor of the exchange then makes a deal with the buyer's broker's representative. If the seller sells short *at the market* he is bound to accept the price arranged by the two representatives. He may, however, place a *limit order* specifying the price at which he will sell short. Later, but before the delivery date, the speculator may decide to buy back, or *cover*, his contract. If market prices have declined meanwhile, he can buy for less than he paid and thus make a profit. If the market went up he will lose the difference. If he does not cover his contract it will be necessary for him to fulfill it by purchasing the commodity in the spot market through his broker and delivering it to the person or company that bought his contract.

Seats on the exchanges are limited and must be bought from retiring members with the consent of the exchange membership.

Individuals or companies desiring to buy and sell commodity futures and commodities must deal in *contracts*, or *round lots*. Some of these are, for example, 5,000 bushels of grain, 100 tons of soybean meal, 15,000 dozen eggs, 50 tons of sugar, and so on.

Commodity brokers deal through their representatives on the floor, much as do stock brokers. Each commodity is traded in a different *pit* or *ring*, where the members with orders to execute shout the details of each order and use hand signals to indicate the prices at which they will trade.

QUESTIONS FOR DISCUSSION

1. With respect to a check, what do the legal terms drawee, drawer, and payee mean?
2. If your credit card is lost without your knowledge and $1,000 worth of goods and services are dishonestly charged by the finder, what must you pay? $1,000? $50? Nothing?
3. What functions are performed by factors?
4. Distinguish between testamentary trusts and living trusts. For what general purposes are they set up?
5. What services are performed by the Federal Reserve banks?
6. What services do stock brokerage companies perform?
7. Distinguish between investing and speculating.
8. A quote from the *Wall Street Journal* is as follows:
   33-1/2 12 Wang Labs 22 110 25-1/2 23-1/4 23-1/4 −2-5/8
   Explain what each figure means.
9. What is meant when a wheat futures speculator says he
   a. Is in a long position?
   b. Is in a short position?
   c. Has covered?
10. What is the difference between a commodity spot transaction and a commodity futures transaction?

SELECTED REFERENCES

Bogen, Jules I., and S. S. Shipman, eds., *Financial Handbook*, 4th ed., Ronald Press Co., New York, 1968, Sections 1, 2, 4, 5, 6, 9, and 10.

Dougall, Herbert E., *Capital Markets and Institutions*, 2nd ed., Prentice-Hall, Englewood Cliffs, N. J., 1970.

Eiteman, D. K., C. A. Dice, and W. J. Eitman, *The Stock Market*, 4th ed., McGraw-Hill, New York, 1966.

Robinson, Roland I., and Dwayne Wrightsman, *Financial Markets*, McGraw-Hill, New York, 1974.

PART III

MANAGERIAL ORGANIZATION

Business management operates within an organization. The first chapter of Part III covers standard organizational structures. Then business administration and management are considered, followed by business information, accounting, and statistics.

CHAPTER 8

THE ORGANIZATIONAL STRUCTURE

When a business operated by a single individual adds an employee, the need arises for having an understanding concerning the division of duties and responsibilities. The new employee takes over certain areas of the business, and authority for accomplishing results is delegated to him, though final responsibility for such accomplishment is retained by the proprietor. If the new employee becomes a partner in the business, and hence a part owner, it still becomes necessary to apportion areas of authority. Generally, one of the owners dominates the other and becomes, tacitly or formally, the senior partner to whom the other partner renders accountability. In the absence of such arrangements the two individuals would constantly work at cross purposes, sometimes duplicating each other's efforts and sometimes leaving essential duties undone.

The Essential Nature of Organization. Presumably each member of a small business enterprise knows what every other member is doing. One individual sees a duty and performs it, while the others observe and avoid repeating it. That such effective communication does not always exist, even in the small unit, is suggested by the story of the man with the long sleeves. He stated at the breakfast table that the shirt on the chair in his room should have the sleeves shortened one inch. Mother, wife, and daughter, each thinking one of the others would do the job, did nothing about it. The next morning the man repeated his request and during the day mother, wife, and daughter, each without the knowledge of the others, shortened the sleeves one inch.

If organization is desirable in the small enterprise it becomes indispensable in the large concern. Organization in the small business tends to promote efficiency, but it is hard to see how the large business could accomplish anything without proper organization. Through organization the manager changes a mob into an orderly corps which is capable of building a bridge, erecting a skyscraper, producing an automobile, winning a battle, or ruling a country. Management, through organization, is able to accomplish far more than could be accomplished by all members of the group working as individuals.

Organization vs. System and Procedure. Although some authorities think of an organization as being both a structure which defines relationships and a process of accomplishing the aims of an enterprise, it seems more useful to restrict the term to the former concept. Nevertheless, the two are closely related and each affects the other. A realistic organization cannot be evolved without having in mind the system and procedures to be employed. Nor can a system be imposed without taking into account the organizational structure. If the nature of the business is such as to require certain types of systems and procedures, it might be that the organization must be changed so as to conform. On the other hand, if certain overriding considerations initially dictate a change in organizational structure it may well be that changes in systems, procedures, and ways of performing duties will be forced.

An organization, to be effective, must be tailor-made for each business enterprise. This is not to deny, however, that there are principles of organization common to all concerns.

PRINCIPLES OF ORGANIZATION

An organization is effective in so far as it embodies the following essentials:

Type of Business as a Factor. Emphasis should be placed upon the needs of the business. The needs of a sales organization differ from those of a transportation company. A manufacturing company has specialized needs differing widely from those of a bank.

There is no standard number of subordinates a supervisor should have. One individual can supervise many people if they do similar work, perform simple operations, and work in a spatially compact unit. It may be harder to supervise a punch-press operator, a tin slitter, a janitor, a baler, a die maker, a cost clerk, a machinist, and a maintenance man than to supervise twenty-five punch-press operators. It may be harder to supervise five tool and die makers doing the same kind of work than twenty-five drill-press operators likewise doing uniformly similar work. And it may be harder to supervise five truck drivers operating over as many states than one hundred ditch diggers or cotton pickers working within an area of four or five acres.

The number of persons one individual can supervise is known as his *span of control.* In addition to conditions peculiar to the industry, spans of control are affected by instruments of communication (telephones and the like), means of transportation (a foreman on horseback or in a jeep can supervise more field hands or road construction men than can one on foot), the content of the supervisory job (specialized production control and dispatching departments, separate inspection, and such staff activities as selecting, hiring, placing, training, counseling, etc., all have the effect of increasing a supervisor's span of control), the state of morale in the department (willing, cooperative workers are easier to supervise), and labor turnover (a stable labor force requires less "breaking in" of new workers). And on the other side of the picture, of course, it is obvious that spans of control must be changed to conform with the varying capacities of those individuals exercising the supervisory function.

Definition of Duties. Every position in the organization should be described so that each incumbent knows exactly what duties he is to perform and where the boundaries of his activities are.

Delegation of Authority. This principle often is violated by making an individual responsible for accomplishing certain matters and at the same time failing to provide for him proper facilities or failing to place certain personnel under his jurisdiction. Examples would include the foreman who is made responsible for keeping machinery in his department in good running order but who has no authority over maintenance men who work in a separate department, the man who is made responsible for answering all correspondence the same day but who has no authority over stenographers who work in a typing pool, and the time-study analyst who is made responsible for obtaining accurate performance standards but who has no authority over the workmen who perform the operations. If it is not advisable to delegate authority to an individual to get specific work done it is not advisable to make him responsible for its accomplishment. As important as personal charm is, a business should not force anyone to rely upon it in order to carry out his duties. In this connection the proper place for personal charm is in exercising existing authority.

Adequate Control. Control is exercised by comparing performance with a standard, and by correcting excessive deviations. Provision should be made in tables of organization for personnel to establish standards, to inspect the results of performance, to make reports, and to follow up orders correcting deviations. The large organization is controlled through a hierarchy of management. The span of control of the person in charge of the concern may not be extensive enough to enable him to supervise all the foremen, in which situation a number of superintendents are used. As a rule, the work of the superintendents is controlled by a general manager, while the president confines himself to overseeing the general manager, the sales manager, the controller, and other major officials.

Coordination of Effort. There is a tendency for the employees of a large concern to pursue the interests of their own departments, often at the expense of the whole enterprise. Generally such apparent selfishness is the result of inadequate communication. A production manager builds up his labor force, orders additional equipment, and otherwise expands his activities, not knowing that the products of his plant are piling up on the shelves of retailers, unsold. A methods engineer incurs considerable expense making a new departmental layout, not knowing that a new design of the product has already rendered the department obsolete. A treasurer denies funds for a new development, not realizing that by so doing he is crippling the enterprise in its struggle for new markets.

As business enterprises increase in size the need for complete distribution of information and painstaking coordination of activities becomes increasingly acute. Customarily, and in the nature of things, policies are determined by top managers and are executed by middle managers and first-line foremen. Such policies, however, are often evolved from incomplete or false information. Orders are easily transmitted along from president to manager to superintendent to foreman, but information is not so easily passed back from foreman to president. A good organization provides sure means of tapping vital information among the rank and file of employees. It reaches out into the market, delves into the company's own records, draws on the experience of others, and engages in original research. Such activities are performed by staff and research branches of the organization, and the results of the work of such departments shoud be discussed thoroughly by policy-making groups, and not be examined passively by a middle manager who, not comprehending the significance of the reports, files them away "for future reference."

Traditionally, great emphasis has been placed upon vertical relationships; that is, the flow of authority from president down through the levels of management to the workers. Increasing importance is now being placed, however, upon horizontal contacts. Foremen are periodically brought together to explain and ask questions; standing committees are set up among representatives of designing and production, sales and credit, engineering and purchasing, efficiency and safety, etc. Temporary committees are set up among production, medical, safety, purchasing, and finance to investigate and report on special health hazards; or among production, designing, sales, finance, motion economy, and engineering for investigating and recommending the use of a new machine, material, or process. Such committees greatly ease the pressure placed upon the line officers of the concern and reduce considerably the misunderstandings and resentments which arise so easily in the large enterprise.

Flexibility of Organization. No organization per se is flexible or inflexible, but some types often lend themselves to change more readily than others. The quality of flexibility actually is more an attitude of management toward the organization than it is an inherent feature of the structure. The high degree of specialization in American business dictates functional forms of organization. Consequently, in practice, an engineer is chosen to head an engineering department, a person with credit experience is chosen to head the credit department, and so on. The requirements of the job, as described in the tables of organization, dictate the qualifications of each incumbent. This is not to say, however, that the organization should never be modified to take into account the peculiar strengths and weaknesses, or likes and dislikes, of individual members of the concern. Safety might be placed under engineering because of the need to construct guards, special ventilation equipment, etc. The safety engineer might not be interested in the psychological aspects of the problem; consequently the personnel department would be forced, more and more, to take a hand. A flexible organization results from a recognition of realities by management. In the situation described, safety would be shifted to the jurisdiction of the personnel manager. Later developments might dictate a further shift of safety into the medical department, or a well-qualified industrial psychologist might become available who will handle safety to advantage as a separate major department. Such changes in the tables of organization are almost forced upon a firm by the loss of a manager with talents which cannot easily be found in another. Too, a person with unusual ability may gradually assume control over areas adjoining his original jurisdiction.

Tables of organization often must be changed when new processes dictate the addition of new departments and the discontinuance of old ones, when new products are added and old ones dropped, when new media of advertising are used and old ones no longer are employed, and when other fundamental changes are made. Regressive personalities have no place in well-managed enterprises. Although stability is exceedingly important, it is transcended in the organizational structure by ordered change.

Recognition of Basic Human Drives. An organization which gives scope to the basic drives of all its personnel is much more effective as a producing force than one which tends to cater to the major executives at the expense of an aggregation of thwarted and frustrated employees. Provision in the tables of organization for numerous committees provides opportunity to many employees to realize a sense of active participation in management. Curiosity is satisfied, and recognition is provided.

Desire for status and the drive to progress are satisfied more fully in an organization with many titles and specialized positions at the rank-and-file level, and with many stages or echelons from laborer to president. When clear lines of promotion are marked out, the organizational structure becomes at once the incarnation of realized ambition and a symbol and challenge for the future.

GENERAL TYPES OF ORGANIZATION

Although every organization differs in some respect from all others, each can be placed in one of three general classes: (1) line, or military, (2) functional, or plural, and (3) line-and-staff.

Line, or Military. In this type of organizational structure the lines of authority ramify at each supervisory level from president to rank-and-file worker. Every person in the organization, except the rank-and-file workers, has one or more subordinates

Line, or military, type of organization.

to supervise; no person in the organization has more than one supervisor; the top official has none.

This type of organization is effective for small concerns and generally is used by them. It requires considerable all-round ability from the supervisors, for there is no provision for the help of specialized assistants other than rank-and-file workers. In other words, what specialization exists is of the departmental type. One department may make patterns, the next may make castings, the next may machine the castings, and the last may assemble parts to the castings. Each department specializes, yet the firm can be organized in the line form. Under this form there are no research or staff departments such as personnel, accounting, time study, etc. Such activities are performed, in addition to his other duties, by each foreman.

In some quarters this form of organization is known as the *military* type. This term is misleading, for no military organization now follows this plan from private up to general, although the Roman army and other ancient military forces were organized along these lines.

Functional, or Plural. The indisputable advantages to business of division of labor were responsible for the development of the so-called *functional* plan of organization. This plan, publicized by Frederick W. Taylor in the 1880s, extended specialization into the ranks of supervision. Taylor divided the foreman's job, for instance, into eight parts, four planning and four performance, and gave each part to a different man. The supervisory functions of all eight foremen then were exercised in common over all rank-and-file workmen, with each foreman restricting his activities to his own speciality. The advantages of this form lie in the increased efficiency resulting from changing eight all-round foremen into eight specialists. The obvious benefits of specialization, however, were canceled out by giving all eight (or whatever the number may be in a given situation) foremen equal authority over the same subordinates. More than the usual number of disputes tend to arise under such conditions, and workmen become confused and resentful when they receive orders from more than one supervisor. The plan was never very widely used, but it is important as a transitional form that pro-

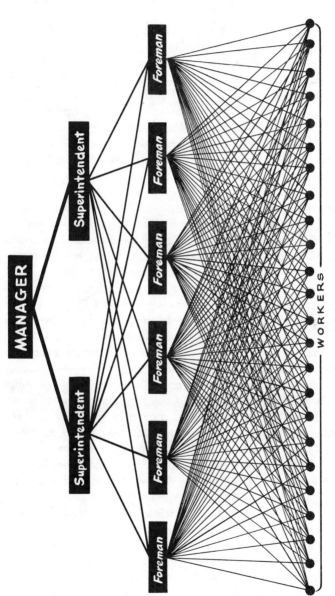

Functional, or plural, type of organization.

vided an impetus toward the more practicable line-and-staff form.

The name by which this plan generally is identified was an unfortunate choice, for nearly all business concerns, regardless of how they are organized, operate along functional lines. If plants, departments, or employees are segregated on the basis of nature of work or nature of service, the concern is functionally organized even though the formal type of organization might be the line or line-and-staff type. The distinguishing feature of the type of organization under consideration is the multiplicity of supervisors to which each worker must answer. Therefore, it would seem to be less confusing to denominate this the *plural* type of organization.

Line-and-Staff. The form of organization most widely used in business (as well as in modern military forces) is known as *line-and-staff*. It uses the good points of the line form and the plural form, and avoids their disadvantages. As in the line form, authority is delegated from president to manager to superintendent to foreman; and, as in the plural form, specialization is provided in all echelons. This form, however, provides that of all the specialists in a given department, one shall stand above the others and he shall be the sole individual to whom his subordinates shall report. Instead of a department having eight foremen it has one foreman and seven staff officers.

The *line-and-staff* form of organization merges imperceptibly into the line form as the size of the firm diminishes. It is not particularly difficult in practice, however, to distinguish so-called production departments from staff departments. A manufacturing organization generally is made up of supervisory and nonsupervisory personnel. The supervisors head either line departments or staff departments. Those who head line departments engage in "productive" work (fabrication, processing, assembly) or "service" work (maintenance, transporting, die-making and setting). Those who head staff departments engage in "research" (time and motion study, statistics, development) or "service" (sales, credit, accounting). The feature in this plan of organization which makes it workable in practice, however, is that no matter whether a given employee works in a produc-

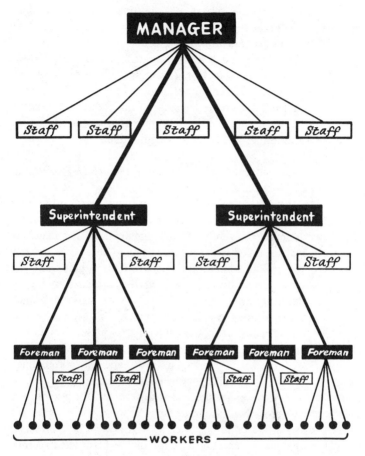

Line-and-staff form of organization.

tion, service, staff, or research department, he never takes orders from or reports to more than one supervisor.

MODIFICATIONS OF STANDARD FORMS

There are many modifications and combinations of the three basic forms of business organization. These are found particularly in the larger business, governmental, and military organizations. Perhaps the two most prevalent variants involve the use of committees and the separation of "line" and "functional" authority. There is little reason for considering a committee form of business organization as a fourth basic type, for it is difficult to conceive of such a form apart from one of the three types previously discussed. But if committees are used as permanent coordinative or functional devices, it may well be that a modification has been created which partakes of the characteristics of a distinct type. Such a modification would be called "line-and-committee," "plural-and-committee," or "line-staff-and-committee."

The two most common uses of committees are (1) coordinative and (2) functional. Although each executive is supposed to coordinate the activities of all departments and individuals under his direction, this task grows in magnitude as the executive ascends in the hierarchy of management. If, for instance, the parts for one product are manufactured in several widely separated plants, the difficulties of coordinating their activities may dictate the formation of a *coordinative committee* made up of middle-management representatives of the various branch plants. The constituting of such committees merely recognizes formally the informal arrangements always made by subordinate officials in response to the pressure of necessity. When informal coordinative arrangements are made they often have the effect of "short-circuiting" the coordinating officer. If two employees wish to make special arrangements for facilitating the functioning of their areas of jurisdiction this is right and proper. But matters of importance should always be passed up to such employees' common superior in the form of a memorandum so he can nullify the new arrangements if they interfere or conflict with company policy. Thus when coordinative committees are constituted, some provision must be made to keep all interested executives apprised of such committees' activities.

The *functional committee* performs one or more of the recognized functions of a business; that is, a committee might replace the purchasing agent, the hiring official, the treasurer, the credit manager, or the industrial engineer. Such committees not only are advisory, they wield genuine power. The president of a corporation puts no policies into effect which are opposed by a substantial portion of the executive committee. Likewise, there must be substantial agreement in the finance committee before action is taken by the treasurer. Educational institutions often are governed by committees: a board of trustees or regents at the top, a committee on committees, a policy committee, a budget committee, a promotion committee, and countless other committees. The use of committees in an organization tends to introduce checks and balances. Their use is time-consuming, but it makes for conservatism and caution.

QUESTIONS FOR DISCUSSION

1. Why is it essential for a business concern, no matter how small, to organize and assign duties to each member?
2. What are the seven principles of organization?
3. What factors influence a supervisor's span of control?
4. In what ways are horizontal organizational contacts of value to a firm?
5. Why is it ever necessary to change an organization once it has been built? Wouldn't change be disruptive and harmful?
6. Describe the line form of organization.
7. The functional form of organization was designed to take advantage of specialization. Why did it fail in practice?
8. Describe the line-and-staff form of organization and state its advantages over the other two forms previously described.
9. In what situations are coordinative committees of value?
10. What are the advantages and disadvantages in the use of functional committees?

SELECTED REFERENCES

Gibson, James L., John M. Ivancevich, and James H. Donnelly, Jr., *Organizations*, Business Publications, Dallas, 1973.

Hall, Richard H., *Organizations: Structure and Process*, Prentice-Hall, Englewood Cliffs, N. J., 1972.

Hicks, Herbert G., *The Management of Organizations*, 2nd ed., McGraw-Hill, New York, 1972.

Hutchinson, John G., *Organizations: Theory and Classical Concepts*, Holt, Rinehart and Winston, New York, 1967.

Koontz, Harold, and Cyril J. O'Donnell, *Essentials of Management*, McGraw-Hill, New York, 1974.

Likert, Rensis, *The Human Organization*, McGraw-Hill, New York, 1967.

Litterer, J. A., *Organizations*, 2nd ed., Vols. 1 and 2, John Wiley & Sons, New York, 1969.

Lorsch, Jay W., and Paul R. Lawrence, *Organization Planning*, Richard D. Irwin, Homewood, Ill., 1972.

Mott, P. E., *The Characteristics of Effective Organizations*, Harper & Row, New York, 1972.

O'Connell, J. J., *Managing Organizational Innovation*, Richard D. Irwin, Homewood, Ill., 1968.

Seashore, S. E., and D. G. Bowers, *Changing the Structure and Functioning of an Organization*, University of Michigan Survey Research Center, Ann Arbor, 1963.

CHAPTER 9

BUSINESS ADMINISTRATION AND MANAGEMENT

Individuals become owners of businesses in the hope that they may make profits. Money is risked in business concerns, which partially justifies the payment of interest and dividends. *Owners* often do not actively engage in establishing or furthering the aims of their businesses. Corporate *stockholders* designate directors to represent them. *Directors* concern themselves chiefly with goals and broad policies. *Top*, or *administrative*, *managers* translate these broad policies into plans for action. *Middle*, or *operating*, *managers* carry out the plans with the assistance of *foremen*, or *first-line supervisors*.

In general, these are the grades and functions in business organizations though the lines of demarcation are not strictly drawn.

Decision Making. Much of the work of managers at all levels involves *making decisions and acting on them*. Every manager must assume responsibility for his own decisions and for the decisions of his subordinates. Unfortunately, most business decisions must be made on the basis of incomplete information. Even though complete information could be obtained, it usually does not pay to take the time and spend the money. Consequently, many mistakes are made in the course of a year. However, the aim of management is to make as many right decisions as possible and not waste time in recriminations when things go wrong.

It would be foolish and wasteful to make repeated decisions in routine matters. Therefore, when it is determined that the same set of circumstances is going to be repeated in the future and to establish a routine pattern of response, a *system* is established. Systems can be simple or highly complex. A departmental work schedule (8:00 to 12:00 and 1:00 to 5:00) is an example of a simple system. The firm's entire organization and the sum-total of its activities is an example of a complex system.

Since much of the work of managers can be reduced to routine standard form and delegated to subordinates, system becomes an important tool of management. Action is induced down through an organization by orders which not only state what is wanted but also act as a release of authority. Fortunately, however, it is not necessary for managers to issue orders for every act performed by their subordinates. When administration converts the aims of ownership into workable plans, management initiates system. A system is a detailed standing order based upon such plans. It foresees certain events and indicates the sequence of acts which shall follow. The existence of system carries with it the authority and responsibility for performing this sequence of acts every time the initiating events occur. Novel situations must be handled by the manager through the use of special orders, after which a new system is created or the old system is modified, if there is assurance that such novel situations will be repeated in the future.

Functions of Management. The functions of management generally are recognized as being organizing, staffing, directing, controlling, and budgeting.

ORGANIZING. The first of the four functions of management, *organizing*, was discussed in the preceding chapter. The products and services to be furnished are listed in detail, the specific duties are described under the proper production and service departments, and lines of authority are drawn.

STAFFING. After the organization has been set up on paper and when the business is ready to commence operations, *staffing* must be undertaken. The details of recruiting, interviewing, placing, and transferring are covered in Chapter 15.

DIRECTING. After operations get under way an important function of management is *directing*. The middle managers tell their subordinates what is to be done and how it is to be accomplished and the first-line supervisors (foremen) see that the workers do it.

Directing is done by training subordinates, by delegating authority, by giving written or verbal orders, and by following up and making corrections where necessary.

The owners of property have the right to use it in any way they wish consistent with law and the rights of others. Among other rights, owners can delegate to others the authority to use their property and give them the right to further delegate authority.

CONTROLLING. Any executive, supervisor, workman, or clerk to whom has been delegated the authority to accomplish certain tasks must assume the responsibility for getting results. He is held accountable to his superior officer. A common error made by managers and supervisors is to tell subordinates that they are being held responsible for results which cannot be accomplished satisfactorily without delegation of corresponding authority. When a manager exercises *control* he observes some act at first hand or by means of a report or a chart; he compares the act with a standard; and if there is significant deviation he issues an order with the purpose of minimizing future similar deviations. Control also involves the establishment, review, and modification of standards as well as the construction, appraisal, and change of organizational structures, personnel relationships, systems, and all other pertinent factors.

Systems must be made to work; the mere existence of system is not enough. Every employee who works within a system must understand it thoroughly and must appreciate the importance of the part he plays. In the absence of such knowledge employees often tend to short-circuit the system by failing to make out forms or by cutting red tape in other ways. If employees are required to follow the system to the letter the manager has the reciprocal obligation to keep the system in line with actual need. Oversystematization and perfectionism should be avoided. The perfect system probably never existed, so only adequacy should be the aim.

Planning for control involves providing for observers, checkers, or inspectors. Workmen may do this work themselves, or foremen may do it. Reports usually must be made, and the results shown on these reports must be compared with a standard. The standard may be imposed by a customer or it may be determined by a staff expert. The comparison may be made directly (as when dimensions are checked by an inspector) or they may be made indirectly (as when a clerk compares actual production with planned production).

It is not enough to establish a system which provides for the gathering of data and the comparing of results with standards. Certain designated managers must make decisions and issue orders when necessary. In the absence of conscious decision making there can be no control. The managerial task of control is not mechanical. It requires reasoning ability and the exercise of mature judgment. Above all, it requires a conscientiousness which urges the investigation of every doubtful and suspicious circumstance. The good manager does not file his report away "for future reference." Neither does he overcontrol. He determines from statistical procedures or from experience the limits of reliability of the processes under his jurisdiction. When performance falls outside these limits he determines the reason and takes steps to prevent a repetition. If the system is at fault, or if it is too costly, he does not hesitate to order changes in its structure.

Control is exercised in two types of organizations: centralized and decentralized. *Centralized* organizations require that most decisions be made by the top operating manager and his staff. Subordinate managers and supervisors are allowed little opportunity to exercise independent judgment. *Decentralized* organizations permit all subordinate managers and supervisors to "run their own show." There is less follow-up, and more responsibility is assumed by those in charge of departments. For this type of organization more responsibility must be assumed by all subordinates and a higher type of supervisors and employees is required. Each manager and supervisor is judged by results.

Control is improved by encouraging coordination among working groups. This requires training as well as the use of mechanical communicating devices. The good of the company must constantly be stressed, sometimes at the temporary expense of the department or even the individual. Secretive, uncommunicative, and uncooperative employees, supervisors, and managers must be made to see the error of their ways or be cleared out if coordination is to work.

BUDGETING. Financial control is accomplished with the help of budgets. It is difficult if not impossible to correct deviations from expectations without first putting expectations into detailed concrete form. Results then can be compared over time by units of output and corrections can be intelligently made.

It should be understood that budgets are guides for the future and since the future cannot be foretold accurately, it is foolish to attempt to live up to them rigidly. But because a budget does not work 100% accurately is no argument for discontinuing the use of all budgets. For good reason, budgets can be adjusted and exceptions can be made without destroying their effectiveness as control devices.

Many firms build budgets each year by estimating sales and then by asking all department heads to submit detailed plans for the coming year based on this expected business. If the requested expenses are greater than expected income less required profits, it becomes necessary to pare down expenses or raise prices, or both. In this event, budget conferences are held between the budget director and each department head in turn. Perhaps a 10% cut in expenses is required to bring the budget into balance. Each department head is asked to make such an adjustment so as to bring his proposed expenditures into line. Initial budget requests must be examined carefully by the budget director to detect evidences of padding. There is a perfectly natural tendency for department heads to request more than they know they will need so as to make any request for trimming less painful and disruptive.

The final budget is based on a sales estimate that may or may not prove to be accurate. Many firms, therefore, set up *flexible budgets*. These simply are a series of budgets based on intervals of sales estimates above and below that of the original master budget. If the various departmental budgets and expenses are then reported and compared cumulatively, very satisfactory control can be maintained. If sales at the rate of the expected $2,000,000 for the year drop to $1,900,000, a new budget automatically goes into effect based on the lower figure. And if sales rise to a higher rate, a correspondingly higher budget is used. A *cumulative budget* shows the managers expectations compared with results not only on a monthly basis but on an accumulated basis from the beginning of the year to date. Cumulative budgets are excellent control devices inasmuch as comparisons between expectations and results are always current, month after month.

Leadership. Inasmuch as managers in an organization must deal with people, an important part of their work involves the exercise of leadership. Although some people, through inherited potentialities and environmental conditioning, easily develop qualities of leadership, it is also true that most of those not so fortunately endowed can train themselves to be successful in this type of activity. Leadership is the ability and willingness to induce a feeling of voluntary cooperation in others. It results from a combination of qualities which tend to inspire confidence among the led. Volumes have been written on the subject, with considerable variation among the writers concerning what should go into the leadership formula. Although the presence or absence of leadership can be detected in a person, the quality is hard to analyze and define because it is made up of so many parts. Nevertheless, an attempt will be made to list the elements of successful leadership.

It is difficult to think of a successful leader as being one who is unwilling to play the part. Successful leaders may be modest, and it may be true that they had to be urged to assume the position, but once in it, they must *willingly assume the duties and responsibilities* of leadership, or they fail. Leaders are *tactful and self-confident*. They have learned what the basic human drives are, and they use this knowledge in motivating their followers. They appreciate *the importance of individual differences*, and they treat their subordinates so as to *enhance the self-esteem* of each. Although leaders may use *fear* as part of their equipment, most followers respond more readily to *kindness, affection*, and *confidence*. Actually, fear, in the absence of practically every other component, will enable a person to attain the results of leadership, but the performance of the subordinates is grudging and unwilling. Hence, domination generally is considered to be less desirable than leadership in business organizations. The best leaders are *consistent* and *well-balanced*, they understand what they want done, and they go about their business in a rational, logical manner. Good leaders *are not selfish*. They listen to the suggestions of their subordinates, they invite participation and cooperation, and they do not resent criticism. *Technical skill often aids* leaders by helping to build respect, but a man may be a successful leader without being able to perform any of the technical work done in his department. It is essential, however, that he shall not bluff, make excuses, or try to hide the fact. And, without exhausting the list, a leader must have the *courage of his convictions*. He is *loyal* to his subordinates as well as to the company, and *he does not vacillate* on important matters.

QUESTIONS FOR DISCUSSION

1. What are the broad, general duties within the organization of (1) stockholders, (2) directors, (3) top managers, (4) operating managers, and (5) first-line supervisors?
2. Your author states that many mistakes are made by business managers. If mistakes can be avoided by taking time to get the facts, why should mistakes ever be made?
3. Define system.
4. What are the five functions of management?
5. By what legal right does your employer tell you what to do and insist that you do it?
6. What is likely to happen in an organization when supervisors are told they are being held responsible for accomplishing certain duties but have not been delegated the authority to get them done? Give an example of this situation.
7. How is the function of control accomplished?
8. Would you rather work in concerns where control is centralized or decentralized? Explain your answer.
9. How can coordination be accomplished in an organization?
10. It has been said that leaders are born, not made. Would you agree that leadership training programs are a waste of time? Explain.

SELECTED REFERENCES

Basile, Joseph, *The Cultural Development of Managers, Executives, and Professionals*, Helicon Press, Baltimore, 1968.

Eilon, S., *Management Control*, John Wiley & Sons, New York, 1972.

George, Claude S., Jr., *Management for Business and Industry*, Prentice-Hall, Englewood Cliffs, N. J., 1970.

Hofstede, G. H., *The Game of Budget Control*, Barnes & Noble, New York, 1968.

Jucius, Michael J., B. A. Deitzer, and W. E. Schlender, *Elements of Managerial Action*, Richard D. Irwin, Homewood, Ill., 1973.

Klein, W. H., and D. C. Murphy, eds., *Policy*, Little, Brown & Co., Boston, 1973.

Koontz, Harold, and Cyril J. O'Donnell, *Essentials of Management*, McGraw-Hill, New York, 1974.

Mason, Joseph G., *How to Build Your Management Skills*, McGraw-Hill, New York, 1971.

Moore, Franklin G., *Management and Organization: Principles and Practices*, Wadsworth Publishing Co., Belmont, Cal., 1975.

Richards, Max D., and Paul S. Greenlaw, *Management Decisions and Behavior*, Richard D. Irwin, Homewood, Ill., 1972.

Van Dersal, William R., *The Successful Supervisor*, rev. ed., Harper & Row, New York, 1968.

CHAPTER 10

BUSINESS INFORMATION

A business concern could not long remain viable without a steady flow of information. Facts in the form of orders, memos, blueprints, specifications, dates, and so on must be sent out through the various echelons of management and supervision to the rank-and-file employees. In reverse, members of management get feedback in the form of written, telephone, and face-to-face reports, and in other ways. The very existence of the firm depends on the ability of managers to exercise control, and control depends on the accessibility of accounting, statistical, and general information. In the absence of reliable external sources of information the planning of top managers must of necessity be based on conjecture and wishful thinking. Furthermore, techniques of executing plans and latest managerial practices cannot be used without the benefit of access to such external sources and the dissemination of pertinent information throughout the organization.

The presentation of understandable internal information by accountants and statisticians is discussed in the next chapter.

EXTERNAL BUSINESS INFORMATION

No business concern could operate long at a profit without recourse by its managers to the technical, managerial, marketing, and personnel facts which aid in solving problems and establishing policies. Journals and technical magazines circulate among those who can benefit from them, and handbooks, manuals, dictionaries, and the like are constantly consulted by secretaries, engineers, department heads, and others. When special problems arise it is good practice to learn how others may have solved similar problems. This often can be done by resorting to a good library where one can learn quickly what solutions to such problems have been published. Basic research and statistical summaries can be invaluable in learning about business conditions and about introducing new products, advertising, modifying budgets, hiring, expanding market areas, and so on.

Library Research. *Library research* starts with the card catalog. All books are listed by author, title, and subject, on cards found in trays at one central point. Each book is referred to by a call number which fits into a classification system that brings books on one subject into the same section on the library shelves. Often current matter is placed together, and usually reference material is collected at another point. Library assistants are always helpful in orienting those seeking aid.

Background Information. General information can be found in the various encyclopedias. Dictionaries, atlases, and year books are available as are the *World Almanac* and the *Reader's Digest Almanac*, the *Statistical Abstract of the United States, Who's Who in America*, regional books on the *Who's Who* principle, and various professional directories. Also, a directory of directories is available.

Indexes. Published *indexes* include the *United States Catalog*, which lists books, and the *Reader's Guide to Periodical Literature, the New York Times Index*, the *Public Affairs Information Service*, and the *Monthly Catalog of Useful Public Documents*, which list current periodical literature.

General Business Information. The *Census of the United States* includes a variety of statistical material useful to business managers. Other collections published by the federal government are the *Census of Manufactures, Domestic Commerce*, the *Survey of Current Business*, the *Monthly Labor Review*, and the *Census of Business*. Publications that contain valuable research materials are the *California Management Review*, the *Harvard Business Review*, the *Journal of Business*, the *Commercial and Financial Chronicle, Dun's Review*, the *Journal of Commerce, Barron's, Business Week*, and the *Wall Street Journal*.

Those interested in foreign trade should consult the *Foreign Commerce Handbook, Foreign Trade—Basic Information*

Sources, the *Exporter's Encyclopedia*, the *Dictionary of Foreign Trade*, the *Rand McNally Commercial Atlas and Marketing Guide*, the *Pan-American Yearbook, Trade Lists*, and *International Trade Inquiries*.

Marketing and Field Research. Much external information vital to the continuing profitable operation of the business concern can be secured by investigation in the field. If the research is conducted properly it probably will disclose central tendencies which are more or less accurate approximations to the true answer. These approximations must, of course, be used with care and only after taking all practicable means of checking their accuracy. All types of market information can be found through field investigations: the kinds, classes, and locations of the firm's customers, and the size of their incomes; whether or not the product is easy to sell and at what seasons and how often it is (or will be) purchased; how the concern's advertising compares in effectiveness with competitors'; what the public thinks of the firm and its products; what channels of distribution should be used; what the prices of products should be; what prospective consumers think of new products; how old products and their packaging can be improved; and so on.

Information secured by field research often results in basic changes in existing policies. Continuing retail inventory studies in key cities can help to adjust a manufacturer's production more closely to actual demand for his products. Such research often detects early signs of style changes, tendencies to prefer one kind of product or material over another, and other types of trends.

The approach to the specific problem, which should be outlined, is that of the scientist. The objective of the investigation, in other words, should be to discover the facts, not to vindicate a preconceived idea. The interviewers must be trained, for untrained field persons often ask leading questions or even record the wrong answers; they may not sample the population properly; they may confuse or antagonize the respondents; and they may not complete the questionnaires properly. Care must be taken in the selection of population areas, and the proper techniques of sampling must be used so as to get representative and adequate interviews. The results must be tabulated accurately and interpreted with judgment. A system of checking the honesty of field interviewers usually is employed. And finally, if a field survey clearly indicates some course of action it would seem to be unnecessary to state that the firm's policies should take that action into account, yet the results of field surveys too often are ignored at the policy-making level.

INTERNAL INFORMATION

Not only does the firm need to know the results of operations; it needs the answers to many other types of questions. Most of these can be solved by questioning employees, by observing operations, and by laboratory research.

Employee Surveys. A valuable source of information is *the employee*. Employees, if approached in the right way, will respond with a wide variety of ideas and suggestions. Management must play fair with the employees, however. When publicity concerning the results of morale surveys have been promised, management has been known to renege. Also, individuals have not always been properly compensated for commercially valuable ideas.

Process Study. A going concern can usually save money by *process study*. Trained operations analysts can streamline production processes; motion study analysts can reduce unnecessary work; time study analysts can establish standard times for various operations; statisticians can set up statistical quality control systems that reduce inspection costs; and so on.

Laboratory Research. Many types of technical problems can be solved by *laboratory research*. Discoveries made in the laboratory can result in slight improvements or fundamental changes in the firm's products. There are three types of research: exploratory, fundamental, and applied.

The *exploratory* type of research might seem to some to be hit-or-miss in nature. It often starts in "think tanks" or "brainstorming" sessions. It may follow up hunches, and have no preconceived objective in view. It is said that Edison often used this approach. Ideas coming out of these sessions often are tested in library research and then, if they appear to be promising, they are taken to the laboratory.

Fundamental research has no predictable outcome. It is slow and expensive, and usually is undertaken only by universities, research foundations, and very large business concerns.

Applied research uses the other two types in trying to solve a pressing problem. How to nullify harmful side effects in the use of a new and promising product, how to catch up with a competitor who has introduced a new or improved product, and how to meet a new need are examples.

Controlling laboratory costs is extremely difficult. How can top management know whether a laboratory is paying its way or not? Obviously, if problems are turned over to the technicians and are solved, one after the other, the cost of the laboratory is justified. But where the research goes on and on without results, what then? The managers may lose patience and abolish the research program just as a world-shaking idea is about to be brought to fruition. Or perhaps the technicians have suspected for a long time that their efforts were leading them nowhere, but have refused to admit defeat and perhaps face discharge. Some firms require monthly progress reports on each project. They estimate in advance the cost of each project and its value to the firm if it works out. They also estimate, all with the help of the technicians, the chances of success. Then the ratio (Estimated value x Probability of success)/(Estimated cost) is worked out. Each project, then, is implemented if it has, say, a ratio of 3 or 4 to 1, and no project is dropped unless a more promising one appears.

A fairly common occurrence in research laboratories is the appearance of promising tangential projects. These should be reported to management and not be explored without permission. Later, after proper evaluation, they may become new projects.

COMMUNICATING

Proper communication is essential to a well-functioning firm, not only for the dissemination of the results of research but for the hour-by-hour flow of orders, reports, production feedback, and general information within the organization, and the correspondence, advertising, and publicity sent out to customers and the general public.

We have, of course, many types of mechanical and electronic

devices for transmitting words and pictures. These are, however, of little use if the intent of the message is not understood by those receiving it. A primary need, then, is to pitch the message to the level of comprehension of the audience. Psychologists have devised *readability* scales which can be used for testing letters and various kinds of copy.

It is important for persons in business to speak in an understandable manner over the phone. But as important as this is, it is even more vital to write or dictate clearly expressed and friendly letters, since about ten times as many transactions are consummated by mail as by telephone.

Attention should be paid to the letterhead. It should, of course, carry the name of the firm, and other important items such as address, telephone number, and possibly the department and name of the executive. Law firms customarily list all the partners and associates on the letterhead. Sometimes a slogan or a list of the chief products is included. A fairly common error is to show both a post office box number and a street number, which is confusing to the person replying. Sometimes only the city and state are given, and frequently the zip code number is left off. Also, a distressing practice, making for inconvenience and error, is that of printing the address in microscopic type with pale, almost illegible ink.

A courteous and clearly expressed letter tends to make friends for the firm. Anger and sarcasm should always be avoided. If the situation seems to require strong language a letter can be dictated and held a day or so. When it is reread later, or read by an associate, more moderate language probably will be indicated.

Attention should be given to logical composition, spelling, and punctuation. Time-worn and stale phrases such as "We beg to inform you" should be avoided. A good handbook of English composition and a desk dictionary are, of course, essential.

Each specialized letter requires varying construction and emphasis, depending on its function. *Sales letters* must attract attention and hold interest, arouse desire for the product or service, and, above all, stimulate action. General *sales promotion letters* are designed to keep in friendly touch with the market. Often such letters are sent with bills or at billing times. *Credit* and *collection letters* require particular attention. They must be carefully and tactfully written. They can be firm in tone if credit is denied or pressure is required in collecting past-due accounts, but they should never express anger. Threats should not be used unless they are to be actually carried out. Last, *adjustment letters* require particular attention. If the adjustment is made, it should be made generously and willingly. The writer should lean over backward in an effort to accept responsibility, and not give the impression that the customer is twisting his arm to get a concession. If the adjustment is denied, clear reasons should be given and friendly relations should be maintained.

QUESTIONS FOR DISCUSSION

1. Why is the flow of effective information important to a business concern?
2. How can a business concern use library research?
3. What types of information can a business concern obtain from field research?
4. What errors do untrained field interviewers frequently make?
5. What precautions should management take in evaluating the results of field research?
6. Name and describe the three types of laboratory research.
7. How can laboratory projects be controlled by the business manager without destroying potential benefits?
8. What is a primary need in communicating with others regardless of the medium used?
9. When should anger and sarcasm be used in a letter?
10. When should threats be used in a collection letter?

SELECTED REFERENCES

Boyd, Harper W., Jr., and Ralph Westfall, *Marketing Research*, rev. ed., Richard D. Irwin, Homewood, Ill., 1964.

Buckley, Earle A., *How to Write Better Business Letters*, McGraw-Hill, New York, 1971.

Churchman, C. West, Russell L. Ackoff, and E. Leonard Arnoff, *Introduction to Operations Research*, John Wiley & Sons, New York, 1957.

deMare, George, *Communicating for Leadership—A Guide for Business Executives*, Ronald Press Co., New York, 1968.

Foltz, Roy G., *Management by Communication*, Chilton Book Co., Philadelphia, 1973.

Haney, William V., *Communication and Organizational Behavior*, 3rd ed., Richard D. Irwin, Homewood, Ill., 1973.

King, Thomas R., *A Program on the Problems of Communication*, Charles E. Merrill Publishing Co., Columbus, Ohio, 1972.

Murphy, Herta A., and Charles E. Peck, *Effective Business Communications*, McGraw-Hill, New York, 1972.

Roman, D. D., *Research and Development Management*, Appleton-Century-Crofts, New York, 1968.

Rummel, J. Francis, and Wesley C. Ballaine, *Research Methodology in Business*, Harper & Row, New York, 1963.

Shurter, Robert L., *Written Communication in Business*, 3rd ed., McGraw-Hill, New York, 1971.

CHAPTER 11

ACCOUNTING AND STATISTICS

Every business must maintain various kinds of records for a variety of reasons. It is desirable to know how much cash is on hand, who owes the company and how much is owed by each debtor, to whom money is owed by the company and the amounts involved, how much money is invested in current and fixed assets, the value of sales in successive time periods, how much money was made or lost through business operations, and so on. Records are kept so the managers of the concern can properly chart its operations; it is necessary to keep records so as to apportion profits among the stockholders; the government compels the keeping of records for tax purposes; and businesses are bought and sold on the strength of their records. The recording of business transactions has been reduced to highly standardized procedures which can be applied to an almost infinite variety of business operations. The procedures of recording and reporting business transactions are known as *accounting*. The analysis, measurement, and interpretation of complex data (including business transactions) constitute the subject matter of *statistics*.

ACCOUNTING

It is thought that systems of accounting existed before writing developed. Be that as it may, accounting certainly is as old as business. As long as business concerns were small and simple in their operations, accounting procedures were relatively simple. Such procedures usually involved setting up an income schedule and an outgo schedule. A comparison of the totals at any given time showed what was owed the business, or what the business owed. One entry was made for each transaction. But as business became more complex it became necessary to develop correspondingly more complex accounting systems. During the fourteenth century an accounting system was developed which involved making two entries for each transaction. This type came to be called double-entry accounting as opposed to the older single-entry type.

Double-Entry Accounting. Double-entry accounting is based on the initial assumption that the *assets* owned by a business equal its *proprietorship*. If a man begins business with a cash capital of $10,000 his first double entry will be

$$\$10,000 \text{ (assets)} = \$10,000 \text{ (proprietorship)}$$

Inasmuch as there are many kinds of assets, the specific account, *cash*, should be used for this entry. Each account has two sides, corresponding to the two sides of the equation. The left side is known as the *debit* side and the right the *credit*. In the language of accounting the first entry involved debiting *Cash* and crediting *Proprietorship*.

Suppose that the new proprietor finds it necessary to have $15,000 before starting business. If he borrows $5,000 the basic equation is

$$\text{Cash} = \text{Notes Payable} + \text{Proprietorship}$$

So *Cash* is debited for $5,000 and *Notes Payable* is credited for the same amount. The books then show

$$\$15,000 \text{ (cash)} = \$5,000 \text{ (notes payable)} +$$
$$\$10,000 \text{ (proprietorship)}$$

Although the books now show assets of $15,000, the equity of the proprietor remains at $10,000. This relationship underlies all double-entry systems, no matter how simple or complex they may be:

$$\text{Assets} = \text{Liabilities} + \text{Proprietorship}$$

As the new proprietor buys a building, equips it, buys merchandise, equips and stocks an office with supplies, sells merchandise, and otherwise carries on his business, he records each transaction in two different accounts. Then at the end of the first month he *closes*, or adds up and balances, each of these accounts. If, for instance, the cash account shows a succession of debit entries which total $2,115.25 and a succession of credit entries which total $1,719.13, the balance or difference is $396.12. The mechanics of closing this account would involve totaling each side and placing the difference on the smaller side. Both sides should be equal. Then under date of the first of the following month the balance is carried to the opposite side, thus:

Jan. 31	Total debits	2,115.25	Jan. 31	Total credits	1,719.13
			31	Balance	396.12
		2,115.25			2,115.25
Feb. 1	Balance	396.12			

If the balance of each account is listed, each on its proper side, the totals of these balances should be equal. If they are not, an error has been made in entering one or more transactions, or in adding or subtracting.

The Balance Sheet. To aid interested parties in obtaining an understanding of the condition of a business, the books are closed periodically and the balances of the various accounts are brought together on one sheet. Properly arranged in the form of the basic formula, assets = liabilities + proprietorship, this report is called a *balance sheet*, an example of which follows:

Assets		*Liabilities*	
Cash	396.12	Notes Payable	5,000.00
Merchandise on Hand	4,500.00	Accounts Payable	2,146.12
Store Equipment	3,000.00		
Office Equipment	1,000.00	Total Liabilities	7,146.12
Building	5,000.00	Proprietorship	10,000.00
Land	3,000.00		
Store Supplies	100.00		
Office Supplies	150.00		
		Total Liabilities	
Total Assets	17,146.12	and Proprietorship	17,146.12

It is possible to apply all sorts of tests to a balance sheet to determine the condition of the business. For instance, compare the two simple examples which follow:

Example A

Cash	10,000.00	Accounts Payable	1,000.00
Merchandise	5,000.00	Mortgage Payable	4,000.00
Building	7,000.00	Proprietorship	19,000.00
Land	2,000.00		
	24,000.00		24,000.00

Example B

Cash	1,000.00	Accounts Payable	4,000.00
Merchandise	2,000.00	Mortgage Payable	1,000.00
Building	18,000.00	Proprietorship	19,000.00
Land	3,000.00		
	24,000.00		24,000.00

The equity of the proprietor is the same in each example, but in one the current position is strong and in the other the current position is weak. In Example A the *current ratio* is $15,000 to $1,000, or 15 to 1; while in Example B it is $3,000 to $4,000, or 3 to 4. In the second example it seems clear that the proprietor will be unable to meet his current obligations as they come due.

Although a balance sheet shows the condition of a business as of a specific date, and is static in nature, it is possible to get a partial picture of the firm as a dynamic concern by examining a series of successive balance sheets. One can trace the gradual reduction of the mortgage, the slow increase in proprietorship, the fluctuating accounts receivable, the accumulation of reserves, and so on. However, a better picture of the dynamic aspects of the concern is provided in the profit and loss statement.

The Profit and Loss Statement. Usually a monthly *profit and loss statement* is also prepared. An example of a simple statement follows:

Sales Income:		
Gross Sales Income		$98,010.90
Less Returns and Allowances		3,862.42
Net Sales Income		$94,148.48
Cost of Goods Sold:		
Previous Merchandise Inventory	$12,110.05	
Purchases	99,771.40	
Total Available for Sale	$111,881.45	
Less Merchandise Inventory	67,220.50	
Cost of Goods Sold		44,660.95
Gross Profit		$49,487.53
Operating Expenses:		
Rent	$ 2,000.00	
Salaries and Wages	10,125.00	
Depreciation on Equipment	2,002.60	
General Expenses	3,141.10	
Total Operating Expenses		17,268.70
Net Profit		$32,218.83
Taxes		3,775.00
Net Profit after Taxes		28,443.83

Control by Means of Financial Statements. By watching the trends of several ratios obtained from the financial statements, the manager is aided in controlling the enterprise. In the profit and loss statement shown above, expenses are about one-third of gross profit. If this ratio increases over the next few months, the manager takes steps to reduce it.

The manager watches the turnover of his stock, found by dividing cost of goods sold by average merchandise inventory. Cost of goods sold is found by adding purchases during the accounting period to the inventory at the beginning of the period, then subtracting the inventory on hand at the end of the period. Average inventory is found by adding the inventory at the beginning of the period to the inventory at the end of the period and dividing by two. In the above example the ratio is $44,660.95 divided by $39,665.28, or approximately 1.13. It is important to keep this turnover figure as high as possible.

Accountants generally believe that the ratio of current assets to current liabilities should be kept at about 2 to 1.

There are many other such indicators which managers watch, and keeping them on an even keel aids considerably in maintaining healthy conditions.

Accounting and Bookkeeping. The routine of making ordinary entries in the books and balancing accounts at the end of each month is known as *bookkeeping*. *Accounting* involves the use of judgment. Bookkeepers can be trained in business schools or can be broken in on the job. Accountants require university training and, if they desire to be certified public accountants (CPA's), they are required to pass state-supervised examinations.

STATISTICS

Statistics puts complex data into simpler and more understandable form. The procedures of statistics are applied to a wide range of subjects: sports, weather, population, psychological tests, business, and so on. We are interested here in the application of statistical principles to complex business data.

Sampling. When it is necessary to know the characteristics of a large body of data, it usually is impractical or impossible to examine every unit. Fortunately, the characteristics of the whole can be very closely approximated by correctly using the techniques of *sampling*. Statisticians call the entire mass of data on which information is desired the *universe*. If the samples taken from the universe are to exhibit characteristics close enough to those of the universe, they must be adequate and representative.

An *adequate* sample has been taken when enough of the universe has been collected so that additional amounts added to what has already been taken do not appreciably change the characteristics being measured.

A *representative* sample involves *random selection*. This means that samples from different parts of the universe are selected in such a way that each sample has the same chance of being selected as any other sample.

Averaging. One figure which is characteristic of many is known as an *average*, or *mean*. There are several types of averages, each having its own peculiarities.

The type of average most frequently used is the *arithmetic average*, or *mean*. It is found by adding all the figures and dividing their sum by the number of figures involved. For example:

$$10 + 12 + 17 + 20 + 26 = 85$$
$$85 \div 5 = 17$$

The *median* is a form of average found by lining all the figures up in order of magnitude (called an *array*) and taking the middle figure as typical of the group. For example, in the array 10, 13, 16, 20, 26, the middle figure is 16.

The *mode* is the figure that appears most frequently in the mass of data. For instance, in the group 10, 13, 18, 18, 22, the figure that occurs most frequently is 18.

Which type of average should be used in a given situation? A certain amount of judgment is required to answer this question. Sometimes more than one should be used for a proper understanding of the data. Arithmetic averages, for instance, give more weight to extremes. So this form would not be appropriate in finding the typical size of an order out of five orders listed as follows: $500, $500, $400, $200, and $10. The typical order as found by the arithmetic method is $322. It may be important to know this, but most statisticians would say that the median ($400) and the mode ($500) were more typical of the group.

Weighted averages reflect the differences in importance of individual items. If some of the items are of more importance they are used more than once in the calculation. For example: assume that two applicants for employment are given five tests on which they make the following scores:

Tests		Applicant No. 1	Applicant No. 2
A	Finger Dexterity	95%	60%
B	Mechanical Aptitude	100	50
C	Intelligence	80	100
D	General Knowledge	70	100
E	Physical Strength	90	65
Totals		435	375
Unweighted averages		87%	75%

It would appear from the unweighted average scores that Applicant No. 1 is the better candidate and should be hired. However, assume that the Personnel Department gives different weights to each test for various occupational groups and that for the job in question the weights are 1, 2, 10, 8, and 1. Weighted averages of the scores made by each applicant are as shown on p. 124.

The weighted averages are found in each instance by dividing the total of the weighted scores by the total of the weights. For the job in question, which might be an executive or sales job, Applicant No. 2 is superior. Applicant No. 1, on the other hand, would rate higher for jobs requiring finger dexterity, mechanical aptitude, or physical strength and where general knowledge and intelligence were not as important.

Less Used Averages. Two other less used and less understood averages should be mentioned. The *geometric mean* should be used for percentages, ratios, and index numbers. It is defined as the nth root of the product of n values. In other words, if ten percentages are to be averaged, they are multiplied and the 10th root of the product is found. Such calculations require the use of logarithms. A simple illustration using only two figures is as follows:

The arithmetic mean of 50% and 100% is 75%. Popularly, this is the way percentages are calculated. The results are not accurate. The correct way to compute the average of 50% and 100% is to multiply them and take the square root of the product. 50% × 100% = 5,000%. The square root of 5,000% is approximately 70.7%.

The *harmonic mean* should be used for averaging rates, such as units per dollar, production per day, or miles per hour. It is defined as the reciprocal of the arithmetic mean of the reciprocals of the figures being averaged. Ask a friend to give you his average round-trip speed per hour if he drives 500 miles at 90 miles per hour and returns at 10 miles per hour. Almost invariably the answer will be 90 + 10 divided by 2, or 50. This is incorrect, as a little reflection will prove.

The harmonic mean gives the correct round-trip speed, as follows (giving the answer the value of x):

$$\frac{\frac{1}{90} + \frac{1}{10}}{2} = \frac{1}{x}$$

Simplifying the left side of the equation: $\dfrac{\frac{1}{90} + \frac{9}{90}}{2} = \dfrac{\frac{10}{90}}{2} = \dfrac{5}{90} = \dfrac{1}{18}$

Since $\dfrac{1}{18} = \dfrac{1}{x}$, $x = 18$ mph.

Frequency Distributions. It is easy to find the means of arrays containing a small number of items. It is more difficult, or it may be impracticable, to deal with large numbers of figures in the same manner. So statisticians find typical characteristics of large masses of data by putting them into groups. Two types of data can be distinguished in this connection: discrete and continuous. *Discrete data* involve sizes or other values that have no continuity or relationship to one another. An item carried in stock might come in five sizes: pint, quart, gallon, 5-gallon, and 10-gallon. There are no in-between sizes. The discrete frequency distribution of such items at inventory time might appear as follows:

Class Intervals (Sizes)	Frequencies (Number in Each Class)
Pint	105
Quart	301
Gallon	447
5-Gallon	263
10-Gallon	27

Continuous data run from low to high without significant breaks. Age groups in a company might, for instance be set up as follows:

Class Intervals (Ages of Employees)	Frequencies (Number in Each Class)
16–26 incl.	193
26–36 ″	281
36–46 ″	677
46–56 ″	345
56–66 ″	209

Tests	Weights		Applicant No. 1 Scores		Weighted Scores	Applicant No. 2 Scores	Weighted Scores
A	1	×	95	=	95	60	60
B	2	×	100	=	200	50	100
C	10	×	80	=	800	100	1000
D	8	×	70	=	560	100	800
E	1	×	90	=	90	65	65
Totals	22				1745		2025
Weighted Averages			(1745 ÷ 22)		79	(2025 ÷ 22)	92

Calculation of weighted averages taken from data on pages 121 and 122.

It will be noted that the discrete class intervals contain only one value for each class interval while continuous class intervals contain two, a lower limit and an upper limit. Each type is used in business, but the continuous form has many more applications in practice than the discrete.

Statisticians can obtain many generalizations from frequency distributions that bring out clear meanings and characteristics of otherwise obscure and meaningless masses of data. Ranges are found from the smallest to the largest item, means can be calculated, distributions can be divided into groups (usually quarters or tenths), measures of *skewness* can be found (whether values are bunched at one end or the other of the distribution), and so on. The results, as calculated for successive time periods or for departments, plants, or other types of divisions, will yield valuable means of control for managers.

Index Numbers. If a firm desires to compare its sales, year after year, with those of its competitors, a series of figures for each firm involved usually will be incomprehensible. However, if a base year common to each of the series is selected and percentage changes from each base are calculated, the results will be comparable and more clearly discernible. An *index number* is a percentage relative to a fixed period in the past. It is calculated by dividing a given figure by the base figure and multiplying by 100. If our sales in the base year had been $1,341,000 and our chief competitor's had been $10,900,000, and if during the past year our sales were $2,115,000 and our competitor's were $13,141,000, did we gain on him? Putting these dollar sales figures in the form of index numbers, it is seen that our figure is 157.7 and our competitor's is 120.6. Although these are percentages, it is customary to leave the % sign off when they are used in this manner. For the years in question our firm did 37.1 percentage points better than our competitor.

The public follows with interest the announcement each month of the Consumer Price Index of the Bureau of Labor Statistics. This index covers a wide variety of prices of goods and services purchased by employees living in cities. The figures are weighted by the results of studies that show how much of each item such wage earners and clerical workers actually buy. The index numbers are based on the average cost of living in the year 1967.

Time Series. A time series is any sequence of values shown over regularly recurring time periods. Many series, when plotted over time, show rhythmic patterns which, when projected into the future, help to forecast events to come. Statisticians have been able to distinguish four types of changes in many time series: seasonal, cyclical, secular, and random.

Seasonal fluctuations occur as a result of many factors that affect the supply of goods and the demand for goods. Regular changes in the supply of agricultural products result, of course, from the changing seasons. Regular changes in the demand for many items also are caused by the seasons as well as by holiday customs. Businessmen know this and plan accordingly.

Cyclical fluctuations can be detected and isolated in many time series. Since the beginning of the Industrial Revolution in England in the eighteenth century cycles in business activity have been experienced. Although they do not recur regularly they average about three years in duration and can be divided into four phases: prosperity, recession, depression, and recovery. Wise businessmen are not hopefully optimistic during the prosperity phase, but conduct their operations so as to be in a strong position when recession and depression come. And during the depression phase they prepare for the prosperity to come. Governments have attempted to deal with the problems caused by business cycles but, although they have been able to soften them, they have not eradicated them.

Secular fluctuations are long-term cycles. They occur in the economy over very long periods of time. They have been isolated in industries and in individual business firms. When a retrograde movement sets in in a business firm it sometimes can be reversed by developing new products and services.

Random fluctuations are deviations from the relatively regular patterns of the other three types. They are caused by political actions, wars, disasters, and unknown factors. They cause more or less temporary dislocations and seldom cause material alterations in the other types of fluctuations.

QUESTIONS FOR DISCUSSION

1. What is a balance sheet? What formula is it based on?
2. What is a profit and loss statement?
3. Explain what adequate and representative samples are.
4. Describe how to find
   (a) the arithmetic mean of a group of figures,
   (b) the median, and (c) the mode.
5. For what types of data is the geometric mean used and how is it calculated?
6. For what types of data is the harmonic mean used and how is it calculated?
7. What are frequency distributions?
8. What are index numbers and how are they used?
9. What is a time series?
10. Name and describe the four types of fluctuations that can be distinguished in the business cycle and other types of time series.

SELECTED REFERENCES

Balsley, Howard L., *Introduction to Statistical Method*, Littlefield, Adams & Co., Totowa, N. J., 1964.

Carson, A. B., Arthur E. Carlson, and Clem Boling, *College Accounting*, 9th ed., South-Western Publishing Co., Cincinnati, 1972.

Clelland, R. C., J. S. de Cani, and F. E. Brown, *Basic Statistics with Business Applications*, 2nd ed., John Wiley & Sons, New York, 1973.

Coleman, A. R., *Financial Accounting: A General Management Approach*, John Wiley & Sons, New York, 1970.

Edwards, Allen L., *Statistical Methods*, 3rd ed., Holt, Rinehart & Winston, New York, 1973.

Finney, Harry A., and Herbert E. Miller, *Principles of Accounting*, 7th ed., Prentice-Hall, Englewood Cliffs, N. J., 1974.

Maxwell, Arthur D., and John H. McMichael, *Elementary Accounting*, Littlefield, Adams & Co., Totowa, N. J., 1966.

Simons, Harry, *Intermediate Accounting*, 5th ed., South-Western Publishing Co., Cincinnati, 1974.

Smith, Lee H., and Donald R. Williams, *Statistical Analysis for Business*, 2nd ed., Wadsworth Publishing Co., Belmont, Cal., 1975.

Stockton, John R., and Charles T. Clark, *Introduction to Business and Economic Statistics*, 5th ed., South-Western Publishing Co., Cincinnati, 1975.

Thomas, Arthur L., *Financial Accounting*, 2nd ed., Wadsworth Publishing Co., Belmont, Cal., 1975.

Vance, Lawrence, and Russell Taussig, *Accounting Principles and Control*, 3rd ed., Holt, Rinehart & Winston, New York, 1972.

Walden, Robert E., and L. Vann Seawell, *Introductory Accounting: A Management Approach*, Houghton Mifflin Co., Boston, 1968.

PART IV

ORGANIZATION FOR PRODUCTION

In the broad sense, production is any activity that adds wealth to the economy. A productive person may pull teeth, engage in farming, cut down trees, seine for fish, teach school, or engage in a great variety of other activities including manufacturing. In the narrow sense, however, *production* means making something, usually in a factory, and most of the other activities are known as *services*. Part IV is concerned with production in this narrow sense. Manufacturing accounts for a large part of the country's wealth-creation each year, but most workers are found in the service industries. Several of the more important service occupations are described in Part VI, under the heading of marketing.

Chapter 12 introduces the reader to modern production methods, beginning with the Industrial Revolution and leading up to the present. Chapter 13 considers some of the problems involved in getting a manufacturing plant under way. And, as the plant goes into production, Chapter 14 describes operating methods and control.

CHAPTER 12

THE NATURE OF
MODERN PRODUCTION

Modern production methods started a relatively short time ago, beginning in England about the middle of the eighteenth century and in the United States 100 years later. As these methods came into being, a fundamental change took place in society—a change which has come to be called the *Industrial Revolution.*

The Industrial Revolution. The causes of the Industrial Revolution have been ascribed to the invention of textile machinery and to the perfection of the steam engine. Actually such inventions constituted the last two logs on the dam which diverted the stream of industry into a new channel. Most of the causes of the Industrial Revolution lie outside the field of technology. They formed the groundwork for the final technological factors which served to touch off these profound changes. One factor goes back to the Crusades when impetus was given to the desire of Englishmen for exotic goods. Further scope was given to this desire by the discovery of new lands, the development of transport facilities, the discovery of new trade routes, and the building of colonial empires. Another important factor involved labor mobility. Persecution of religious groups on the Continent caused them to emigrate to England, where they settled in cities and formed pools of skilled labor. Skilled and unskilled labor moved from the country to the cities, and the guild system of handicraft control was unable to cope with the situation. The advent of the entrepreneur and the new form of cottage production under which capitalists undertook to buy raw materials, put them out where skilled craftsmen could process them in their own homes, and collect and sell the finished products, led directly to the capitalist system which provided the favorable climate in which the Industrial Revolution flourished. Not the least of the factors was a new way of thinking about economic matters—a violent reaction from the existing concept of mercantilism under which government control throttled productive enterprise. This new way of thinking came to be called *laissez faire*, a philosophy which relegated government to the spheres of external security (armies and navies), internal security (police forces), the enforcement of justice and contracts (criminal and civil courts), and to some extent public information and education. The popularity of this philosophy reacted to the advantage of industry by relieving it from practically all governmental restraint. Many writers give the impression that division of labor, factory production, and the use of machinery all were suddenly invented about the middle of the eighteenth century and that these caused the Industrial Revolution. Actually all three had been used since antiquity, and in the absence of the more profound causes they could never have caused the industrial changes which took place. Factories, automatic machines, organization, and managerial skill cannot be used to advantage without mass markets. Nor can mass markets be developed without efficient methods of mass production. The beginnings of *mass markets* are found in the large orders given for identical goods by monarchs and by the great joint-stock companies. Perhaps the first such order was placed by King Louis XIV for uniforms for his army. The demands for textiles grew by leaps and bounds as trade with new countries developed. But if there is a key to the Industrial Revolution, a factor which was the turning point, it can probably be found in the invention of *interchangeable parts. Mass production* had to await this relatively simple concept which was based upon the dual necessities of *standardization* and *precision*. Once this idea (which originated in France) permeated the thinking of industrial producers, handicraft production as the characteristic mode of manufacturing was doomed.[1]

Characteristics of Modern Production. Factories had been used

---

1. Although interchangeable parts were used in France and Russia in the eighteenth century, they were hand produced and their use was not practical. One of the first successful uses of interchangeable parts took

before the Industrial Revolution. Abandoned monasteries often were used for the purpose in England. Isolated instances of factory production can even be traced to the days of the Roman Empire. Although *factory production* was used prior to the Industrial Revolution, it became afterwards the characteristic mode of production.

Power-driven machinery was not unknown prior to the Industrial Revolution, but afterwards two significant differences may be noted. First, there was relatively less use of wind and water power. The use of the newly perfected steam engine permitted entrepreneurs to build factories at more favorable points: in the midst of a pool of displaced foreign labor particularly skilled in certain ways, or in the midst of a rich market area. Second, machines reached a point in their development when they no longer were mere adjuncts to the skill of the craftsman; the skill of the craftsman had finally been transferred to the machine. Production no longer had to await the slow training of masses of skilled workmen; it now could function with a relatively small number of highly skilled craftsmen (who built and maintained machines) and with relatively larger numbers of unskilled machine tenders. The workmen had now become a mere adjunct to the machine. Even children, who could be taught to stop and start machines and to tie knots in broken threads, could be used to advantage in the textile mills.

Sociologically, the Industrial Revolution instigated profound changes. Workmen no longer had any roots. Under the *manor system* of society which existed in the Middle Ages, most people in England were serfs or slaves. They had something more than the security and peace of mind of a man who has been committed to prison for life. Each man's future was assured from birth. Under the *guild system* which followed the manorial system, the workmen had the security which goes with: a home and workshop; the skill of a mastered craft; the tools of his trade; the materials and finished products which he owned until they were sold; a semimonopoly on business in his area; protection (largely through custom) against changes in prices, rents,

---

place in Eli Whitney's Connecticut firearms plant about 1800, where the parts were machine produced.

and wages; and membership in a powerful employers' association (the guild). With the advent of *capitalism*, in the form of the *cottage* or *putting-out system,* the producer lost control over his materials and his markets. He lived in his own home and worked with his own tools, but he was at the mercy of powerful marketing interests who gave and took away work as they pleased. The Industrial Revolution completed the process of taking security from the worker. He now had to work in an employer's factory, with an employer's tools, on materials owned by an employer. The employer even owned most of the skill, which now was an inherent part of the machine. All the average worker had to sell was a highly perishable commodity, his physical labor, and that was purchased at the whim of a soulless organization or an employer so far removed from his underpaid workers as to be little affected by their sufferings.

The deplorable conditions which followed the advent of modern production resulted in a reexamination of the philosophy of laissez faire and the gradual reimposition of government controls on business. Through the activities of unions, humane and socially minded employers, and the general public, a sane middle course has been followed which has given industry sufficient freedom to provide the inhabitants of the United States with the highest level of living the world has ever known. The problem facing capitalistic society now is how to increase the security of the masses of people without at the same time reducing them to the status of serfs. Most American workers seem to want a medium amount of security and a medium amount of liberty and opportunity; they appear not to want more of one at the expense of the other. Efforts are being made to preserve the advantages of modern production methods and at the same time to find ways of overcoming its weak points. The strides which are being taken in this direction are discussed in Part V.

Modern production is characterized by its use of *scientific method*. Changes are based upon objective evidence. Pure research in physics, chemistry, psychology, etc. is underwritten by foundations, by industrial concerns, by public appropriations, and by popular subscriptions. Applied research deliberately attempts to use the results of pure research so as to develop improved methods of production, safe conditions under which people must labor, and more products for satisfying the desires of consumers.

Although *division of labor* was practiced before the Industrial Revolution, it has been refined to a high degree since. Along with the removal from the worker of the ownership of his tools and place of work, this factor has contributed much to the discontent of the modern worker. It tends to violate such basic human drives as the desire to create, pride of workmanship, feeling of accomplishment, feeling of making progress, curiosity, and the like. Specialization is desirable. It provides interest and makes for pride in being able to do what most other people cannot do. But if it is so refined that all the worker does is to tighten nut No. 5 on an endless stream of machines rolling along a conveyor, there is little pride of accomplishment, and furthermore, the job can get very monotonous.

Modern production typically is *large-scale* in nature. Although there are still many small businesses, some even handicraft in nature, most American goods are made in large factories.

Modern production turns out great quantities of *duplicate products*. A die is made and attached to a punch press; thereafter, identical blanks are stamped out, hour after hour, day after day. Standardization is the key to low-priced, high-quality merchandise. A single book can cost $5,000 to produce; but because fixed, or nonrecurring, expense is relatively high, a run of one million books can get the price down to 50 cents each (the cost of materials, labor, and overhead per book; plus nonrecurring costs, which now become insignificant: $5,000 ÷ 1,000,000). Most people like to be different from others, but not too different. Modern industry caters to this basic desire of customers by producing goods which basically are identical, but which superficially are different. A million identical automobiles can be given the illusion of variety with little additional expense, by using different paint colors and combinations of colors, and by changing from time to time hood and fender shapes, grillwork styles, and the like.

More Recent Developments. As production has become more

and more complex, developments in production organizations have taken the form of more simplification and control. Only a few of such innovations can be mentioned here.

The *systems concept* treats the organization as an integrated whole instead of as an assortment of more or less unrelated activities. Many years ago a foreman told the writer: "I don't care what the rest of the organization is doing—I'm just interested in my own department."

The systems approach seeks to keep every department head interested in his own area, but at the same time to make him aware of his obligations to the firm as a whole. Writers on this subject express the concept in terms of receiving inputs and using them to create values, which then become outputs for the use of customers.

Subsystems are integrated departmental organizations which, when tied together, form the *total system*, or the functioning whole. Planning and coordinating, with the aid of computers and the flow of informational reports, permit smooth and positive performance in highly complex and intricate situations.

In connection with scheduling and controlling individual projects or activities within large undertakings, two techniques were developed in the 1950s which proved to be effective. These have become popular under the acronyms of CPM and PERT, which stand for *Critical Path Method* and *Program Evaluation and Review Technique.*

These procedures were developed in connection with *Monte Carlo simulation techniques,* which attempted to imitate business situations by the use of "models." A variety of situations were set up and tested, usually with the help of computers, thus allowing executives to learn what might happen under varying conditions without having to experience such conditions in real life. These procedures also lean heavily on work done by H. L. Gantt, who devised "machine loading charts" early in the present century.

CPM and PERT techniques involve drawing diagrams representing projects that must be accomplished both successively and concurrently so as to complete a comprehensive undertaking. When the expected performance times are added for each activity, three alternative routes are drawn. The longest path is known as the pessimistic or critical path and the shortest the optimistic path. The middle path is the most probable. The time factors are usually determined with the aid of a computer. From these data over-all performance schedules can realistically be calculated. The CPM technique uses fixed performance times and thus lends itself to routine plant activities. PERT, however, is designed to deal with uncertainty. The same procedures are followed except that performance times are calculated in terms of probability.

Speed and accuracy in planning and control have been greatly improved by *electronic computers*. Almost instantaneous answers are found for a great variety of planning problems, and *real time* data processing takes place in situations where the data are used concurrently with the process.

Automation began to be used widely in the 1950s. Mechanization characterized the beginnings of the Industrial Revolution. This involved transferring the skills of the workmen to machines, converting him to a mere machine tender. A story that illustrates the beginnings of automation is that in the early days of the reciprocating steam engine, which usually was located outside the walls of the factory, a boy was hired to throw the lever that changed the direction of the piston. The lever controlled the flow of steam from one cylinder to the other and back again, forcing the piston back and forth and operating the machinery inside. This task proved exceedingly monotonous to one of these boys until the thought struck him that if he tied one end of a rope to the lever and the other to the middle of the piston, the movement of the piston as it reached the end of each stroke would tighten the rope and pull the lever over, thus automatically reversing the direction of the piston. The story goes on to say that the boy continued to check in, tie the rope securely, go fishing with his friends, and return in the evening to check out. We are not told how long this boy was able to have his cake and eat it, but we may be sure that when he was found out the engineers incorporated self-reversing devices on all steam engines and that the position of lever boy soon passed into oblivion.

One distinguishing feature of automation is *feedback*. If the process gives signals that require adjustments by the operator, it is known as an open-loop process. If the signals are acted on by the mechanism without human intervention, it is a closed-loop process. Another feature is that automation is applied in *sophisticated situations*. The term is applied, for instance, to machines that electronically register dimensions or hues and immediately make corrections if there are variations outside set tolerances; it is not applied to reversing mechanisms on reciprocating steam engines or to alarm clocks.

QUESTIONS FOR DISCUSSION

1. What was the Industrial Revolution, where did it start, and what caused it?
2. What effect did the Industrial Revolution have on the handicraft skills of workers?
3. Modern production is characterized by the use of scientific method. Explain and give illustrations.
4. Modern production is also characterized by division of labor and specialization. What is good about this, and what is bad?
5. Describe the systems concept as it applies to business organization.
6. Describe the techniques of CPM and PERT. Distinguish between the two.
7. What is meant by real time data processing?
8. What is mechanization?
9. One characteristic of automation is feedback. Explain.
10. Another characteristic of automation is its application to sophisticated situations. Give examples.

SELECTED REFERENCES

Abramowitz, Irving, *Production Management—Concepts and Analysis for Operation and Control*, Ronald Press Co., New York, 1967.

Bain, Joe S., *Industrial Organization*, 2nd ed., John Wiley & Sons, New York, 1968.

Chase, Richard B., and Nicholas J. Aquilano, *Production and Operations Management*, Richard D. Irwin, Homewood, Ill., 1973.

Horowitz, Joseph, *Critical Path Scheduling—Management Control through CPM and PERT*, Ronald Press Co., New York, 1967.

Leone, William C., *Production Automation and Numerical Control*, Ronald Press Co., New York, 1967.

Mann, Floyd C., and L. Richard Hoffman, *Automation and the Worker*, Henry Holt & Co., New York, 1960.

Moore, Franklin G., *Production Management*, 6th ed., Richard D. Irwin, Homewood, Ill., 1973.

CHAPTER 13

PLANT LOCATION AND LAYOUT

The problems of plant location and plant layout are somewhat similar. Basically, proper plant location reduces to a minimum the costs of getting raw materials to the plant, of fabricating them, and of getting them to the customer. Proper plant layout reduces to a minimum the costs of receiving materials, moving them through the plant, and shipping the finished products. Plant location is concerned with externals, plant layout with internals. The solution of each type of problem is nearly always a compromise, for arranging an ideal situation seldom is possible in practice. In each problem, too, one must think in terms of the future, which makes the evaluation of conflicting factors particularly difficult.

PLANT LOCATION

Plant location involves two separate sets of problems: (1) establishing the geographical area and (2) determining the site.

Establishing the Geographical Area. Most business enterprises are either market oriented or raw materials oriented. *A market oriented* business is one which, for one reason or another, belongs close to the place where it markets its product. If transportation cost is the chief factor to be considered, a market oriented business is one in which the transportation cost of finished product per mile, per unit of finished product, is greater than the transportation cost of raw materials per mile, per unit of finished product. For example, bottling operations should take place near the market, for it usually is cheaper to ship the liquid in bulk than to ship it in bottles. If freshness is a factor, the plant should be near the market to avoid spoilage. For example, bakeries usually find it advantageous to allow flour and other ingredients of bakery products to be shipped long distances, and to ship their bread and other products short distances. If the process of manufacture makes the materials more bulky, fragile, or harder in other ways to ship, the plant should be near the market. For example, automobiles, furniture, machinery, and other such products often are manufactured near the source of the raw materials but are shipped in knocked-down form to assembly plants located near the market.

A *raw materials oriented* business finds it more economical to locate plants near the sources of raw materials. The reasons for thus locating a plant generally are the reverse of those mentioned in the foregoing paragraph. Whereas it would not pay to locate a plant near the source of raw materials if the process of manufacture added weight, it would if the process removed weight. For example, copper refining is done near the mine, for it costs less to ship copper than to ship ore.

Several factors tend to upset the rules with respect to location near or away from the market. One is the practice followed by transportation agencies of charging what the traffic will bear. Mere bulk or weight cannot be used as the sole criterion; value must also be considered. Another factor involves techniques of keeping products fresh. Fruit, milk, ice cream, and other perishables, if properly refrigerated, can be shipped great distances.

If more than one raw material is used, and if sales are made in more than one market, the problem of plant location becomes more complex, and its proper solution depends mostly upon the ability of the officers to forecast typical proportions of materials to be used and products to be sold. Once these proportions are established the problem is solved, as far as shipping costs are concerned, by assuming various possible localities and determining total shipping costs for each. It is interesting to note the reason for so many steel mills being located along the southern shores of the Great Lakes. Iron ore comes by boat from the Mesabi Range in northern Minnesota, and coal and limestone come by rail from various points south of the shoreline. Present locations avoid transshipping costs. If navigable rivers extended into the coal and limestone country, the mills (so far as raw materials are concerned) could be located either in the coal fields or at the iron mines. But to locate them at either point under existing conditions would require the additional cost of loading cars with ore from the ships, or loading ships with coal from the cars.

Factors Which Influence Plant Location. Besides transportation costs, there are several factors influencing plant location which are of greater or lesser importance depending upon the industry.

A concern contemplating alternative prospective localities for a plant would do well to investigate the *labor supply* at each point. Not only should labor be plentiful, but the correct trades and skills should be represented adequately. There have been many examples of firms being forced to close newly located plants because of inability to secure the right kinds of labor. After World War I a decentralizing tendency resulted in considerable ruralization of industry. This movement of industry to the country was soon reversed, due largely to the unwillingness of workers to leave the cities. Industry has, however, shown a marked tendency to move out of cities, but plants are now being located increasingly in suburban areas.

Very real difficulties have been encountered when firms in certain specialized industries have tried to locate in new areas. Such areas do not have required labor and services found in the old established locations. It is true that rubber companies have pulled away from Akron and have successfully operated in Los Angeles, and shoe companies have moved from New England to St. Louis, but it was necessary to move workers with required skills to the new locations, and there were many failures for each success.

Parasitic industries usually are found in specialized industrial areas. Such industries take advantage of the surplus labor that cannot be absorbed by the primary industry. Insurance company offices, dress-making shops, and mail-order houses are examples. On the other hand, certain *complementary* and *service industries* must locate near the primary industries if their owners wish to engage in these types of occupations. Examples of these industries and occupations are almost limitless. If the primary industry uses special types of containers it might be mutually advantageous for a company making such products to locate nearby. A few other such businesses are waste-disposal companies, specialized machinery manufacturing and servicing, electronic experts, printing plants and binderies, and training centers and bookstores.

Another factor which some industries find to be limiting is the effect of *climate*. Notable examples taken from the past are the cotton textile, cigar rolling, and motion picture industries. The development of air-conditioned factories has enabled the cotton textile industry to locate outside New England, and the cigar industry to locate away from Cuba and Florida. Although the film industry left Long Island to seek more days of sunshine in Hollywood, the changes in production methods which have taken place since the move have lessened greatly the reliance of this industry upon sunny weather.

Power is another factor of importance. Some industries, such as aluminum refining, require great quantities of electric power, whereas many other industries are not so dependent upon this factor.

There are many other factors which influence the location of manufacturing plants, but for most industries they exert a minor effect. *State laws* differ in many respects, and may exert some influence. The enactment of a particularly onerous statute has resulted in the movement of certain types of businesses into neighboring states. *Local enticements* in the form of a free site, relief from local taxation for a period of years, capital raised from stock-selling campaigns among residents of the locality, etc. often influence plant location. Care must be taken to keep such enticements in their proper perspective, and managers should not allow such factors to blind them to the presence of factors less favorable but more important to the concern in the long run. A last factor, *personal preference of the manager*, also is mentioned with a word of warning. A substantial number of factories have been given locations because personal inclinations dominated. In such instances, the choice is good or bad depending upon whether the other more rational factors tend to be favorable or unfavorable. Managers often deliberately accept the penalties of keener competition and lower profits in order to live in areas congenial to their inclinations.

Site Selection. A primary limiting factor in site selection is *rent*. This factor tends to level off at the maximum ability to pay. Firms do not locate in high-rent areas unless it is necessary and when this element of expense rises beyond their ability to pay, they move or go out of business. *Cost of land* and *taxes* are also limiting factors.

Some types of business organizations must consider ready *access of customers*. Gasoline service stations must locate where their customers can easily find them. Stores carrying shopping goods must locate near their competitors, as shoppers will not go to remote areas to compare prices.

There are, of course, many limiting factors in site selection such as *zoning laws; access to rivers, harbors, or railways*; and *need to dispose of waste products*.

Most companies give some thought to *convenience of employees*. Just as a company requiring specially trained employees finds it difficult if not impossible to operate in isolated areas, so any company will encounter more trouble finding and keeping employees if the sites selected make it difficult for such employees to live near transportation, schools, churches, shopping centers, fire and police protection, and recreation.

A difficult factor to evaluate is rapidity of growth. When a site is selected considerable thought must be given to providing *room for expansion*. Overoptimism could result in initially acquiring too much space with attendant heavy overhead expense. Too little space could result in the necessity for moving to a new site within a few years unless adjacent properties were available. Some firms have handled this problem by leasing excess capacity to other firms on short-term bases.

Obtaining Information and Evaluating Alternatives. Information obtained from federal government sources, consulting companies, and construction companies usually is factual. Information from chambers of commerce, trade associations, local governmental bodies, and other "interested" sources is, for the most part, factual but expressed in enthusiastic terms.

A simple way to select the best location or site from among many alternatives is, first, to evaluate the factors involved and, second, to rate each site with respect to each factor. Third, ultiply each factor evaluation in turn by the site rating and add the results. To illustrate, assume three alternate sites for a men's tailoring company: *A*, *B*, and *C*, and four pertinent factors: cost, transportation, customer convenience, and employee convenience.

A is downtown, *B* is in a suburban shopping area, and *C* is on a main highway just out of town.

Weights of the factors range from 10, meaning vital, to 0, meaning no importance. Cost is vital, with a weight of 10. Transportation is very important, with a weight of 8. Customer convenience is rated 10 and employee convenience 5.

An oversimplified analysis might go as follows:

A downtown site is not very desirable from the standpoint of cost. Thus site *A* is rated 2 for the factor of cost. Site *B* is rated 5 and site *C* is rated 8, reflecting the lower costs.

Transportation (by truck) is about equal for each site: *A*, 5; *B*, 7, and *C*, 6.

Customer convenience is rated 6 for downtown, 9 for the shopping area, and 3 for the edge of town.

Employee convenience is given 6 for downtown, 10 for the shopping area, and 4 for the edge of town.

When both scales are taken into account by scoring each site (factor weight times site rating) and the figures are put into a table, as follows, it is seen that site *B* definitely has more in its favor than the other two.

Analysis of Factors in Site Selection

	A	B	C
Cost	$10 \times 2 = 20$	$10 \times 5 = 50$	$10 \times 8 = 80$
Transportation	$8 \times 5 = 40$	$8 \times 7 = 56$	$8 \times 6 = 48$
Customer convenience	$10 \times 6 = 60$	$10 \times 9 = 90$	$10 \times 3 = 30$
Employee convenience	$5 \times 6 = 30$	$5 \times 10 = 50$	$5 \times 4 = 20$
Weighted totals	150	246	178

PLANT LAYOUT

The ideal layout provides for an orderly flow of materials, supplies, products, and paperwork in a direct line, with a minimum of doubling back and crossing traffic.

Requirements of a Layout. Every layout must meet four requirements:

1. The demand for available space.
2. The requirements of the processes involved.
3. The requirements of the personnel.
4. The policy respecting methods of handling materials.

The Nature of Layout Problems. We know what an ideal layout is, but conditions never permit such a layout. Every solution of a layout problem represents one or more compromises between desired and actual conditions. Some factors which must be compromised are:

1. Space that could be used conveniently and the cost of space.

2. Space occupied by materials and that used by the machine and the operator.

3. Cost of moving machines to better locations and the advantages of maintaining flexibility and of keeping the layout up-to-date.

4. Needs of the layout and the desire to make the layout look conventional and orderly.

5. Efficient arrangement of machines and a less desirable arrangement caused by obstructions, the need for accessibility to machines, or the need to maintain visibility for proper supervision.

6. Direct-line layout and special conditions which often make it desirable to take a process out of its logical place and put it elsewhere in the plant.

Diagrams, Charts, and Models. It often is wise, if possible, to build a plant around a carefully designed layout. Perhaps most concerns can fit their processes, departments, and offices into existing conventional buildings, with a minimum of remodeling, but if a new building is being constructed anyhow, the architect can, with only a little more work, design it to conform with the peculiarities of the required processes. This should be done only if it is anticipated that the layout will not be changed materially in the future.

Original layouts and improvements of existing layouts generally are made first in the form of a chart, then in the form of a scale diagram.

The needs of a process can be visualized clearly if *operation charts* are drawn. These simply show along a vertical line from top to bottom the things which are done to one type of material. If many materials are involved, each is shown separately. If two or more materials are assembled, the point at which assembly takes place is indicated by horizontal lines connecting at the proper places. A simple operation chart follows:

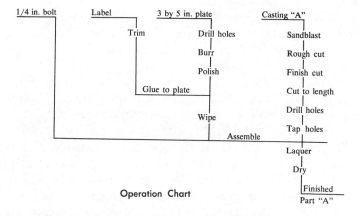

Operation Chart

If the concern manufactures only one product and if it is made up of few materials, and furthermore if the process is *synthetic* (that is, the various materials are put together to form one product), the process chart will indicate clearly the general nature of the layout desired. Reference to the illustrated operation chart shows that a production line should be set up for Casting "A" as follows:

1. Storage space for castings
2. Conveyor
3. Sandblasting equipment
4. Conveyor
5. Machine lathe which will rough cut, finish cut, and cut to length
6. Conveyor
7. Drill press where holes will be drilled and tapped
8. Conveyor
9. Assembly bench
10. Conveyor

11. Lacquer booth
12. Conveyor (but a different kind)
13. Infrared drying equipment
14. Conveyor
15. Storage

Similarly, a line for the 3 by 5-in. plates must be set up. If a direct-line layout is desired (and this generally is preferred) an additional drill press will be provided.

The *analytic* type of process follows the same procedure, except that it begins with one material which is broken down into several finished products. Meat slaughtering, petroleum, and coke production are examples.

Before a flow diagram can be constructed, certain supplementary information must be compiled. It is necessary to establish plant capacity, and this can be expressed in terms of units of product per hour. The allowed speed of each operation must be determined and expressed in terms of finished units per hour. Such speeds can be obtained from the manufacturers of the required machinery and equipment, from workmen skilled in the operations, or from manufacturers performing similar operations. The allowed time per unit of finished product, multiplied by required capacity per hour, will give the number of pieces of equipment or machines needed for that operation. For example, if a maximum flow of 100 units per hour of finished product is desired, and if the lathe work will require 0.05 hour (three minutes) per unit of finished product, 0.05 times 100 will give 5, the number of lathes required. If the drilling can be done in 0.02 hour, 2 drill presses will be required.

The amount of floor space required by the machine or equipment, or the amount of floor or bench space required to perform each operation, is next determined. Dimensions are secured from the catalogs of suppliers. Care must be taken in estimating additional space required by the machine in use, and by the material. A machine may be 2 by 5 feet, but if a table extends 2 more feet the long way and if an arm swings 1 foot each way to the sides, the floor space required will be 4 by 7 feet. A 10-foot paper-tube winding machine may produce 12-foot tubes which extend as many feet beyond the end of the machine before they are cut off. It is necessary, therefore, to allow at least 22 feet of floor space. The same precaution must be taken for machines which process long pieces of bar stock, pipes, and other such materials. Space must be allowed, of course, for the operator and possibly for temporary storage of materials. If materials are transported in trucks, sufficient aisle space must be provided. There must be clearance space around and above each machine for dismantling and replacing worn parts. The question of floor strength must be investigated for each piece of equipment, and such matters as possible interference with light sources, overhead obstructions, elevator landing space, etc., must be studied. After having taken all these matters into account the layout man is ready to make a flow diagram.

Customarily, the *flow diagram* is made by placing templates representing all the pieces of equipment and the various elements of required space (all cut to scale out of heavy paper, and properly labeled) on a large piece of paper on which is drawn a scale floor plan of the building. When a desirable arrangement is made, the templates are glued down with rubber cement. Then lines are drawn representing the flow of materials. Materials difficult to transport are shown with heavy lines, and materials easy to move are shown with light lines. If the building is not yet constructed, considerable readjustment of the positions of walls, elevators, columns, windows, doors, etc. can be made. Otherwise, the layout must be made with reference to existing conditions.

Those charged with making the layout attempt to improve the tentative arrangement by studying the flow diagram. Always the aim is to eliminate or reduce switchbacks, crossing traffic, and bottlenecks. If possible, the heavy lines on the diagram are shortened even though this might result in lengthening somewhat the light lines. When the diagram is as good as it can be made for the time being, it is put into more permanent form (perhaps photographed) and the physical layout is begun. Sometimes three-dimensional scale models of equipment are constructed and put into a model of the factory. This procedure often is justified when the equipment is heavy and expensive to move, for no matter how carefully the layout men plan, there always seems to be something they could not foresee. If the machinery lends itself to the procedure it is well to operate the production line a few days before the equipment is bolted into place to be sure that everything is arranged properly.

Layout Types. When one product is manufactured, or when one raw material is introduced into the process, or when products and procedures are fairly well standardized and are stable in nature, the direct-line type of layout is undoubtedly best. This is the type which has been described in the foregoing material. Such a layout is known as *product grouping*. The arrangement of all processes defers to the requirements of the product, which travels in a direct line through the plant. If, as a result of a design change, an additional operation is required, equipment for performing that operation is moved into the line at the proper point. If an additional product is manufactured, requiring a different sequence of operations, a new production line is set up, even though the machines are identical with those in the first production line. If frequent design changes are required, and if the machines are light, the line is changed for every change in operational sequence. But if the equipment cannot easily be moved, or if there are many different products and if new products are constantly being added and old ones dropped, it is better to use the *process-grouping* type of plant layout. Under this type, all similar machines and processes are grouped, and the materials are *routed* from machine to machine. It is necessary to *schedule* each job lot so as not to overload some machines and allow others to remain idle. *Dispatchers* are needed to keep the flow of materials up to schedule, to explain deviations, and to deal with emergencies. The flow of production must be controlled regardless of the type of layout, but the difficulties are greatly multiplied in the plant where machines are process-grouped. Routing, scheduling, and dispatching are considered in more detail in the next chapter.

There are a few industries where the machines must be taken to the material or the product, which remains stationary (as in shipbuilding), although this type of layout closely resembles process grouping. In a given plant one may find all sorts of modifications of the two basic types. Machine parts may be processed, for instance, in process-grouped departments, while the parts may be assembled in a product-grouped department. Or the reverse may be true in the sense that from the standpoint of the plant as a whole the *departments* are product-grouped while within each department the *machines* are process-grouped. More special machines and more narrow specialization are found in product-grouped departments, while more general-purpose machines and more versatility are found in the process-grouped departments.

QUESTIONS FOR DISCUSSION

1. Explain the difference between a market oriented business and one that is raw materials oriented. Give an example of each.
2. What is a parasitic industry? A complementary industry?
3. How important in site selection are rent, cost of land, and property taxes? Would it be wise to locate in a high-rent area if other factors were favorable?
4. How reliable are Chambers of Commerce as sources of information in solving location and site problems? Are there better sources?
5. State in general terms how masses of facts and claims concerning alternate locations and sites can be put into understandable form.
6. What four requirements must every plant layout meet?
7. State five compromises that must be made between ideal and practical plant layouts.
8. Why is it often desirable to design a building around the layout? What are the dangers in following this procedure?
9. Distinguish between synthetic and analytic industries. Give an example of each.
10. Distinguish between a product-grouped layout and a process-grouped layout. When should one be used rather than the other?

SELECTED REFERENCES

Apple, James M., *Plant Layout and Materials Handling*, 2nd ed., Ronald Press Co., New York, 1963.

Ireson, Grant, and Gene Grant, *Handbook of Industrial Engineering and Management*, 2nd ed., Prentice-Hall, Englewood Cliffs, N. J., 1971.

Moore, Franklin G., *Production Management*, 6th ed., Richard D. Irwin, Homewood, Ill., 1973.

Muther, Richard, *Practical Plant Layout*, McGraw-Hill, New York, 1956.

CHAPTER 14

PRODUCTION METHODS AND CONTROL

The broader aspects of management were discussed in Chapter 9. In this chapter, the more specific aspects of management, as they apply to factory production, will be covered.

Use of the Term "Production." The economist uses the term "production" as meaning all economic activity. In this chapter the concept generally followed in business is used, that of making things.

It is true that one can "produce" services. Nevertheless, an insurance company generally is not referred to as a production enterprise—it is a service enterprise.

A lawyer or an accountant working for an automobile manufacturing concern does not consider himself to be "in production." He is a professional employee. Even those who work closely with production employees (designers, engineers, inspectors, and so on) do not consider themselves as production persons. Those who route, schedule, and dispatch are in production, but they add a qualifying word, and call the occupation "production control." Again, foremen generally do not claim to be production workers: they are "blue-collar" supervisors. The rank-and-file worker is the true "production employee," though many other persons in supervision, control, planning, accounting, law, sales, advertising, transportation, and so on are needed to make the results of his efforts effective.

Production Processes Classified. On the basis of their predominating processes all manufacturing concerns fall into one of the following types: analytic, synthetic, or conditioning.

Analytic production breaks one raw material down into two

or more finished products. A good example is petroleum, from which are derived heating oil, lubricating oil, kerosene, gasoline, and many other products. These products are vital to the well-being of the country, and the present shortage of this one raw material is keenly felt.

Synthetic production puts two or more raw materials together to form one finished product. An example of this form is automobile production.

Conditioning production neither takes things apart nor puts them together. It involves seasoning, shaping, drying, molding, pressing, and so on. A few examples of such industries are: brickmaking, wire drawing, steel rolling mills, forging mills, ham and bacon smoking, lumber seasoning, and liquor aging.

Another way of classifying industries is on the basis of continuity.

Continuous production refers to production-line operations involving the manufacture of many identical or similar products day after day. Frequently successive numbers are stamped on the products as they come off the line—hence the term *serialized production* also is applied to this form.

Intermittent production refers to the job-order type of manufacturing. Orders go through the plant in lots, each of which differs in some respect from others. To process these products it is necessary to shut down the plant, or sections of it, periodically for basic adjustments or retooling.

Production Control. Production would be chaotic without plans and adherence to them. Usually it is important to get orders out on time. Accomplishing this cannot be left to chance. Planning the flow of materials and following them through the various required processes is the job of a specialized department called *production control*. The work of this department is divided into four parts: routing, scheduling, dispatching, and follow-up.

Routing involves determining from the work that must be done where the raw materials, parts, and subassemblies must go to be processed. In product-grouped departments routing is accomplished when the layout of machines and equipment is first made. In process- or machine-grouped departments it is necessary to get the materials and parts through the successive steps in orderly fashion without interfering with other orders being processed simultaneously.

In centralized routing the machines and equipment are designated on cards attached to each item or batch of items. Movemen then take the materials from station to station as shown on the cards. In decentralized routing the successive operations are specified initially, but a departmental dispatcher determines when each order is to go into the process. Usually the oldest order goes next unless there are rush orders waiting.

Scheduling is setting up timetables for the various lots of materials, parts, and subassemblies to be processed. Working from engineering specifications and blueprints or from standard lists of processes, the schedulers usually work backward, beginning with the promised delivery date of finished product or lot of products. In the following table, for instance, the finished product was promised August 29. Shipping time is two days, so the product is scheduled to leave the plant August 27. Final inspection and crating take one day, so these operations are scheduled for August 26. Moving requires one day and painting and drying require three days. Taking advantage of a weekend for drying, the product goes to the paint shop on the 22nd. Final assembly is done on the 21st and Part A with clamps, bolts, and nuts (all purchased outside) and the subassembly of two Part Bs and one Part C are moved to the Assembly Department August 20. Two Part Bs are assembled and welded to one Part C on the 18th, and Part A (with clamps, bolts, and nuts) are ordered on the 15th. Part C is machined on the 14th. Two Part Bs are moved to the Welding Department and the sandblasted casting C is moved to a lathe for machining to dimensions on the 13th. Part C is sandblasted on the 12th and operations are scheduled to begin on the order by moving the part requiring the most work out of the stockroom on August 11.

This procedure does not avoid all rescheduling and congestion, but it reduces them significantly.

Dispatching is the term applied to putting plans into action. The dispatcher keeps each order on a board or chart broken down by processes and dates. It is his job to assign the work to the correct place at the planned date, or as close to it as possi-

Date	Part A	Part B	Part C
Aug. 11			Move casting from Stockroom to Sandblasting
12			Sandblast
13		Move 2 steel bars from storeroom to Welding	Move to Lathe #10
14			Machine to dimensions and move to Welding
15	Order Part A with clamps, bolts, and nuts		
18		Weld bars to Part C	
19	Receive Part A		
20	Move to Assembly	Move to Assembly	
21	Final Assembly. Clamp Part A to Parts B and C		
22	Move to Paint Shop and paint		
25	Move to Crating Department		
26	Final inspection. Crate and move to Shipping Department		
27	Ship to customer		
29	Delivery date		

ble. Dispatchers' desks are located in cages at certain points throughout the plant. These cages hold the paperwork for production control and frequently, also, special tools required for each order. They can be locked so as to keep possible intruders out.

The dispatcher records the starting and finishing times for each job together with the station and the employee who worked on it. He also sees that finished parts are promptly inspected and moved, and if there are absent employees or materials shortages he notifies the office. Although the foreman manages his department, the dispatcher handles the moving of materials and assigning workers to do the work.

Frequently things go awry. Cards, materials, and tools are misplaced and mistakes are made in planning, routing, scheduling, and dispatching. Sometimes dispatchers or even workers take it on themselves to make changes. It is necessary, therefore, to *follow up* so as to ensure correct functioning of the system. As the follow-up officer traces the trouble he straightens things out himself, if possible. Otherwise he reports the trouble to those who can.

It must be recognized that production control is costly and should be used sparingly. The aim here is not perfection but, rather, only enough system to keep adequate control.

Materials Control. Materials control is closely connected with the system of production control. However, it usually is considered to be a separate activity with its own techniques.

The first step in the control of materials is *receiving*. When materials are ordered, a copy of the order is sent to the receiving department. When the materials arrive, they are inspected and weighed or counted. Some companies omit the quantities on the copy of the order sent to receiving. Quantities received are entered by the checker, and the copies are returned to the office where comparisons are made between what was received and what should have been received. This procedure, known as *blind checking*, forces employees in the receiving department to be extra careful.

Receiving notifies the laboratory when materials arrive that must be tested. Inasmuch as laboratory technicians prefer to take their own samples, receiving furnishes such information as nature of the materials, quantities received, and location. Since the technician must certify as to the quality of the materials, he must secure adequate and representative samples of the correct shipment.

If the materials are not up to specifications the shipment can, and often is, rejected. To avoid the expense and trouble of getting a rejected shipment back, the vendor often makes a price concession which may be accepted by the purchaser.

When the materials are accepted after being inspected, they are moved to the storeroom. From here they are moved out onto the production floor as needed. An important function of materials control is that of making management aware of where all materials are at any given time.

Storekeepers and *movemen* make reports, which form the basis of perpetual inventory systems. Storekeepers usually make periodic physical counts of materials in their custody, and their accounts are subject to regular audits. Often storekeepers re-order previously calculated economical lots of standard materials when the quantities on hand reach the ordering point.

Those in charge of materials control usually are also interested in *materials handling*. Since a substantial percentage of production costs involves picking materials up, carrying them, and setting them down, it is important to shorten lines of travel and to use the cheapest forms of handling equipment.

Other Specialized Departments. There are, of course, many specialized departments in most companies. Those most closely associated with production control include the following:

The *sales department* usually originates the order. Often the order goes first to the *credit department* where arrangements are made for payment by the customer. The *order department* then gets it and types it up in appropriate form, sending copies to those who record, bill, and control. The *traffic department* usually specifies the most satisfactory way of shipping incoming materials and sometimes determines methods of shipping to customers. The *shipping department* prepares bills of lading and sometimes orders trucks or freight cars. Loading is supervised by this department and, as a rule, it keeps records of shipments.

Supervisors. *Supervisors* represent management in the various departments. Each is in charge of his own department. Many *staff employees* work in each department with the permission of the foreman. They cannot ignore or supersede the foreman and they should never come into a production department without notifying him. Some of these staff activities are *personnel*, which hires, trains, transfers, disciplines, and discharges employees; *timekeeping*, which records the time each employee spends at work; *payroll*, which prepares periodic pay checks or envelopes; *methods*, which works out techniques to be used in production; *motion-study*, which reduces wasteful motions; *time-study*, which sets time standards; *safety*, which tries to eliminate hazards; *maintenance*, which keeps machines and equipment in repair; and *industrial relations,* which deals with employee grievances.

Foremen are responsible for the smooth functioning of their departments, so they are given the authority to issue appropriate orders. They do not perform specialized functions but they do coordinate these activities.

QUESTIONS FOR DISCUSSION

1. Persons in business attach a somewhat different meaning to the term "production" than do economists. Explain.
2. Give examples of the three types of production processes: analytic, synthetic, and conditioning.
3. Describe and give examples of continuous and intermittent production.
4. Name and describe the four activities that make up production control.
5. What should a dispatcher do if the foreman of the department in which he is working disagrees with the order in which jobs are being assigned?
6. Why is it not advisable to design a production control system as close to perfection as possible? What should be the aim?
7. What does "blind checking" mean?
8. What precautions should the receiving department take when materials come in that must be tested?
9. Who is responsible for keeping management informed as to how much of all materials are on hand and where they are located?
10. Name five specialized, or staff, departments that operate in production departments. How can they function effectively if foremen are in charge?

SELECTED REFERENCES

Abramowitz, Irving, *Production Management—Concepts and Analysis for Operation and Control*, Ronald Press Co., New York, 1967.

Apple, James M., *Plant Layout and Materials Handling*, 2nd ed., Ronald Press Co., New York, 1963.

Biegel, John E., *Production Control*, 2nd ed., Prentice-Hall, Englewood Cliffs, N. J., 1971.

Bock, Robert H., and William K. Holstein, eds., *Production Planning and Control*, Charles E. Merrill Publishing Co., Columbus, Ohio, 1963.

Buffa, Elwood S., *Production Inventory Systems: Planning and Control*, rev. ed., Richard D. Irwin, Homewood, Ill., 1972.

Chase, Richard B., and Nicholas J. Aquilano, *Production and Operations Management*, Richard D. Irwin, Homewood, Ill., 1973.

Greene, James H., *Production Control: Systems and Decisions*, rev. ed., Richard D. Irwin, Homewood, Ill., 1974.

Hopeman, Richard J., *Production: Concepts—Analysis—Control*, 2nd ed., Charles E. Merrill Publishing Co., Columbus, Ohio, 1971.

Moore, Franklin G., *Production Management*, 6th ed., Richard D. Irwin, Homewood, Ill., 1973, Chap. 18.

Niland, Powell, *Production Planning, Scheduling and Inventory Control*, Macmillan Co., New York, 1970.

PART V

PERSONNEL ORGANIZATION

Part V is concerned with three aspects of human beings in the business setting. Chapter 15 deals with the effective utilization of employees, Chapter 16 provides an account of how employees have increased their bargaining power through mutual organization, and Chapter 17 is concerned with management-union relations.

CHAPTER 15

PERSONNEL MANAGEMENT

Personnel management as a specialized function in business organizations started to emerge after World War I. It began by relieving supervisors of details that detracted from the main job of getting production out. As time passed, many additional duties were placed in the hands of the personnel manager, duties that probably never would have been thought of as appropriate for foremen and superintendents to discharge.

Historical Aspects. The earliest employees, outside of family and clan relationships, were *slaves*. From the earliest days of recorded history down to modern times slavery has existed. Slaves had no rights, no incentive, no hope. They could be bought cheaply and it did not pay the master to treat them well. It was more profitable to wear them out and buy replacements than to house, clothe, and feed them decently.

Ancient Egypt and early Greece depended on slave labor, though in Greece free men often worked beside slaves.

Slavery existed in the Roman Empire and was common throughout Europe in the Middle Ages. In Rome, animals were treated better than slaves. However, during the Middle Ages a new type of labor-master relationship developed—*serfdom*.

Serfdom had its beginnings in the latter days of the Roman Empire. Masters of landed estates gradually found it desirable to allow their slaves to settle on the land. From the eighth to the eleventh centuries throughout Europe life was almost wholly agricultural. Feudal lords owned the land. Each such holding was known as a *manor*, and the economic and political organization of that day came to be known as the *manorial system*.

In this period of time there were *free tenants*, men who

rented substantial plots of land, and *cotters*, who rented small plots. Most, however, were *serfs*, known also as *villeins*. These were half free. They could not be sold by the master, but they were bound to the land. Most of what they produced went to the lord of the manor, but they kept part for themselves. Under this system there were also slaves. These, mostly, were craftsmen owned by the lord. It was possible for a slave to buy his freedom, by producing extra goods or by borrowing the money and working off the debt. However, slaves increasingly ran away and found employment in a distant town. So, in this period of time in rural areas there were free men, serfs, and slaves.

In the towns there were master craftsmen, journeymen, and apprentices who operated under the *guild system*. Guilds were associations of *master craftsmen* who governed the employment relationships in their town. Each master contracted with parents of one or more boys to teach the boys his trade in return for what the boys produced over a period of 4 to 10 years. Usually these *apprentices* lived in the master's home, were clothed and fed by him, and sometimes were given a small wage. On completion of the term the apprentice became a *journeyman craftsman* and could hire himself to a master for wages. Usually, after a year or so in this position, the journeyman sought admission to the guild and, after being examined and paying a fee, he became a master and set up in business for himself.

Many writers in this field contend that craftsmen of that day enjoyed economic privileges such as they never enjoyed previously or since. They began in a secure and congenial atmosphere as apprentices. As journeymen they were almost certain to become masters. And as masters they owned their own shops, tools, and equipment and, if they were industrious, could look forward to a lifetime of prosperity. There was little or no friction and frustration in the employment relationship and there were minimal social class distinctions among apprentices, journeymen, and masters.

As the years passed, there was an increasing shift of population from rural areas to the towns. In England the king raised money for waging war by granting political independence to urban centers. Increasing demand for goods increased the demand for labor. In the fourteenth century, the Black Death wiped out one-third of the population. Then came the Hundred Years' War and a series of famines and droughts, all of which caused radical changes in the economy. Journeymen craftsmen found it more and more difficult to go into business in the face of rising costs. They sought higher wages, but Parliament enacted laws freezing wages and providing prison sentences for those who refused jobs at the old customary rates. As a permanent class of laborers developed, *journeymen guilds* were formed for protection. These were the precursors of modern unions.

In the fifteenth and sixteenth centuries economic protectionism grew and labor relations were rigidly enforced by the central government. This form of economic system was known as *mercantilism.*

In the seventeenth and eighteenth centuries the *domestic system* was typical. Capitalist producers sent materials to the homes of workers where they were processed. Then, near the end of the eighteenth century the Industrial Revolution began making itself felt and the *factory system* came into the picture. As machinery took over the skills of the workers, employment conditions fell to a new low. Wages were at a subsistence level and young children were widely used as machine tenders.

Meanwhile, labor in the American colonies was largely agricultural. But as the colonies developed and as workers moved west seeking personal independence and more favorable living conditions, opportunities for employment along the seaboard increased. Immigrants from Europe filled this need. It has been estimated that at least half of all immigrants during the colonial period were *indentured servants*. These laborers signed agreements to serve masters in America for a number of years in return for their passage. Most came voluntarily, many had the choice of coming in lieu of prison sentences or execution for crimes committed in England, and many were brought over by kidnappers. In any event all generally were treated harshly by their masters.

Slave labor, which never had disappeared in the rest of the world, was introduced into America during colonial days. Its desirability in the Northern states diminished gradually but it persisted on the large plantations of the South until abolished by Presidential proclamation during the Civil War.

In the years prior to the Civil War thousands of skilled workers came to the United States from Europe to fill the demands of expanding industry. Although wages were relatively high, living expenses also were high. A few unions were formed but individual bargaining between employees and employers persisted. Employment conditions were bad but not as bad as they were in Europe. Disaffected employees in the United States could always move west to the frontier.

In the period between the Civil War and World War I unionism became stronger, but so also did employers. There was much consolidation of business concerns, some collective bargaining, and frequent violent clashes between workers and plant guards.

In the early days of the Industrial Revolution a British employer, Robert Owen, introduced paternalistic practices into his textile mills. His employees responded favorably, but few other employers followed his example. In 1825 he founded a communal settlement at New Harmony, Indiana, but after three years it failed. During the years prior to World War I employers became increasingly paternalistic. They organized company unions and systems for discussing, if not settling, employee grievances. Employees and the general public were suspicious of independent union organizers and the attitude of most persons was that unions were unnecessary.

Working conditions were good, wages were high, and unemployment was low as the decade of the 1920s came to a close. Then the Great Depression of 1929 struck. In 1929 there were 31,339,000 wage and salary workers in the United States. In 1931 the low point of 23,628,000 was reached. Not until 1940 was the 1929 figure reached again. Much prolabor legislation was passed during this period, most of which had the effect of granting hourly-paid employees the right to organize and bargain collectively with their employers regarding wages, hours, and working conditions. Over the years these laws, together with bettering economic conditions, have given hourly-paid workers an economic status they never before enjoyed. Unfortunately, however, unemployment has continued to plague the country off and on. In 1940 it was 14.6% but in 1953 it fell to 2.9%. In 1969 it was 3.5% and in 1970, 4.9%. In 1975 it was rising rapidly, reaching 8.9% in April. Mostly it ranges from 6.8% to 4.3%. The unemployed receive compensation under federal and state laws.

Today the average American firm treats its employees well and provides good working conditions. Most hourly workers are limited to 8 hours per day and 40 hours per week, above which overtime wages must be paid.[1] Most union-management agreements provide for grievance procedures including the arbitration by an impartial third party of unresolved disputes. Workers still have the right by law to strike, but only as a last resort. Usually, by agreement, unions agree not to strike and employers agree not to lock out employees during the term of the contract, which generally is three years.

The Personnel Department. Just as many other staff departments have been introduced by business concerns to take burdensome detail off the hands of supervisors, so has the *personnel department* been developed. Timekeeping departments have been in existence for many years as have hiring offices. Other similar specialized offices have been introduced over the years, such as payroll, safety, pension, recreation, and health and welfare. During the 1930s many firms began consolidating these departments into personnel divisions, and new activities were added from time to time. Many firms, however, have kept timekeeping and payroll as separate departments. At first, collective bargaining was handled by the company executives; then it was delegated to personnel. Today it is usual for this activity to be handled, at least by larger firms, by a closely related division often known as the *labor relations department*. It is customary, also, for the union-company grievance procedure to be administered by this division. This activity is discussed in the next chapter.

Recruitment and Hiring. It is customary in industry to fit the person to the job. Jobs are designed to perform a needed func-

---

1. Based on a minimum rate per hour of $2.10 effective January 1, 1975, and $2.30 January 1, 1976. Variations based on unusual conditions must be approved by the National Labor Relations Board.

tion and, while some can be modified somewhat to match the qualifications of an available applicant, usually it is necessary to search until someone is found who can meet all the demands.

Where does the personnel department look for recruits for new or vacant jobs? There are two broad sources: internal and external.

Internal sources for recruits are found within the firm. A common method of locating qualified employees for new job openings is known as the *post and bid* procedure. A description of the job is posted on the bulletin board with room below for the signatures of applicants. After a few days the applicants are interviewed and selected. If two or more are equally qualified, the senior employee in point of service is selected and the job he vacates is similarly filled. If no one is qualified, it becomes necessary to seek applicants from outside the organization. It is more expensive to follow the post and bid procedure, but it tends to build security and high morale in the work force. Some unions insist on the procedure and it is written into the union-company agreement.

External sources include former employees, files of job applicants, employment agencies, schools, and many others. The advantage of using *former employees* is that they know the job, and everything surrounding it is familiar. There is no expensive period of breaking in. This source is, however, limited and difficult to use.

Many new employees are selected from *applications on file* in the personnel office. Timing, of course, is a factor in matching jobs and persons, and the unsolicited applicant often is out of a job and cannot wait for a vacancy in the firm of his choice. When the right job opens up he may be working elsewhere. Nevertheless, most concerns like to hold application forms made out by likely future employees and often such individuals make themselves available when suitable openings occur.

Most new employees are obtained from private and public employment agencies. Much of the work of interviewing and selecting is done by the agencies. *Private employment agencies* charge fees for matching jobs and applicants. Whether the employer or the applicant pays depends on who benefits the most. *Public employment agencies* are operated by the states under the general control of the United States Training and Employment Service and with federal financial support. Unemployment insurance benefits are payable only to individuals who register with the agency and accept suitable work found for them.

Many firms send personnel representatives to *schools* where they interview students who are about to finish their courses. *Unions* are a source for likely employees. As a matter of fact, in some industries (waterfront is one) hiring through the union hall is mandatory.

Some firms find it advantageous to hire some workers from among *discharged prisoners*. These persons, if carefully selected, usually make excellent employees. They are grateful to the company for helping them at a critical time, they know that they must make good, and they usually work harder than other employees.

All through the hiring procedure and after the new worker has been assigned to the job, care must be taken not to discriminate against any person because of race, sex, color, religion, national origin, or age. The Civil Rights Act of 1964 (amended in 1968 and 1972) makes most of these forms of discrimination illegal and the Equal Employment Opportunity Commission administers its provisions. The Age Discrimination in Employment Act of 1967 (amended in 1974) protects persons from 49 to 65. Sex discrimination is prohibited by the Act of 1964 (amended in 1972). The 1972 Equal Rights Amendment to the Constitution provides that equality of rights under the law shall not be denied or abridged by the United States or by any state on account of sex. On April 1, 1974, 33 states out of the required 38 had ratified the amendment for adoption.

Selection. After a sufficiently large number of applicants for the open job or jobs has been recruited, it is necessary to narrow the field. Often this is done through a series of *interviews*. The candidates may be sent, one at a time, to the supervisor so he can "size them up." In most cases this is not advisable at the outset unless appearance is very important. Department stores find that it is best to judge the appearance of applicants for sales jobs at what is called the *rail interview*. Sloppy persons or those with objectionable mannerisms are eliminated at this time from further consideration. If *physical fitness* is of primary importance the applicants are given physical examinations first, and the unfit are rejected. Likewise, if specialized knowledge and skills are required *psychological examinations* and *trial runs* will serve to confirm claims of experience made on the application blanks.

If the new employees will be expected to learn theory and will be trained in new techniques, *tests* may be administered.

Intelligence tests indicate the person's ability to learn as compared with the average. *Aptitude tests* show a person's potential in given types of activity. *Performance tests* indicate a person's present skills.

Only a person trained in administering tests should be allowed to do this work. Only *validated tests* should be given. These are tests that have been tried out and have proved to be capable of performing their functions. Tests are validated best by being given to employees now doing the work. Supervisors rate these employees as, say, (1) best, (2) almost best, (3) medium, (4) poor, and (5) poorest. If (1) makes the highest test score and (5) the lowest, and if the others come out second, third, and fourth, then the test is valid. If a new job is being filled, applicants are given the aptitude test, then, after having been on the job a few weeks, they are rated by the supervisor. If the ratings check with the test scores, the tests are valid.

To avoid discrimination it has been the practice to give the same tests to all applicants for a given job, and this has been used as proof that there was no discrimination in filling the job. It is not true, however, that a given test will accurately place all persons in the proper category, and a fully qualified psychologist knows this. An intelligence test validated on white, 20-year-old male Kansans might give wholly erroneous results when administered to blacks, young white New Yorkers, women, 50-year-olds, foreigners, and so on. So giving the same test to all comers is not necessarily the right procedure. The answer, when validity is in doubt, usually is to hire persons with a variety of backgrounds and drop those who do not make the grade. Unions do not object to this procedure if the period of time involved is relatively short.

Training. When new employees are hired or when employees are put on new jobs or their jobs are changed in any respect they must be trained or retrained. As the years go by some jobs seem never to change while others require constant study and practice to keep up to date. Except for the introduction of the triphammer, blacksmithing is much the same as it was two hundred or more years ago. On the other hand, engineering graduates in electronics are considered by many firms to be untrained unless they have had further training during the past ten years.

New employees, if hired in groups, frequently are given *vestibule training*. This is a form of off-the-job training given in a quiet room equipped with the machinery that will be used on the job after the training is completed. A variety of this form is *classroom training*, where lectures, audio-visual equipment, and demonstrations are used.

The most commonly used form of training is *on-the-job training*. In this form the trainee is put on the production floor under the direction of a supervisor or another employee, who observes the learner and corrects his mistakes. Care must be taken, when this form is used, to select good instructors. Too often the older employee designated to instruct a trainee resents the interruption of his routine, his demonstrations are dazzling exhibitions of his own skill, and his "instruction" consists of a series of reprimands. The personnel department, by selecting good instructors (who are not necessarily the best performers) can help greatly in upgrading the quality of this type of training. To be of value, demonstrations must be understood by the trainee. Good instructors tell trainees what to look for in demonstrations; then if they fail to perform satisfactorily the first few times, they are not reprimanded but are told what to do to perform properly. They are watched while they perform on the job until their work is acceptable. Thereafter, the instructor leaves for longer and longer periods of time until the new employee is considered to be fully trained.

Young persons desiring to learn a trade are trained by some companies over longer periods of time, with the cooperation of the union concerned, in *apprenticeship training* programs. After sufficient preparation they work on the job, but with reduced wages and always under supervision.

When theory, methods, policies, and improvements are involved, *conference training* is often used. Accidents and other problems can be discussed and ideas for improvement thrown out for discussion. This form of training, which sometimes includes *role playing*, usually is reserved for supervisory, staff, and executive employees.

Trade schools and some companies use teaching machines for *programmed training*. A small portion of the entire lesson is presented on what appears to be a television screen. A question follows and the student responds. If he is wrong the material is repeated and explained further. If he is right the next segment of the lesson is presented. This method of training is thorough and fast.

Some firms encourage their employees to engage in *correspondence training* to qualify for possible upgrading. Many professional correspondence training schools provide practical and valuable courses. Also, leading universities offer through their extension divisions a great variety of courses. Some companies pay their employees' tuition for each course satisfactorily completed.

Motivation and Performance. The personnel department is concerned with what makes employees want to produce. Attempts are made to keep employees, from the time they are hired and trained, content with their jobs and willing to work hard at them. For many years some employers assumed that a happy work force should be a productive work force. Others forgot the frills and assumed that money was all that counted. However, it gradually became apparent that high morale does not necessarily encourage high productivity and that money is not always the strongest motivating force. Furthermore, employers discovered that some employees responded to certain forms of motivation and others did not. One investigator[1] in attempting to explain the many inconsistencies of employee behavior discovered the existence of a *hierarchy of needs*. Employees who must give primary attention to satisfying elementary physiological needs are motivated most strongly by money.

---

1. A. H. Maslow, *Motivation and Personality*, Harper & Brothers, New York, 1954.

Wage incentive plans are effective for such employees up to the point where the income reasonably satisfies these needs and increased production is not worth the additional effort.

Once the physiological needs are substantially satisfied, the employee gives more weight to "safety" needs. When these are relatively satisfied, he becomes cognizant of "social" needs. He next wants "esteem," and the highest plane of motivation is "self-fulfillment."

The specific factors that motivate individuals are almost infinite in variety. The personnel department can help clarify in the minds of employees what it is they want from their jobs and then, through training or transfers, help them to achieve their goals. They might even help such workers as the one who told the writer the motivating force that drove him the strongest was the desire to show a mother-in-law, who believed he could never succeed at anything, that she was wrong.

Change. Much of the time of the personnel department is devoted to problems involving *change.* Supervisors are as much of the problem as are rank-and-file workers. Some individuals welcome change and some resist it. One of the biggest mistakes management can make is to decide on a change and not tell the employees. Often the employees hear of a change, such as extensive automation of the plant, from a newspaper announcement or from company or community rumors. To build loyalty among the labor force every change of consequence should be disclosed to the employees. This can be done in group meetings, on the public address system, or on bulletin boards. The advantages and disadvantages of the change should be clearly explained as soon as feasible to prevent the exaggerated interpretations that invariably follow such announcements.

Individuals and small groups are involved in promotions, transfers, demotions, layoffs, separations, and recalls. If a union is involved, the procedures usually are spelled out. But the personnel department can do much to ease the transition.

Strangely enough many individuals resist *promotion.* Although higher pay is an attraction, it may not be enough to offset increased responsibilities, new and strange surroundings, jealousy of coworkers, fear of failure, and so on. The personnel department can do much to overcome such resistance as well as the frequent objections of the supervisor involved who will lose a good worker.

Transfers are lateral moves involving no pay-rate change. They are caused by a great variety of reasons. The employee may welcome the move. If he does not, a personnel representative may be able to convince him that the change is for the best. When an employee is moved from a job that is at the top of a wage scale to another job that is at the bottom of a higher wage scale with no change in wage, some employers call this a "lateral promotion." Even though opportunities have improved, such a move is still a transfer.

Demotions, layoffs, and *separations* (discharges) usually are painful for all concerned. Some firms make it a practice never to demote an employee, for, no matter how much personnel tries to make it palatable, there is a tendency for the employee to become morose and disaffected. Some will quit rather than submit to the lower income and loss of face.

Layoffs usually are necessary in the face of temporary reductions in business. Many firms have standby work for such occasions, such as painting, roof repairs, cleanup work, and so on. If possible, manufacturing is continued for stock. As a rule layoffs are made on the basis of seniority, the most senior employees being laid off last and recalled first. Some concerns lay employees off on the basis of seniority and recall them on the basis of merit. Often the process of *bumping* is followed under which an employee slated for layoff is allowed to select a lower-rated job and displace the incumbent if the latter is junior in point of service. The *post and bid* procedure is also frequently opened to laid-off employees, who are allowed to apply for jobs as they are vacated. The most proficient employees usually are selected for the position, but if several of equal merit apply, the senior employee gets the position. As a rule a laid-off employee does not lose his seniority until a given period of time has elapsed.

Both unions and managers insist that employees be separated only for just cause and not at the whim of the foreman. Companies subject to cyclical demand must, of necessity, discharge employees. Unions are not so much concerned with this type of separation (provided bumping and seniority rules are observed) as they are with disciplinary discharges. Often the company sets up rules which, if broken, carry varying degrees of penalties. Some offenses such as fighting or theft would result in immediate discharge, whereas smoking in forbidden areas might bring a reprimand and a warning notice with a repetition resulting in discharge.

Absenteeism and Tardiness. Two ever-present problems that must be faced by the personnel department are *absenteeism* and *tardiness*. It is recognized that few individuals can maintain perfect records indefinitely. Illness and various emergencies inevitably come to all, and missed busses, flat tires, traffic jams, and so on tend to confound the most punctual employee. However, every firm must deal with employees who are chronically absent or tardy.

As a rule an employee who knows he must be absent is required to phone the office. Some companies will dispatch a company nurse at once if the employee reports he is ill. Since this smacks of spying, it has become the accepted practice to wait a day or until the nurse is requested. Most firms provide sick leave arrangements, either voluntarily or as part of a negotiated labor agreement with a union. Briefly, such arrangements give each employee pay for an additional number of days above the number of working days in the year. Each day of absence will then be deducted from this extra allowance. Unclaimed days are either paid for in cash to the employee or added to his paid vacation time.

Tardiness is handled in a variety of ways. Some firms remove time cards from the racks fifteen minutes after starting time and force late employees to come to the office to make their excuses. Often pay is deducted in fifteen minute increments. The seriousness of tardiness varies from company to company. Where straight-line production is used and where the absence of an employee could tie up production, tardiness is more serious than situations where the employees work independently.

Employees who are chronically absent or tardy usually are discharged from the work force.

Labor Turnover. There are several ways of calculating *labor turnover*. The most commonly used formula is separations divided by average force for a given period of time. Multiplying this ratio by 100 will express turnover in the form of a percent.

Turnover can also be expressed as additions to the force divided by the average force, or replacements divided by the average force. Still another method uses the average of separations and accessions divided by the average work force.

Any company can compare its turnover figures with those published for the same industry in the *Monthly Labor Review*. If the company's figures are unfavorably high, investigation can disclose the reason and measures can be taken to correct the situation.

Other Activities of the Personnel Department. The personnel department is also actively concerned with wage policy, fringe benefits, financial incentives, health, safety, and other factors involving the work force.

QUESTIONS FOR DISCUSSION

1. Describe briefly the manorial system of the Middle Ages.
2. Describe briefly the guild system. What forces in the fourteenth century caused a decline in this system?
3. What were the chief differences between the domestic system and the factory system?
4. Tell something of Robert Owen's employee practices.
5. Name a few sources for employee recruits and mention some possible advantages and disadvantages of each.
6. What advantages are found in the use of tests in selecting new employees? What precautions must be taken?
7. Name a few methods of training employees. Why not hire trained employees and save the expense of setting up training programs?
8. What motivates employees to work? Explain Maslow's theory.
9. Why should news of consequence involving the company be disclosed to the employees first?
10. How would you deal with the problem of absenteeism and tardiness?

SELECTED REFERENCES

Chruden, Herbert J., and Arthur W. Sherman, Jr., *Personnel Management*, 4th ed., South-Western Publishing Co., Cincinnati, 1972.

Crane, Donald P., *Personnel Management: A Situational Approach*, Wadsworth Publishing Co., Belmont, Cal., 1974.

Pigors, Paul, and Charles A. Myers, *Personnel Administration*, 7th ed., McGraw-Hill, New York, 1973.

Strauss, George, and Leonard R. Sayles, *Personnel: The Human Problems of Management*, 3rd ed., Prentice-Hall, Englewood Cliffs, N. J., 1972.

Yoder, Dale, *Personnel Management and Industrial Relations*, 6th ed., Prentice-Hall, Englewood Cliffs, N. J., 1970.

CHAPTER 16
LABOR ORGANIZATION

Except during periodic business depressions businessmen are convinced that the labor market always is characterized by more or less acute scarcity. They think not so much in terms of absolute numbers of laborers as in terms of the cost of keeping each individual on their payrolls. Inasmuch as labor costs more than they would like to pay, businessmen feel certain that it must be scarce. Actually, the desired pool of unemployed has with a few exceptions never had much influence in keeping wages at the levels desired by employers. Until the turn of the century there was always a frontier, which drained off surplus Eastern labor. Then, when the frontier disappeared, more stringent immigration laws were passed and more reliance was placed by labor upon unionization.

The Beginnings of Unionization. Although there were many isolated cases of disputes between employers and organized groups of employees in colonial America, the real beginnings of unionization had to await the industrialization of the country. One of the first strikes occurred in New York in 1768, when journeymen tailors "turned out" against their employers. During the Revolutionary War, the rapid increase in prices encouraged an organized protest (1778) by the journeymen printers of New York against existing wages. There were other similar disputes during this period, but in each instance the organization of employees was undertaken for the temporary purpose of striking, or the organization which undertook the wage protest was a philanthropic group. Perhaps the first American trade union was the Federal Society of Journeymen Cordwainers. This group of Philadelphia leather workers organized themselves in

1794, but disbanded in 1806 with the declaration by the United States Supreme Court that such organizations were against the public interest. Other societies, nevertheless, were formed and gradually they came to be accepted, both by the public and in the eyes of the law. The depression of 1819 all but wrecked existing unions, and thereafter the strength of their membership waxed and waned with business cycles.

In 1866 steps were taken to form a general labor organization on a national scale. The National Labor Union worked for the eight-hour day, the promotion of cooperatives, the reform of currency and banking practices, the abolition of convict labor, the restriction of immigration, restriction of land grants to actual settlers, and a department of labor in the national government. This organization collapsed in 1872 after engaging too extensively in national politics. Efforts immediately were begun to organize a national union which should be dedicated to economic rather than political action, but the panic of 1873 provided an insuperable barrier for several years.

The decades of the 1870s and the 1880s were characterized by violent disturbances among working people. Out of the Tompkins Square riot in New York (1874), the railroad strikes of 1877, the criminal activities of the Molly Maguires in the coal fields, and the Haymarket Square riot in Chicago (1886) came the conviction on the part of the public that labor unionism was dominated by foreign anarchists and Communists. Although these elements used the labor unrest of the times to serve their own ends, the great bulk of laboring men remained conservative. All through these troublous times two developments were slowly taking place which were to have a profound influence upon the future of unionism: (1) the Knights of Labor was gathering strength and (2) the craft unions were being formed which later would unite to form the American Federation of Labor.

The Knights of Labor. Nine tailors formed the Knights of Labor on December 9, 1869. It was a secret order with an elaborate ritual and idealistic aims. For about five years the society remained localized in and near Philadelphia, but in 1874 groups began to "swarm" and new assemblies were formed in the West. A national organization was set up in 1878.

Its membership was composed of all who engaged in "honorable toil." Lawyers, physicians, bankers, liquor dealers, stockbrokers, and professional gamblers were excluded.

The purposes of the organization never were very clear and often were conflicting. Paradoxically, the organization, which was outspoken in its opposition to strikes, won the first great national strike and concluded the first industry-wide labor contract in 1885. This great victory over Jay Gould and his railway system sowed the seeds of dissolution, for workers joined the organization by the thousands and made absurd demands upon their employers in the expectation that the all-powerful Knights of Labor would back them up. Discipline was nonexistent and the leadership was weak and vacillating. Consequently, the organization was unable to control the rash of unauthorized strikes which broke out all over the country. The union was branded as irresponsible, and when its president disavowed such strikes and urged the participants to go back to work the membership became disaffected and accused the officers of selling out to the employers. Membership dwindled rapidly, and the employers took full advantage of the situation to discharge Knights and replace them with nonunionists.

One element of weakness in the Knights of Labor was their policy of admitting all labor—skilled and unskilled—as well as former laborers and even shopkeepers and employers. The leadership doggedly insisted upon the solidarity of labor, while farmers pulled against industrial workers, unskilled workers pulled against skilled, and shopkeepers and employer members pulled against the rest of the membership. While labor solidarity seemed to be a desirable goal, it actually was unattainable and of doubtful value socially. Many leaders of the day were outspoken in their denunciation of the organization's nondemocratic tendencies. They felt that one gigantic labor organization would, in the hands of a strong-willed leader, actually result in a dictatorship, especially in view of rumors that its head was seeking the presidency of the United States.

By 1893 the Knights of Labor had dwindled to a mere 75,000 members from a peak of close to 700,000 reached in 1890. In desperation the organization turned to the political arena. The leaders of the union were overthrown when the farmers gained control, and in 1894 the Knights took a stand for the abolition of the wage system and the substitution for capitalism of an economic system based upon common ownership of the means of production by the workers. The craft unionists had already left the Knights and now most industrial workers quit, for what they wanted most was wages—higher wages. Meanwhile, another form of unionism was gaining strength.

The American Federation of Labor. Although the American Federation of Labor was founded in 1886, its genesis properly goes back to the establishment in New York in 1875 of a local chapter of the all-but-extinct International Cigar Makers' Union. The president of this local union was Samuel Gompers, a young man who was convinced that unions would have to be organized on sound business principles if they were to succeed. Gompers' union became a model of responsibility and efficiency. It held no brief for revolutionary theories and Utopian societies, but simply fought for higher wages and shorter hours. The ideas impressed by Gompers upon the Cigar Makers' Union were carried over to the American Federation of Labor, which he helped to found. In 1881 a Federation of Organized Trades and Labor Unions was formed in Pittsburgh. This organization included the Knights of Labor, along with a number of independent craft unions. (A craft union is made up of members who work at the same craft or trade, such as carpenters, cigar makers, or bricklayers.) Samuel Gompers participated in the Pittsburgh meetings as a delegate of the Cigar Makers' Union. Efforts were made by the delegates of the Knights to make their organization the basis for the new federation. Some of the craft unionists, however, felt that to do so would be to drag them (the skilled workers) down to the level of the unskilled workers who comprised much of the membership of the Knights. After a period of rivalry between the Knights and the national craft unions the Federation of Organized Trades was reorganized in 1886 as the American Federation of Labor, with Samuel Gompers as president. Although the new organization was a continuation of the old, the reorganization marks the beginning of the policy of noninterference by the federation in the internal affairs of member unions. Each member union was autonomous, but the executive council proposed to build up its financial resources so as to lend aid to any member who was called upon to conduct a strike or resist a lockout. Through education it was proposed to weld all craft unions into a close-knit federation. The success of this organization is largely a tribute to the ability and diligence of Samuel Gompers, who, with the exception of one term, was reelected president year after year until his death.

With the death of the Knights of Labor, the A.F. of L. came to dominate the picture, but it never monopolized the labor movement. Craft unions drifted into the federation and out of it; the railway brotherhoods always remained aloof; and several strong and successful industrial unions developed, especially in the clothing and coal mining industries. (Industrial unions are made up of members who work in a given industry, i.e., all mine workers, all steel workers, etc.)

From 1905 to about 1920 the A.F. of L. had as a rival the revolutionary Industrial Workers of the World, an organization which developed in the West. Its strike tactics were aggressive and its leadership was bold, but in spite of several spectacular victories over employers, it proved to be too radical for the great bulk of American workers.

During World War I the A.F. of L. supported the great national effort. However, as prices rose without corresponding wage increases, labor discontent began to spread. With respect to unionization, the (first) War Labor Board promulgated the policy of maintaining the *status quo*. Works councils for settling disputes were urged and soon were in common use. After the war, labor aggressively went to work to gain what they felt was rightfully theirs. Although Gompers was outspoken in his denunciation of Communism, the wide publicity given by the press to a few instances of Red-inspired and Communist-led strikes had the effect of marshaling public opinion against all strikes and all labor, whether radical or conservative. As a consequence, few strikes were won by the A.F. of L. or by any of the independent unions in the postwar period. This adverse public feeling, coupled with growing antagonism on the part of the federal administration and the courts, set the stage for a period of stagnation among unions. During the ensuing years of prosperity, workers received good wages, and the opinion was widely held that workers no longer needed unions.

Then, after 1929, workers suddenly began feeling the need for unions, but industry was prostrate and workers were too desperate for employment at any wage to consider joining a union. Meanwhile, in 1924 Gompers had died and was replaced by William Green, who held views as conservative as those of his predecessor. Green, a former United Mine Workers officer, seemed to favor industrial unionism over craft unionism. For this reason he was supported by John L. Lewis, but as time went by the A.F. of L. showed no evidences of a change in its traditional craft-oriented policies.

The A.F. of L. had always held aloof from political action, and in the campaign of 1932 it refused to endorse either Herbert Hoover or Franklin D. Roosevelt. Neither would it advance a program for dealing with the depression. Nevertheless, the exigencies of the times began bringing prolabor legislation into being even before sweeping a prolabor administration into power. The Norris-La Guardia anti-injunction law was passed while Hoover was still president. This was to be followed in the next few years by a host of prolabor statutes and court decisions, all of which encouraged labor organizations to rise once again and soar to unprecedented heights.

The new gains of labor were made with governmental assistance against the stubborn resistance of many large employers of labor. One of the most effective weapons against unionization had been the yellow-dog contract (an undertaking by a prospective employee to stay out of unions in consideration of employment) coupled with the injunction, or court order. The contract was of little value directly, but if a union organizer came to the area, an employer could obtain an injunction against his activities on the ground of "inducing breach of contract." Then if the organizer persisted in his attempts to persuade employees to join his union the organizer could be held to be in contempt of court. This technique of preventing union organization was blocked with the enactment of the Norris-La Guardia Act in 1932.

Another technique used by employers grew out of the efforts

of the (first) War Labor Board to promote works councils. These councils were expanded by many employers into company unions. Employers voluntarily gave their employees wage increases and other benefits, then told the employees that these concessions had been forced by the new societies. When government policy envisaged a prairie fire of unionism as one means of combating industrial depression, employers worked desperately to set company-union backfires. Little by little, however, the courts eradicated company-dominated unions—but employee-dominated company unions have remained legal.

In four short months after the National Industrial Recovery Act was passed, A.F. of L. membership jumped from 2,500,000 to close to 4,000,000. The federation began the organization of unskilled workers and a rapid drift toward industrial unionism developed. These new industrial unions were affiliated with the federation through so-called federal charters. Due partly to the traditional antipathy of the A.F. of L. toward industrial unions, this new activity soon bogged down. When a dissident element demanded more aggressive tactics in organizing the great masses of labor in the automobile, rubber, steel, and other unorganized industries, a serious split developed. This group set up within the A.F. of L. a Committee for Industrial Organization. Again efforts were made to organize the mass-production industries and assurances were given that the privileges of existing craft unions would be respected. However, the problems of resolving jurisdictional claims proved to be formidable, and at the Atlantic City convention of the A.F. of L. industrial unionism was voted down. Nevertheless, another Committee for Industrial Organization was set up and efforts were made to educate the membership of the A.F. of L. These efforts were attacked by Green as contrary to the sense of the convention, whereupon John L. Lewis tendered his resignation as vice-president of the A.F. of L.

During the subsequent months the C.I.O. went ahead with its organizing plans. Demands were made upon the A.F. of L. for industrial charters. The A.F. of L. demanded that the C.I.O. cease its activities. Then, finally, the A.F. of L. suspended the ten unions comprising the C.I.O. Valiant efforts continued to be made by individuals on each side to prevent a final split, but delegates from the ten suspended unions did not attend the Tampa convention of 1936, so the A.F. of L. voted to keep the suspension in effect until they should be reinstated on terms laid down by the Executive Committee of the A.F. of L. During the following two years the breach grew wider and seemed to be more and more a struggle for power between Green and Lewis. In May of 1938 the split was confirmed by the formation of the Congress of Industrial Organizations, now a federation with membership exceeding that of the A.F. of L.

The A.F. of L. had always opposed governmental meddling with union matters such as minimum wages, old age pensions, and unemployment insurance. But when as a result of depressed business conditions federal legislation was proposed in these fields the traditional attitude of the A.F. of L. was modified, and to a greater extent than ever before organized labor swung behind one political party. This support of labor was instrumental in returning Franklin D. Roosevelt to office in 1936. Although efforts were made at this time to set up a third party dedicated to furthering the interests of labor, neither the A.F. of L. nor the C.I.O. would endorse it. In the 1940 elections the A.F. of L. wholeheartedly supported Roosevelt, while the C.I.O. leadership supported Wendell Willkie. Much of the C.I.O. rank and file, however, continued to support the Democratic administration, which again was returned to power.

At the outbreak of World War II organized labor pledged itself not to strike, a pledge which was kept to a remarkable degree. There were strikes, some deliberately called by labor and some forced on labor by unbearable managerial attitudes, but in spite of the wide publicity given to such walkouts by "antilabor" newspapers the ratio of hours lost to available hours of work averaged less than one to one thousand, or about one day per worker for the three-year period January, 1942, to December, 1944. But with the end of the war, work stoppages rose to staggering proportions. During this postwar period, during which the A.F. of L. continued its policy of neutrality in political matters, labor steadfastly supported the Democratic administration. From depression days the Wagner Act (1935) had thrown the weight of the government onto the scales in favor of organized labor, but with the revival of employment, the war, and the postwar rush to replenish depleted stocks of consumers' goods, public opinion began to swing away from its prolabor attitude. But instead of releasing the restrictions on employers, the new federal legislation embodied in the Taft-Hartley Act (1947) imposed similar restrictions upon labor. Apparently public opinion believed that labor finally had reached a position of equality with business management, and that both should be restricted in the interests of the public.

The Congress of Industrial Organizations. The foregoing discussion has shown how the C.I.O. began as a movement within the A.F. of L. toward granting charters to groups of workers in entire industries irrespective of the nature of work performed by the individuals involved. There were difficulties in the way of this movement. For instance, assume that the C.I.O. should institute a membership drive at a plant where the truck drivers belonged to one A.F. of L. affiliate, the electricians to another, and the machinists to still another. Actually the A.F. of L. extended its blessing to a type of organization drive which should respect these existing jurisdictions. But in practice, the C.I.O. tried to take into the new unions *all* employees in the plant, and the A.F. of L. union members attempted to discourage these incursions. Such matters might have been adjusted amicably, in spite of the traditional antipathy of the A.F. of L. toward industrial unionism, had not personal considerations of the union leaders entered the picture. The public speeches of Green and Lewis showed little but antagonism each toward the other.

The C.I.O. emerged gradually, but in May, 1938, its name was formally changed from Committee for Industrial Organization to Congress of Industrial Organizations. This congress of unions differed little from the older federation except that it did not recognize craft lines. Although some Communists got into positions of responsibility in the organization there is no evidence that its long-term objectives were revolutionary as were those of some of the earlier unions. It even proved to be more conservative in some ways than the federation, for its leaders urged its membership to increase (not restrict) labor productivity as the only sound means of justifying wage increases. The structure of the congress was somewhat similar to that of the federation. However, the congress showed stronger centralized control, and, as will be shown, engaged more actively in national and local politics.

John L. Lewis was the first president of the C.I.O. Under his guidance and that of his lieutenants (and with the assistance of the law of the land) the new organization made phenomenal progress. One of the first of the antiunion strongholds to fall was "Big Steel." Under the direct leadership of Philip Murray the Steel Workers' Organizing Committee succeeded in rolling up a membership of 100,000. With the recognition of the S.W.O.C. as the bargaining agent for its employees the United States Steel Corporation granted a wage increase and accepted the eight-hour day and forty-hour week. Other steel companies fell into line, and the membership of the S.W.O.C. quickly trebled. Although "Little Steel" was able to defeat the S.W.O.C. its resistance proved to be temporary. By 1941 the S.W.O.C., now the United Steelworkers of America, had organized practically the entire industry and had reached a membership of 600,000.

The C.I.O. similarly organized the automobile and other mass-production industries. While organizing the automobile workers, the C.I.O. made wide use of a new technique, the sit-down strike. Eventually the courts, although not antagonistic toward labor, ruled that sit-down strikes went too far. In its work of organizing the unorganized, the C.I.O. more and more met resistance from the A.F. of L. In trying to keep pace with the C.I.O., whose membership exceeded that of the A.F. of L., the federation tended to depart somewhat from its policy of neglecting all but craft workers. Soon the National Labor Relations Board was busy deciding whether workers within bargaining units were to be represented by the A.F. of L. or by the C.I.O. Too, many hapless employers were caught in the crossfire of jurisdictional strikes, fought not as in the past with union against employer but with union against union. Ultimately the N.L.R.B. recognized the position of employers and amended its rules to permit them to petition for employee-representation elections, even though the rival unions elected to fight the matter out on the picket line. But this concession provided only a permissive privilege which finally was changed to a legal right with the enactment of the Taft-Hartley Act.

The C.I.O. engaged actively in politics, and after the elections of 1936 Lewis took much of the credit for re-electing Roosevelt. This credit Roosevelt refused to acknowledge. Consequently in the next four years there was considerable friction between the C.I.O. and the administration. When it became clear that Lewis would not be given the place he thought he deserved in the 1940 elections he sought to throw the weight of the C.I.O. to the Republicans. He made it clear that the election of Roosevelt would be considered as a vote of no confidence in John L. Lewis. When the Democrats won once more, Lewis, true to his word, resigned as president of the C.I.O. He was succeeded by Philip Murray.

During the 1944 election campaign the C.I.O. undertook an educational campaign. A Political Action Committee was formed, under the direction of Sidney Hillman, for the purpose of ringing doorbells and mailing out campaign literature. At the national level the C.I.O.-P.A.C. supported the Democrats, but at the local level the branches were allowed to recommend any candidate they desired. Many citizens were confused by the existence of a National Citizens Political Action Committee which disclaimed any connection with the C.I.O., but which had similar aims and which supported substantially the same candidates.

The C.I.O. admirably supported the national effort during World War II. At the war's close its membership was almost 6,000,000. Although it had outstripped its older rival in the early days, the A.F. of L. now had a membership of about 6,800,000.

The postwar scene was characterized by the government trying to stem inflation while labor demanded round after round of wage increases. This problem had arisen during the war when the (second) War Labor Board was faced with a demand from the employees of "Little Steel" for a dollar a day increase. The Board pointed out that prices had begun climbing in January of 1941 and that they had risen about 15 percent when the government's anti-inflationary program had been put into effect. Consequently, the Board argued, "Little Steel" workers were entitled to a corresponding increase in pay, which amounted to 44 cents instead of $1 a day. This line of reasoning was used in other cases and it came to be called the "Little Steel Formula." In the postwar era a large number of wage contracts were concluded which tied wages to the Bureau of Labor Statistics cost-of-living index. During this period there was much useless speculation over matters of cause and effect. Employers followed each round of wage increases with a price increase, maintaining that wages constituted an element of cost. But unions stoutly held that their demands for wage increases were for the purpose of catching up with prior price increases, and they loudly demanded that they be given access to the employers' books so as to prove that wage increases could be given without employers being forced to raise prices. Then, with the invasion of South Korea by the Communists of North Korea and the intervention of the United Nations, wartime controls over price and wage increases were reimposed.

In 1955 the A.F. of L. united with the C.I.O. to form the AFL-CIO. In 1970 the new organization's combined membership was something over fifteen and one-half million. At the same time, approximately four and one-half million persons belonged to unaffiliated unions.

Labor Legislation. Federal and state labor legislation has affected the status and growth of unionism as well as the relationships unions bear to business organizations.

The *Wagner Act*, upheld by the Supreme Court in 1937, gave employees working for firms engaged in interstate commerce the right to organize and bargain collectively.

In 1947 the *Taft-Hartley Act*, amending the Wagner Act, was passed. It added certain unfair practices which unions were forbidden to use and retained the employer unfair practices (except that employers were no longer forbidden to express their opinion on the issues of disputes). The National Labor Relations Board was increased in size from three to five members and the position of General Counsel of the Board was established. The closed shop (one in which only union members may be employed) was outlawed and the practice of deducting union dues from wages (the checkoff system) was forbidden except with prior consent of the union members concerned.

In 1959 the *Landrum-Griffin Act* was passed. The first six titles of the act clarified internal union behavior. The seventh amended the Taft-Hartley Act. The regulation of internal union affairs was aimed at preventing racketeering and financial irresponsibility found in some labor organizations.

The impact of these and other laws on joint relations will be discussed in the following chapter.

QUESTIONS FOR DISCUSSION

1. Why did the first American union, the Journeymen Cordwainers, disband?
2. Did the Knights of Labor oppose or encourage strikes?
3. Was the American Federation of Labor a craft union or an industrial union? Explain the difference between the two types.
4. How were yellow-dog contracts and injunctions used to combat union organization? What did the Norris-LaGuardia Act say about this technique?
5. Tell briefly how the C.I.O. was formed.
6. The Wagner Act placed certain restrictions on employers. To remove the imbalance what did the Taft-Hartley Act do: remove these restrictions or place similar restrictions on labor?
7. What new technique did the C.I.O. use in organizing the automobile industry? What did the courts say about it?
8. How did the War Labor Board adjust wages during the early days of World War II? What was this formula called? Was this procedure followed in the postwar era?
9. How did the Taft-Hartley Act deal with the checkoff (deduction of union dues from wages)?
10. What was the Landrum-Griffin Act chiefly concerned with?

SELECTED ᴿEFERENCES

Chamberlain, Neil W., *Sourcebook on Labor*, McGraw-Hill, New York, 1964.

———, *The Labor Sector*, 2nd ed., McGraw-Hill, New York, 1971.

Cohen, Sanford, *Labor in the United States*, 3rd ed., Charles E. Merrill Publishing Co., Columbus, Ohio, 1970.

Heneman, Herbert G., and Dale Yoder, *Labor Economics*, 2nd ed., South-Western Publishing Co., Cincinnati, 1965.

Miller, Robert W., Frederick A. Zeller, and Glenn W. Miller, *The Practice of Local Union Leadership*, Ohio State University Press, Columbus, 1965.

Peterson, Florence, *American Labor Unions*, 2nd rev. ed., Harper & Row, New York, 1963.

Tyler, Gus, *Labor in the Metropolis*, Charles E. Merrill Publishing Co., Columbus, Ohio, 1973.

CHAPTER 17

JOINT RELATIONS

Since the beginnings of this country, employees have sought the right to bargain with their employers over wages, hours, and conditions of work. Labor has been treated as a commodity, to be purchased in a competitive market along with raw materials and supplies. Individuals have always had the *privilege* of bargaining with their employers. Those with unique talents and training could do so successfully. Those less favored persons could always quit (except, of course, the slaves of pre-Civil War days). Employers have emphasized this freedom workers have to accept what is offered or leave. Workers have felt, however, that it was unfair to expect an individual to "bargain" with, for instance, a New York Central Railway or a General Motors Corporation. True bargaining can only be achieved between two parties of approximately equal economic strength. Therefore, employees who saw the futility of individual bargaining tried, in the early days of the Republic, to present their demands as a group. Soon, however, the courts declared this tactic to be an unlawful combination in restraint of trade. But gradually the courts relaxed this position as it became clear that the prevailing policy of laissez faire often gave aggregations of economic power unfair advantage over individuals and groups with fewer resources. Over the years the courts stopped labeling labor organizations as conspiracies in restraint of trade and began allowing them to match their strength against the business organizations in which their members worked. Meanwhile, many business concerns combined and began monopolizing certain segments of the economy. This development caused a shift in governmental policy from repression of labor organizations to the regulation of business organizations.

Joint Relations and Governmental Policy. Before 1842 unions could not legally exist in the United States. In that year the Massachusetts Supreme Court decided (in *Commonwealth* v. *Hunt*, 45 Mass. 111) that strikes for closed shops were not crimes and that there was nothing illegal per se in employees combining to refuse to work. It reasoned that such combinations might have worthy as well as unworthy objectives. This decision had the effect of reversing the practice courts had had of identifying all unions with criminal conspiracies.

Although unions began gaining the privilege of bargaining collectively in 1842, the *right* (privilege enforced by law) did not come into being until 1930 when the United States Supreme Court ruled (in *Texas and New Orleans Railway Co.* v. *Brotherhood of Railway and Steamship Clerks*, 50 Sup. Ct. 427) that the Railway Labor Act of 1926 restricted the right of interstate carriers to discharge their employees for union membership and union activity. The right of employees of companies in interstate commerce to bargain collectively was granted in 1935 when the Wagner Act was passed. This statute was validated by the United States Supreme Court two years later.

The Taft-Hartley Act, passed in 1947, further strengthened the policy that unions and companies should deal jointly with their mutual problems.

The Employee Representation Election. Before an election to decide which union shall represent the employees can be held, the bounds of the jurisdiction must be determined. This is the task of the National Labor Relations Board. Either the employees or a company can petition the Board for an election. A representative of the Board then investigates the situation, whereupon it is decided whether the bargaining unit will be a craft within the company, within a branch of the company, or within a limited geographical area, or all employees in a department, a branch, the company, or a limited geographical area. When the unit has been set, a list of eligible voters is prepared and an election is announced to be held under the auspices of the Board. The names of alternate unions are placed on the ballots. Employees may vote for one of these, or for "no union." A company-dominated labor organization cannot qualify as one of the alternatives.

To win an election one of the alternatives must get a majority of the votes, not just a plurality. If no union gets a majority, a run-off election is subsequently held between the top two choices. The winner of this election is then certified by the Board as the official representative of the employees within the bargaining unit. If the election was close, those losing might wish to try again after an intensive recruiting campaign. However, the rules of the Board prohibit another election until a year has elapsed. Groups and individuals not belonging to the union representing the majority are permitted by law to bargain with the company separately provided a member of the official union is present and provided the separate arrangements are not inconsistent with existing arrangements made with the official union.

The Taft-Hartley Act permits individual states to pass "right-to-work" laws, giving individuals the right not to join any union. In those states not having such laws it is possible for a union in power within a given company to create a *union shop*. Under such an arrangement a new employee has a limited time to join the union, after which if he does not do so the company must drop him.

Some labor agreements permit a *maintenance-of-membership shop* under which employees may voluntarily join the union but once they have joined they must remain members in good standing for the life of the contract. Some arrangements permit employees to stay out of the union but require them to pay dues to it. This is the *agency shop*. The *closed shop* requires the employer to hire only union members. Although this arrangement is forbidden by the Taft-Hartley Act, a few unions still require employers to hire through their hiring halls which, in effect, results in closed-shop conditions. No action has been taken to date changing this long-standing practice.

Collective Bargaining Procedure. After a union is certified as the official bargaining agent for the employees within a given unit, representatives of the union and the company arrange for contract negotiations. Usually several individuals are present at each session and as a rule one person speaks for each side. The union begins by presenting a list of demands. The law requires the company to bargain seriously. The company does not have to agree to anything, but to avoid the accusation of refusing to bargain they must agree to study the demands and set a date for resumption of the talks. Meanwhile, each clause should be labeled as to its acceptability. Many clauses will be satisfactory if rewritten and changed in some respect. The changes wanted should be clearly written out and the reasons stated. The remaining clauses will be unacceptable. Some of these will be fundamentally objectionable to the company and others will probably be *trading clauses*. These are demands the union does not expect to get, but will "reluctantly" drop in return for a concession made by the company.

At the next bargaining session the parties get down to business. As clauses are agreed on, they are tentatively accepted. It may be that one party will later wish to withdraw approval of one of these clauses as a bargaining tactic.

As the business of shaping up an agreement proceeds, it is inevitable that differences will develop. To prevent serious friction it is important to stick to facts and avoid personalities. Deadlocks should be prevented by keeping the sessions relatively brief. If neither side will yield, it helps to call a recess or a postponement. Often the chairmanship is passed back and forth from session to session.

It is important for the representatives of both sides to know, or have available, the company's wage rates as well as rates paid by competitors and by other companies in the community. It may be useful for each side to have an attorney present and to know the applicable federal and state laws and court decisions. Normally it is best if the lawyer does not bargain.

After the negotiators have finished their work, long delays in finally signing the agreement should be avoided. Local plant managers should have authority to bind the company, and if the local union president cannot bind the union without approval of the membership, a special union meeting should be called immediately.

After the agreement has become effective, copies are printed and distributed to the employees. Since experience shows that few employees more than glance through the agreement, it is suggested that series of joint meetings be held for the purpose of informing the employees of their rights under the new contract.

Pressure Tactics of Employees. If the union feels that a show of strength would aid the negotiators, a strike vote can be taken and, if approved, authorization can be given to the union president to call out the employees in case of a deadlock or if the contract is not completed before a given deadline. A *strike* is a temporary refusal to work. Strikes are forbidden by law among government employees and are somewhat restricted or delayed in the transportation industry. But employees of business organizations have the legal right to strike. *Sit-down strikes* and *slowdowns* have been declared unlawful by the courts and their use has all but disappeared. Employers may continue operating, if they can, with supervisors and nonunion employees. If the employer needs more workers he can bring in *strikebreakers*, called *scabs* by union members. Federal law forbids an employer to import strikebreakers from another state. A *wildcat strike* is one called by a local union against instructions of the national or international union.

Picketing and *giving information to the public* attempt to keep persons other than the strikers from entering the place of business. *Mass picketing*, in which those trying to enter are physically prevented, is frowned on by the courts.

A concerted refusal to have business dealings with a business concern is a *boycott*. Union members can legally refuse to buy from (or sell to) a firm with which they are having a dispute. They can also persuade others by word of mouth or by advertising. This type of action is a *primary boycott*. It is not lawful to engage in a *secondary boycott*, which involves refusing to have business dealings with those who buy or sell from the employer in question. For example, if the employees of a baking company wished to boycott its products they could advertise the dispute and picket the bakery, but they could not legally picket and organize a boycott against a store selling the products of the bakery. They could try to dissuade a wholesale flour company from selling to the bakery, but they could not legally organize a boycott against the flour company.

Employees can *use propaganda*, try to *influence public elections*, and *lobby* among state and federal legislators. Where the feelings become bitter, unions and individual employees have engaged in *sabotage* and *physical intimidation,* both of which, of course, are illegal activities.

Pressure Tactics of Employers. The tactic of employers which corresponds to the strike is the *lockout.* Although a company can close its doors and quit operating, it cannot legally move away to avoid performing under a contract with a certified union.

Courts frown on the use of *blacklists* of active union members. These have been widely used to prevent the inadvertent hiring of an active union organizer.

Prior to 1932, one of the most effective tactics used by employers to resist the incursions of unionism was the *individual nonunion agreement* (called a *yellow-dog contract* by unionists) in connection with *court orders* or *injunctions.* It was perfectly legal for an employer to ask a prospective employee to sign a contract stating that in consideration for employment he would not join a union and that if now a member he would resign from it. Employers were not interested in prosecuting or even in discharging employees who violated this contract. They *were* interested in prosecuting union organizers. Since inducing breach of contract is actionable under the law it was reasonably easy to have the local judge issue an injunction against organizers persuading employees to break their contracts. Organizers who persisted could be found in contempt of court and jailed without trial. Although they would eventually be brought to trial, they usually took the judge's advice and left the county when released. This whole procedure was made unlawful (with exceptions) by the Norris-La Guardia Act passed in the Hoover administration (1932).

Just as unions do, employers can try to influence the public by *advertising* and *lobbying.*

Grievance Procedure. A *grievance* is a claim by a member of a union, or by the union, that the company has violated the labor agreement in some respect. Grievances are handled in a series of steps. Step one usually involves the presentation of a filled-out form, dated and signed by the employee or a representative of the union, stating the nature of the complaint, the clause or clauses allegedly violated, and the remedy desired.

This form is presented to the immediate supervisor, who sits down with the employee to work out the problem. The employee's union representative (the *steward*) may or may not be present. He must be called in if the employee so desires. Usually the grievance must be filed one month or less after the occurrence.

If the supervisor grants the employee's wishes, that is the end of the matter. If he does not, the union may take the grievance to step two. This must be done within, say, ten working days after rejection by the supervisor.

Some agreements call for a special meeting of representatives of the labor relations department of the company, the president of the local union, and the appropriate steward each time a grievance reaches step two. Larger companies, with more grievances to process, handle all step two grievances in regularly scheduled meetings. Some demands may be granted, while others are rejected at this stage.

Grievances not appealed to step three within the time limit are considered to be waived by the union. Those appealed are discussed by a joint committee made up of a middle manager, a representative of the labor relations department, the supervisor concerned, and the union representatives: the steward, the local president, and, perhaps, a district union representative. If the dispute cannot be settled at this stage it can be appealed, within a time limit, to arbitration. Although the parties usually stipulate that the arbitrator's decision will be final and binding, such decisions occasionally are taken to the courts if the arbitrator is believed to have been biased, if he rejected or ignored evidence, or if he engaged in misconduct in any way.

Arbitration. Most union-management agreements include an arbitration clause which permits any unsettled union or individual grievance to go to arbitration if the employer is notified within the time limit.

An *arbitrator* is an impartial outsider who is called in to listen to both sides: to take testimony (usually sworn), to receive exhibits, and to listen to argument. In many such proceedings a court reporter records everything that is said and prepares a transcript, copies of which go to the two parties and the arbitrator. After the transcripts are delivered the representative of each side usually prepares a post-hearing brief which reviews the evidence and argues the case. The arbitrator then studies the material, reviews the arguments, and decides, usually within thirty days, which side is right. He then puts his decision and reasons in writing. The decision is called the award and the reasons constitute the opinion. The *opinion* shows the names of the parties and of the arbitrator, date, identification names and numbers, place of the hearings, a review of the facts, the submission agreement (question to be decided), positions of the parties, and the arbitrator's findings. The *award* states whether the grievance is sustained or rejected and what remedy is ordered. Copies of the award and opinion are then sent to each of the parties and to any others who might be concerned. If the parties agree, copies are also sent to reporting agencies which print and distribute them in bound volumes or loose-leaf form to libraries and other subscribers.

To be acceptable as an arbitrator an individual must have technical knowledge of the subject matter involved in the dispute and enjoy the confidence of both parties as to his impartiality, fairness, and analytic and reasoning ability. Perhaps half of all arbitrators in the field of labor relations are lawyers, while professors of labor relations come second. It is common for lawyers to represent the parties and for a nonlawyer with industrial experience to act as the arbitrator.

Parties to a labor dispute can find arbitrators in several ways. If they like a person who has served them previously he may be used again. He may subsequently be named as a "permanent" arbitrator and be used exclusively. Panels of "permanent" arbitrators often are named by a company and a union, the members of which are used in rotation from case to case. Many contracts specify that any arbitrator chosen by the parties must be selected from the membership list of the National Academy of Arbitrators. This is a professional organization of approximately four hundred top arbitrators in the United States and Canada. On request to the Federal Mediation and Conciliation Service by the parties, the names of seven or so experienced arbitrators from their roster will be sent. Customarily the parties look over the names and the data sheet sent for each and select one. If none is acceptable the Service will send one more list of names. If the parties cannot agree on a name, many contracts provide that one party (selected by lot) shall strike a name. The other party then strikes a name, and so on. The person remaining on the list then must be used.

The American Arbitration Association, with branch offices in most large cities, maintains rosters of arbitrators for commercial as well as labor cases together with hearing-room facilities as well as hearing officers who handle the administration of oaths and other details and secretaries who prepare and mail notices.

Most states, also, furnish names of approved arbitrators and many have hearing rooms available.

In most cases only one person serves as arbitrator. In many cases a tripartite arbitration board is used. In very few cases are three neutral persons used. Usually a tripartite board is made up of one neutral and two partisans. Rulings are made by the neutral during the hearing and decisions are made by the neutral, after which one or more executive sessions are held during which the decision may be modified. The award is then written up and signed by the neutral, with the other two usually signing under "concur" and "dissent."

No charges are made by the agencies for sending panels of names. The American Arbitration Association makes a small charge for the use of its hearing rooms. If a hearing officer goes into the field there is a charge for his time and travel expenses. The AAA handles mostly commercial cases, i.e., disputes over the performance of contracts in construction, etc., the fairness of charges made by physicians, hospitals, etc., settlements in automobile and other types of insurance claims, and so on. Arbitrators in commercial cases receive expenses but customarily charge no fees. Labor arbitrators receive expenses plus a per diem fee averaging $200 for hearing, travel, inspection, study, and writing time. Nearly always the parties share costs, but occasionally the loser pays all. If one party wants a court reporter he hires him directly, or through the arbitrator, and pays for two transcripts, one for the arbitrator. If the other party wants a copy of the transcript he pays the reporter for it.

Arbitration is much like a court proceeding except that it is more informal. Arbitrators are not bound by precedent, that is, by the decisions of other arbitrators in similar cases. Their decisions are based on the submission agreement, though if the parties cannot get together on the wording of the dispute the arbitrator usually is given the right to frame the issue or issues after he hears the case.

Arbitrators cannot change the contract in any respect, though they can interpret or construe the clauses in conflict. As a rule, if such clauses are vague or contradictory they can look for the intent of the parties in minutes of negotiating sessions or in past practice within the firm or the industry.

Arbitrators primarily are used in settling grievance disputes though they are increasingly used to assist in negotiating new agreements and in fact-finding and mediating activities.

Mediation, Conciliation, and Fact Finding. A *mediator* tries to find some common ground on which contending parties can agree. A *conciliator* simply brings the parties together. A *fact finder* presents the situation in a factual manner. Mediators and fact finders may or may not be asked to make recommendations. Conciliators try to create an aura of good feeling so as to encourage the contending parties to work out their own solutions.

The Federal Mediation and Conciliation Service sends experts into disputes that threaten interstate commerce. If these individuals fail, the Service recommends arbitration and furnishes names of arbitrators if the parties agree to follow this course.

The process of mediation consists in obtaining the demands and concessions of each party separately, then of fitting them together in a workable whole. The process often works like magic when an outsider writes up a proposed settlement free from the hampering restraints of emotion, personal animosity, and pride. This tactic is frequently employed in public service disputes.

Another procedure frequently used in public service disputes is fact finding. The Railway Labor Act provides for a tripartite board to be appointed by the President in case of a railway stoppage. It is made up of members representing the carriers, the union, and the public. During thirty days allowed for deliberations striking is forbidden, as it is for thirty days after the facts are publicized. Thereafter the union may strike, but frequently the force of public opinion causes the impending strike to be called off. In some instances, when the unions actually called a strike after the sixty-day period, the President has ordered the Army to operate the railroads.

Fact finding without recommendations has frequently forced adjustments on the part of either one side or the other, or both sides, when the facts were made public.

QUESTIONS FOR DISCUSSION

1. What is wrong, if anything, with individual bargaining, a worker against a corporation, with the option open to the worker to quit his job if not satisfied?
2. In what case did a court first open the gates to collective bargaining? What statute gave employees in interstate commerce the legal right to bargain collectively?
3. How is the unit within which employee elections are held determined? Who conducts employee representation elections?
4. What are: (1) Union shops? (2) Closed shops? (3) Maintenance-of-membership shops? (4) Agency shops?
5. Distinguish between primary and secondary boycotts? Are they legal?
6. Explain why the use by employers of the individual nonunion agreement (the yellow-dog contract), in connection with injunctions, was so effective in fighting unionism. Is this tactic legal?
7. Describe briefly the general outlines of a typical union-management grievance-settlement procedure.
8. In what way is the Federal Mediation and Conciliation Service connected with arbitration?
9. In what ways does arbitration resemble court procedure? In what ways does it differ?
10. Describe mediation, conciliation, and fact finding.

SELECTED REFERENCES

Chandler, Margaret K., *Management Rights and Union Interests*, McGraw-Hill, New York, 1964.

Davey, Harold W., *Contemporary Collective Bargaining*, 3rd ed., Prentice-Hall, Englewood Cliffs, N. J., 1972.

French, Wendell, *The Personnel Management Process*, 2nd ed., Houghton Mifflin Co., Boston, 1970.

Prasow, Paul, and Edward Peters, *Arbitration and Collective Bargaining*, McGraw-Hill, New York, 1970.

Robinson, James W., *Labor Economics and Labor Relations*, Ronald Press Co., New York, 1972.

Simkin, William E., *Mediation and the Dynamics of Collective Bargaining*, Bureau of National Affairs, Washington, D. C., 1971.

Sloane, Arthur A., and Fred Witney, *Labor Relations*, 2nd ed., Prentice-Hall, Englewood Cliffs, N. J., 1972.

Ulman, Lloyd, ed., *Challenges to Collective Bargaining*, Prentice-Hall, Englewood Cliffs, N. J., 1967.

Wiggins, Ronald L., *The Arbitration of Industrial Engineering Disputes*, Bureau of National Affairs, Washington, D. C., 1970.

PART VI
MARKETING ORGANIZATION

Part VI covers the distribution of goods and the methods of making services available.

Chapter 18 classifies commodities, describes the processes of standardization and grading, indicates the costs of distribution as compared with production, traces the channels of distribution, and outlines the various marketing structures.

Chapter 19 describes the wholesale trade, indicates variations in practice at this stage of distribution, and covers the most important types of retailing organizations.

Chapter 20 is concerned with buying: for resale and for consumption.

Chapter 21 emphasizes the importance of selling and advertising in moving goods from the producer into the channels of trade and to the user.

Chapter 22 covers two important aspects of distribution: transportation and storage. Producers must move their products to areas of consumption and store them until they are needed. It is then necessary to move them from storage into the hands of specific users.

International trade is the subject of Chapter 23. Many complex problems arise when goods are produced in one country and sold in another. Not only are there legal restrictions, but there are many complications arising out of moving products great distances, being paid in foreign currencies, and advertising and selling to persons of diverse backgrounds and social customs.

CHAPTER 18

THE MARKETING PROCESS

The assumption Emerson made that the world would beat a path to the door of the inventor of a better mouse trap certainly is not true today. It is true that the world wants novel, unique, and exotic goods, but today it is necessary to test new products in market research projects to be sure they will be accepted. The new items then may be modified in the light of suggestions made by prospective users and produced in large quantities for the sake of economy. Thousands of dollars are spent telling consumers the new product is just what they have been waiting for. The correct channel of distribution is selected, salesmen persuade dealers to stock the item, and arrangements are made to transport and stock it in correct quantities. Some new products can be put onto the market without undue haste, but others require crash programs to saturate the market before competition gets serious.

Goods Classified. On the basis of the use to which goods are put they can be classified into producers' goods and consumers' goods. Such items as machines and hand tools of various kinds, used in making other goods, are *producers' goods*. Goods such as bread and clothing that are used up by the individual buyer are *consumers' goods*. An item such as fuel oil can be classified either way depending on whether it is consumed in making electricity or used in the home for heat.

Producers' goods can be broken down into:

1. *Raw materials*. Flax, sugar beets, sand.
2. *Semifinished goods*. Steel rods, plastic sheets, lumber.
3. *Supplies*. Lubricating oil, writing paper, ink.
4. *Installations*. Furnaces, air-conditioning equipment, elevators.

5. *Accessories*. Filing cabinets, desks, chairs.

Consumers' goods can be broken down into:

1. *Convenience goods*. Chewing gum, newspapers, matches.
2. *Shopping goods*. Automobiles, dresses, jewelry.
3. *Specialty goods*. Coffee, shoes, vacuum sweepers.

These classifications are not exact, but they help to determine how and where to market the items concerned. A given consumer item might be placed in any one of the three classes depending on the economic status and conditioning of the buyer. A shirt might be considered to be a convenience item by some men, to be picked up without regard to brand or price. Other men would shop around and then buy the one costing the least. Still others might insist on a given brand and hunt until it was found. Market research discloses how most buyers probably would treat a new item. If it will be treated as a convenience good it should be sold to and displayed in stores that provide ready accessibility. If it will be treated as a shopping item it should be placed for sale in stores located in areas where competing items are sold, thus making it easy for shoppers to compare values. If it appears that most customers will ask for it by brand name it can be stocked by stores in less expensive areas since buyers will go to more trouble to obtain it.

Standardization and Grading. A *standard* is a measure of qualities and characteristics. It may be expressed either objectively or subjectively. *Grading* is the process of assigning lots of a product to their appropriate standards. Standards have been established by the United States Bureau of Standards for many types of products. The Bureau's Division of Simplified Practice has made considerable progress in reducing the variety of manufactured products.

Manufacturers can hold their products to given standards, but farmers must take what the weather, insect pests, and the like give them. Their products are graded and sold for what they bring.

Many manufacturers, canners, and other types of producers establish more or less fixed standards for their products, brand them, and advertise the brand. Many producers also place on their labels the specific standard designation, for the convenience of their customers.

Marketing Costs. Over the years the real price of manufactured goods has dropped. During this time the proportionate costs of manufacturing and marketing have changed places. Before the days of mass production, manufacturing costs were high per unit of product and marketing costs were low. But as marketing distances from producing areas increased, distributing costs increased. And as the demand from larger marketing areas increased, the cost per unit of more production dropped. In most situations it would be false economy to cut advertising and sales budgets, for the eventual drop in demand for the product would bring about a disproportionate rise in unit costs of manufacturing.

Distribution Channels. A distribution channel governs the flow of products from producer to consumers. There are many services that must be performed during the marketing process.

The orthodox channel of distribution is: Producer to wholesaler to retailer to consumer.

In recent years this channel has been changed. There are, for instance, paper wholesalers that handle practically everything in the paper line. Certain specialized paper houses, called jobbers, have entered the picture. They buy from both producers and wholesalers and sell to retailers. One example of such a jobber handles only paper items used by grocery stores: wrapping paper, paper bags, and other paper items.

Makers of industrial installations usually sell directly to the user because most of their production is made to the order of the buyer. Manufacturers of industrial supplies and machines sell both to middlemen and to users. Middlemen in this area often handle single lines of merchandise, such as wrenches or pipes, particularly for the convenience of small manufacturers or service shops. These middlemen buy directly from manufacturers.

Efforts have been made over the years to eliminate one or more of the middlemen for various reasons. When supermarkets first began developing they bought in carload lots from producers and sold to consumers.

It must be remembered that each middleman performed certain functions and that the elimination of middlemen did not eliminate the functions. The supermarket buys from producers and sells to consumers. But it performs its own transporting, financing, warehousing, and wholesaling functions. And the customer, in effect, buys directly from a wholesaler since many of the former functions of a retail grocer are now performed by the consumer. A number of years ago it was customary to phone orders to the retail grocer, or, more commonly, he made the rounds of his customers' homes each morning taking orders; later in the day they were delivered by the grocer's boy who brought them in and left them on the kitchen table. Bills were paid monthly, and there were no interest charges on late payments. Today, customers go to the store, wait on themselves, stand in line to be checked out, pay cash, and deliver their own groceries.

Chain stores have been in existence for many years. They have developed in opposite directions at the same time. Wholesalers developed retail outlets while retailers combined to perform their own wholesaling functions.

Some producers have been able to sell all or the bulk of their output to one buyer. Some avoid this for fear the larger buyer might dominate them, dictate prices and terms, take them over, or suddenly drop them. Some producers prefer to sell directly to retailers since wholesalers usually carry competing products and cannot be relied on to carry out the producers' policies.

Marketing Structures. Several kinds of marketing structures can be distinguished. *Agency structures* are found in each industry. They include the organizations that perform the functions necessary to move the products from producer to user: the middlemen, the contacts with the customers, and the information, transportation, storage, and financial services required.

Area structures are more or less well defined for *selling* and *buying*. Producers of similar products in given geographical areas send them, as a rule, to the same central markets. Here, buyers compete in their purchase. These areas are fairly well delimited by transportation costs. Wholesalers sell in much larger areas than retailers.

Buying areas vary from one purchaser to another and from one product to another. Some purchasers may restrict all their clothing needs to the county or the neighborhood. Some may patronize the mail-order stores. And some may go international by buying suits in Hong Kong and dresses in Paris. Automobiles and better roads extend buying areas. Fairly well-defined areas can be drawn for a relatively small number of classes of purchasers and for large groups of items.

Price structures are series or systems of prices. Seasonal fluctuations are evident for some products as are cyclical prices. The general price level shows a long secular uptrend with cyclical waves above and below it. Wars and catastrophies cause temporary dislocations in prices.

Of course, prices reflect freight costs as well as temporary shortages. National self-sufficiency may be smart policy so as to avoid shortages in wartime and dependency on foreign suppliers (e.g., the Arab petroleum experience). Self-sufficiency in the long run causes higher prices.

The present price of a commodity may vary with delivery dates. As a rule *spot prices* (those delivered now) are lower than *future prices* (those purchased now for future delivery) since costs of storage, interest, and insurance must be added to the price of the product.

QUESTIONS FOR DISCUSSION

1. Why is it so hard to introduce new products?
2. What is the difference between producers' goods and consumers' goods?
3. What five ways can producers' goods be classified?
4. Differentiate the three classes of consumers' goods and give an example of each.
5. Why has the proportionate cost of marketing increased over the cost of producing most items?
6. What is a distribution channel?
7. What is the orthodox distribution channel?
8. How much truth is there in the claim that elimination of middlemen results in substantial savings? Who performs the middleman's functions if he is eliminated?
9. What limits the area within which a person may buy for his household needs?
10. What are your arguments for and against national self-sufficiency?

SELECTED REFERENCES

Buskirk, Richard H., *Principles of Marketing*, 3rd ed., Holt, Rine-
    hart & Winston, New York, 1970.

Cundiff, Edward W., Richard R. Still, and Norman A. P. Govoni,
    Fundamentals of Modern Marketing, Prentice-Hall, Englewood
    Cliffs, N. J., 1973.

Davis, Kenneth R., *Marketing Management*, 3rd ed., Ronald Press
    Co., New York, 1972.

Dodge, H. Robert, *Industrial Marketing*, McGraw-Hill, New York,
    1970.

Shultz, William J., *Outline of Marketing*, Littlefield, Adams & Co.,
    Totowa, N. J., 1961.

Stanton, William J., *Fundamentals of Marketing*, 3rd ed., McGraw-
    Hill, New York, 1971.

Stuteville, John R., *Marketing in an Affluent Society*, Wadsworth
    Publishing Co., Belmont, Cal., 1974.

CHAPTER 19

WHOLESALE AND RETAIL TRADE

The flow of goods from the producer to consumers takes place through two agencies, wholesaling and retailing.

WHOLESALING

Typically, wholesalers assemble a great variety of products in a general line by purchasing them from the producers and then selling in smaller quantities to retailers. However, there are many exceptions to this procedure.

Full-Function Wholesalers. The great majority of wholesalers are *full-function* or *full-service* dealers. They take title to the goods they buy; they take possession, transport, and store them. They usually pay cash and often extend credit when they sell. *Full-line wholesalers* are declining in number and importance. Increasingly wholesalers are handling specialized subdivisions instead of broad commodity lines. However, those handling broad lines tend to persist because retailers would rather place one large order than place many small orders with a variety of specialized firms. Wholesalers provide frequent delivery service, help retailers with sales-promotion ideas, and provide expert accounting suggestions. Producers object to the failure or inability of wholesalers to push their lines, since full-line wholesalers customarily carry several competing lines.

Limited-Function Wholesalers. Some full-function wholesalers operate cash-and-carry departments. Many wholesalers, however, do all their selling on this basis. They require cash immediately and the retailer must come for the merchandise. They sell for less but, of course, the finance and delivery functions are shifted to the buyers.

Drop shippers operate in the coal and lumber fields. They take orders from retailers, then buy from producers who deliver directly to the retailers. They take title to the goods but they do not store or transport them. Drop shippers are also called *desk jobbers*.

Truck jobbers and *truck wholesalers* do not store. They pick up the products at the producers' places of business, pay cash, deliver to their customers, and collect cash. A variation of this type is the *rack jobber*, who puts the merchandise on the retailers' shelves and maintains attractive displays. Rack jobbers operate chiefly in the cosmetics field.

Mail-order wholesalers are found chiefly among voluntary retail grocers' associations. Daily orders are sent by mail to the association-owned wholesaler. Orders are also sent in by telephone.

Most wholesalers are *local* in nature. Some can be called *regional* in that they operate in several states. *National* wholesalers are few in number and handle mostly drugs and hardware. They have salesmen who cover the country and shipments are made from strategically located warehouses.

Agent Middlemen. *Merchandise brokers* find buyers for producers and find sources of merchandise for sellers, either jobbers or retailers. They also act as agents in buying and selling and for both types of service they usually charge a fee, which varies with quantities involved, or receive a commission. They do not take title to the merchandise they buy and sell nor do they take possession.

Selling agents usually have the responsibility of disposing of a producer's entire output. Although they are independent firms, they work closely with their principals. Some agents receive merchandise on consignment and store it in their own warehouses.

Commission houses receive in central markets and sell agricultural products shipped to them from farms. They take physical possession but do not accept title. Retail buyers come to these markets for their daily requirements, pay cash, and transport the merchandise. The commission house pays the producer immediately. Occasionally the farmer receives cash payment prior to sale of his product. The commission house, as the name indicates, is paid a percentage of what it sells.

Manufacturers' agents operate in more or less fixed territories where they sell complementary, noncompeting products of several producers. Their discretion as to prices and terms are more restricted than the authority granted to selling agents and their commissions are lower. Most manufacturers' agents operate out of a small office with a secretary and perhaps one or two salesmen.

Resident buyers operate as agents for retailers in purchasing their stock. They also provide a center where out-of-town buyers can receive salesmen. They give advice with respect to styles and sources of merchandise and serve as representatives of their clients in all matters concerning relationships with suppliers. They are paid on either a fee or a commission basis.

Auction companies dispose of certain farm products for the producers. Bidders attend the auctions, inspect samples of the products, then compete with others during the bidding process. The goods go to the highest bidders.

Wholesalers' Brands. If a wholesaler sells articles bearing manufacturers' brands he may be in an insecure position. It is possible for him to build up a demand for the articles only to have them taken away. He has no control over the manufacturer, who may wish to change to another wholesaler or who may wish to develop his own wholesale department. Although it generally costs more, wholesalers that are able to use their own brands to be used on all merchandise they sell are in a very secure position. The acceptance they have built for their own brands cannot be taken away from them by the producers. Wholesalers selling goods under their own brands can change their suppliers at will without disturbing their retailer and consumer relationships.

RETAILING

Retailers place goods where ultimate consumers can conveniently buy. There are exceptions, where retail food stores sell to restaurants or where hardware stores sell to contractors. Also, producers frequently sell directly to ultimate consumers. However, the typical situation is where a store stocks and displays goods for sale to final consumers. There are approximately two million such retail outlets in the country.

Retail Stores. Historically, the *general store* should be mentioned first. These stores supplied most of the needs of early Americans. Other kinds of stores developed as urban centers grew, but general stores followed the frontier across the country and have persisted to this day in rural areas. In the early days general stores were called *trading posts*. They still go by that name on Indian reservations. Small-town general stores carry many lines of merchandise from matches through groceries to clothing. Some general stores accept for credit such items as milk, eggs, and fruit.

Single-line stores have replaced most general stores and are now the most prevalent type. They handle only one general type of merchandise, such as groceries. Most buy from wholesalers though some of the larger stores buy from producers. Formerly, the proprietors of single-line stores waited on customers, made deliveries, and extended credit. The trend in recent years, however, has been away from these services. It is difficult to generalize when describing this category since a single-line store owned and operated by a single individual differs in many respects from those owned by a chain-store corporation, and operating procedures differ substantially among restaurants, clothing stores, and art and antique shops, to name a few.

Specialty stores carry a narrow line of merchandise and customers tend to make extra effort to patronize them. A given brand of shoes, for instance, may be sold only in a store that restricts its business to this brand and not in stores that carry competing brands. Other examples are suits, dresses, and watches. These stores are given exclusive rights within fairly large territories. They may advertise in local newspapers, but they usually lean more heavily on window displays for reaching consumers.

Variety stores display a wide variety of merchandise on counters within easy reach of customers. Formerly these were the 5-and-10 stores, later dollar stores. Now, because of inflation and changing operating policies, most of these stores have no fixed upper prices, but they retain their traditional modes of displaying merchandise. Sales personnel are restricted to wrapping items selected by the customers and receiving cash. They make little or no effort to sell anything.

Department stores display and sell a large variety of merchandise. Formerly, they were located in downtown shopping areas of cities. In the 1920s, J. C. Nichols developed the Country Club Plaza at the south edge of the two Kansas Cities (Kansas and Missouri). This area quickly grew into a popular shopping area. In the following years similar projects were developed in suburban areas throughout the United States. Although all types of retail stores, together with gasoline service stations, restaurants, beauty and barber shops, theaters, and office buildings, moved to these shopping areas, large downtown department stores began putting branch stores here, also. Even big department stores associated with New York shopping areas put branches in these new shopping "plazas" throughout the United States. New, independent department stores also sprang up in these suburban areas and in recent years many old, established stores in city shopping districts have either moved to outlying areas or quit business.

As the name indicates, department stores are divided into departments, each of which handles a single line of merchandise. The department manager usually is the buyer and he is in charge of the salesmen and responsible for departmental results. Many departments are leased to outside companies. These companies pay rent to the store management. Although it is only a book transaction, all departments owned by the local store are also charged rent. Such charges vary from floor to floor and from front to rear. Highest rent charges are made for first floor front locations, and very high charges are made for window display space. Relatively low charges are made for storage and "behind the scenes" work and office space, which generally requires more than half the space in the entire store.

Supermarkets handle a variety of groceries, dairy products, meats, bakery items, and convenience goods. Their gross sales usually are well in excess of one-half million dollars per year. They usually are located in outlying shopping areas and cater to the "automobile trade" by providing spacious parking space. They make shopping convenient for their customers by providing carts as well as carry-out boys. They entice heavy patronage by advertising *loss leaders*, branded items sold at cost or even lower. Buying as they do in carload lots from producers, these stores can undersell smaller stores.

The Piggly Wiggly chain stores were the first to initiate a supermarket characteristic: self-service. This was in 1912 when the Alpha Beta chain, the ABC Stores, and stores in Texas and California also began self-service operations. The cash-and-carry concept was also initiated in 1912 by the Great Atlantic and Pacific Tea Company.

The first supermarkets developed in Los Angeles in 1929. Although many were being started at that time, the Chapman Park Drive-In Market was the most elaborate. It cost, initially, $400,000. At the same time several movie stars invested some of their excess cash in these new drive-in, self-service, cash-and-carry stores. In the middle 1930s one of these stores was opened in Hollywood. Its financial backer gave it a typical movieland title; he called it a "supermarket." The name soon was used to describe all such stores.

Meanwhile, in August of 1930, the King Kullen Store was opened in Jamaica, Long Island. In the following years several more stores were established in the area. The owner, Michael Cullen, called them "The Price Wreckers." Many writers give Cullen credit for being the true originator of the supermarket.

In December of 1932, Roy Dawson and Robert Otis opened their Big Bear Market, advertised as "The Price Crusher," in the abandoned Durant factory in Elizabeth, N. J. (The author and his wife frequently shopped there amid much confusion and excitement.) A circus atmosphere pervaded this market as well as similar stores being opened in the New York metropolitan area. Some were opened in warehouses, others in tents, and a few even operated on vacant lots. Crates of widely assorted goods were dramatically pushed into sales areas on hand trucks and, as sales clerks opened them and loudly hawked their contents, customers rushed in to buy. As the years passed, however, supermarkets moved into cities and outlying shopping areas and took on their present complexion. Goods are displayed on shelves where customers can make their selections and put the items in their shopping carts. Overhead signs help customers find what they want. There are no salespersons; only stock clerks, butchers, checkout cashiers at the exits, and the manager. Some stock clerks open crates of packaged and canned goods, price-mark them, and move them to the display shelves. Prices are also shown on the shelves. Clerks in the vegetable and fruit sections must sort, trim, and freshen their products. Some items are prepacked in transparent plastic bags, sealed, and price-marked. Again, prices of vegetables and fruits are shown on shelves, bins, and tables.

Employees in the meat department are more stock clerks than butchers, though they do some cutting. Most meat cuts and meat products are packaged elsewhere and brought to the store's cold-storage room in transparent plastic bags. They are weighed, price-tagged, and placed in cooled bins for customer selection. Customers desiring special cuts are served by the butchers.

One of the most difficult problems faced by supermarket managers is making it easy and convenient for customers to pay for their purchases. It is necessary for the manager to balance the number of checkout cashiers to the number of customers in the store and to the varying quantities purchased by each. Since it is wasteful to have an adequate number of cashiers on the job as some of them would inevitably be idle part of the time, it is rare for a customer to get out of a supermarket without having to stand in line and wait his turn to be checked out. Many managers attempt to partially solve this problem by using an "express line" which moves faster since it is restricted to customers with, say, six items or less. Another partial solution is to require cashiers to double as stock clerks. If cashiers can be put on standby jobs when customer traffic is light, more of them can be used during rush periods.

A comparatively recent development in the supermarket field is represented by K-Mart, a sort of super supermarket, which is a cross between the conventional type of store and a department store. In addition to the usual lines stocked by supermarkets it handles clothing and footware, sporting goods and firearms, photographic equipment and supplies, paint, drugs, garden supplies and nursery stock, automobile supplies, jewelry, rugs and bedding, pictures and frames, and many other items. Customers select their purchases and take them either to the departmental cashier or to the exit cashiers. An exit inspector quickly passes those with receipts clipped by departmental cashiers to their packages.

Many types of stores are operated by *chain-store* companies. Ownership and management are centrally located but the stores are widely scattered and each stocks the same line of goods. They have standard fronts and layouts. There is disagreement among the authorities as to what actually constitutes a chain. There are many examples of individuals owning and operating two to five or six stores in a small area. Some would say these are not chains. The *Progressive Grocer* has set eleven stores as the minimum.

Prior to the 1920s variety and grocery chains were rapidly expanding throughout the country. Their great volume and progressive merchandising methods posed serious problems for local merchants. Eventually many privately owned stores were able to compete successfully with the chain stores by using their layout methods, by reducing the items stocked to those most profitable and fastest selling, and by substituting personal interest and service for the lower prices chains could charge because of quantity buying. Local merchants appealed, also, to community pride by advertising "spend your money in locally owned stores and keep it at home."

In some states, the first efforts made by local merchants to compete with chain stores were made through state legislatures. Some states imposed occupational taxes on stores owned by out-of-state owners, and some taxed chain stores as such. One state taxed chain-store companies progressively on the number of stores owned in that state, i.e., $100 on the first, $200 on the second, and so on. And, finally, one state imposed a flat tax on each store owned by the company, regardless of the number of stores located in that state. Twenty-nine states enacted tax laws, but fifteen subsequently repealed them.

In the 1930s federal and state *fair trade* laws were passed making it legal for producers to enforce resale price maintenance contracts with retailers. The state *unfair trade practice* laws forbade sales by retailers below cost. These laws struck at the practice of enticing customers into stores by advertising *loss leaders*, well-known branded items at very low prices. Chain stores were prevented from obtaining lower prices than other types of stores could get under the federal Robinson-Patman Act (1936) which outlawed *price discrimination*. In many areas of the country these laws, in recent years, have been only sporadically enforced. In some areas chain stores regularly sell below cost, and small fines that do not deter the practice are regularly imposed.

Several cases charging chains with violation of the antitrust laws went to the United States Supreme Court, but over the years chain stores have managed to survive, and local merchants have learned to live with them.

Not only have local merchants aped chain stores with respect to layout, display, and merchandising policies; they have formed *voluntary chains*. These chains have adopted uniform store-front styles, uniform layouts, and cooperative advertising programs. They have pooled their resources for many purposes and have engaged in cooperative purchasing, transporting, and storing.

Cooperative purchasing associations pool the buying power of consumers. They have set up department stores, general stores, and other types of retail outlets. Generally they charge competitive prices and then rebate "profits" to members on the basis of patronage.

Discount houses deal in fair-traded durable consumer goods. They advertise and sell well-known trade-marked items at substantial discounts, ignoring the fact that other merchants feel obligated to maintain the prices fixed by the manufacturers. Although other retailers sometimes cut prices and give other inducements to customers, the discount houses consistently follow this practice. Although manufacturers spend much money and time in building acceptance for their branded products and although they know that to permit retailers to cut below the advertised prices will cheapen their products and arouse resentment among other retailers who must maintain these prices, the producers continue to sell to the discount houses because of the large size of their orders.

Many discount houses sell only to organized groups such as clubs, schools, and so on. Others organize such groups by requiring customers to purchase a "membership card." All emphasize low prices and keep their overhead low by locating in cheap rental areas and by using few salespersons. They sell for cash and charge for delivery services.

Store Location and Layout. The question of *store location* is a serious one, inasmuch as considerable money must be put into the operation before it gets under way. Supermarkets, department stores, and chain stores locate in areas where potentially high volume can support them. New, rapidly growing areas are always attractive. Diversified industry in the area makes for relatively steady sales and freedom from wide-swinging business cycles.

The specific site can be downtown, in a secondary shopping area, on a main street through town, in a small outlying residence area, or in a planned shopping plaza. The latter is nearly always safe, if one can be found. Investigators have learned that such planned shopping plazas draw shoppers from as far away as ten miles, whereas single stores usually draw trade within a two-mile radius.

In recent years downtown locations have become more attractive due to the creation of malls along closed-off streets.

The first step in designing *office and store layouts* is to build on a floor plan. For offices, the flow of paper work, the relationships and varying sizes of departments, needs for communicating, and so on, are considered. Often scale models of desks, filing cabinets, and office machinery are used to find the best arrangement.

Store layouts must take into account the flow of materials and stock from storerooms to display and sales areas but, more importantly, customer traffic must be considered. Department store operators have learned that more aisle space is required in the front of the ground floor than in back and on other floors. Plenty of space must be allowed, also, in front of elevator doors. Usually attractive and flashy merchandise is displayed in front to draw customers into the store and make a good first impression. Certain convenience goods are placed to the rear in the hope that customers in going for such items will be exposed to other merchandise on the way and may buy it.

Other Types of Retailers. Not as numerous as they once were, *public markets* are found at the edge of many cities. They are operated for the convenience of produce farmers and of consumers who desire fresh vegetables and fruit. Commission merchants rent stalls in most of these markets where they sell the products of more distantly located farmers.

Resembling public markets, but on a much smaller scale, are *farmers' roadside stands*. They sell fresh produce, usually at bargain prices. Buyers must beware, however, for the operators of these stands sometimes sell not-so-fresh produce they buy from wholesalers in nearby cities.

Some companies successfully employ *door-to-door selling* directly to housewives in their homes. In some communities *hucksters* still operate, though they have diminished in number over the past fifty years. Mostly they sell farm produce and ice cream.

Peddlers were common in the early days of the country. A few still operate in cities but most of those left sell in remote areas. They carry their merchandise in cases or in wagons or pickup trucks. *Lunch wagon peddlers*, operating in small manufacturing areas, are becoming more numerous. They carry a variety of sandwiches, pies, rolls, coffee, soft drinks, milk, ice cream, candy bars, and sometimes hot soup and other items. The driver props the sides of the truck up, permitting customers to help themselves. The hours of service are short since the peddlers can do business only during lunch hours and coffee breaks.

Order-takers go from house to house displaying sample merchandise and taking orders. Sometimes the same person returns later with the items ordered; sometimes the articles are mailed C.O.D.

Many door-to-door retailers operate both as peddlers and order-takers. They sell what they have with them and take orders for other items they do not have in stock. The best-known merchants of this type sell brushes, toilet articles, and kitchen ware.

The percentage of retail business done by *direct mail* is relatively small, although a few of the concerns that operate in this field as general-line houses are very large. These concerns follow one or more of the following procedures. *First*, they mail catalogs to prospective customers and fill orders by mail as they are received. Either payment is made by check in advance, or the merchandise is received C.O.D. *Second*, small catalog and sample offices are located in smaller cities and towns. Customers place orders in these offices and pick up the merchandise when notified it has arrived. Payment is made either when the order is placed or after the goods are inspected. *Third*, retail outlets resembling other chain stores are placed in busy downtown locations or in shopping plazas. Some of these stores provide delivery service.

There are several thousand smaller special-line mail-order concerns that sell books, clothing, and gadgets of all sorts. Some use catalogs but most use mailing pieces and newspaper advertisements.

Many persons, living in country and city areas, consistently patronize the catalog houses for several reasons. Although it is inconvenient to fill out order blanks and mail them in, although it is not possible to shop and compare values before ordering, and although there is often a long wait before the merchandise is received, there are compensating advantages. Usually dissatisfied customers can return merchandise for credit without question, prices generally are a little lower, and mail-order customers can avoid long drives to shopping areas (or short drives through heavy traffic) and the exhaustion that often results from fighting crowds of shoppers in stores.

A method of retailing which accounts for less than 1% of all retail sales but which is growing in popularity is *automatic vending*. Children have dropped pennies into gum and peanut vending machines for many years, and coin-operated telephones have been around a long time. Although the Automats have been in existence in New York for quite a while, the principle of coin-operated lunch rooms in factories, offices, and schools has developed on a large scale only comparatively recently.

There are close to 3,000,000 vending machines in operation in the United States today. Most of them dispense candy bars, with cigarettes a close second. Vending machines sell a great variety of products including soft drinks, postage stamps, travel insurance policies, newspapers, ice cream bars, coffee, hot soup, and milk. They are used for such services as typing, shaving, transportation, washing clothes, using telescopes, making voice recordings, playing records, taking pictures, making Xerox copies of documents, and even gambling.

It is said that a Greek invented the first coin-operated dispenser about 2000 years ago. It released holy water. In modern times the first coin-operated machine was produced in 1882 in Germany. It was a scale on which a person stood to see how much he weighed. This machine spread rapidly throughout the United States and soon afterward chewing gum dispensers appeared.

Dispensing-machine operators have had their troubles, not all of which have been overcome. At first, clever thieves were able to induce the machine to give up its store of coins. When this defect was corrected, it was common for thieves to break into the coin receptacle. When the coin boxes were made stronger, the glass fronts were broken and the merchandise was taken. This has been corrected, and the machines have been made slug-proof. Many of these dispensers have been placed where they can be watched by attendants who are available should the mechanism fail to work or should a customer have a complaint about the merchandise.

QUESTIONS FOR DISCUSSION

1. What functions are performed by full-function wholesalers?
2. What is a rack jobber?
3. Do merchandise brokers specialize in buying or selling? How are they paid?
4. How do commission houses operate? Do they physically handle the merchandise?
5. Why should a wholesaler promote the sale of goods under his own brand name? Which are gaining over the other: producers' brands or wholesalers' brands?
6. Describe department stores. What location problems have they had in recent years?
7. Explain why supermarkets, which depend on mass demand, should have developed in the early days of the Great Depression of the 1930s, when money was so scarce.
8. Operators of supermarkets admit that their present method of checking customers out is not good. What have they done to reduce waiting time? Can you think of a better way of handling this problem?
9. How do discount houses differ from supermarkets?

10. What are the advantages and disadvantages in buying from mail-order houses?

SELECTED REFERENCES

Beckman, Theodore N., Nathanael Engle, and Robert D. Buzzel, *Wholesaling*, 3rd ed., Ronald Press Co., New York, 1959.

Beckman, Theodore N., and William R. Davidson, *Marketing*, 9th ed., Ronald Press Co., New York, 1973, Part III.

Brann, Christian, *Direct Mail and Direct Response Promotion*, John Wiley & Sons, New York, 1972.

Corbman, Bernard P., and Murray Krieger, *Mathematics of Retail Management*, 2nd ed., Ronald Press Co., New York, 1972.

Darrah, L. B., *Food Marketing*, Ronald Press Co., New York, 1971.

Jones, Fred M., *Retail Management*, rev. ed., Richard D. Irwin, Homewood, Ill., 1967.

Magee, John F., *Physical Distribution Systems*, McGraw-Hill, New York, 1967.

Markin, Rom J., *The Supermarket*, Washington State University Press, Pullman, Wash., 1968.

Pintel, Gerald, and Jay Diamond, *Retailing*, Prentice-Hall, Englewood Cliffs, N. J., 1971.

Ryans, John K., James H. Donnelly, Jr., and John M. Ivancevich, *New Dimensions in Retailing*, Wadsworth Publishing Co., Belmont, Cal., 1973.

Shultz, William J., *An Outline of Marketing*, Littlefield, Adams & Co., Totowa, N. J., 1961.

Wingate, John W., Elmer O. Schaller, and F. Leonard Miller, *Retail Merchandise Management*, Prentice-Hall, Englewood Cliffs, N. J., 1972.

CHAPTER 20

BUYING

We can distinguish three types of buying: for resale, for the use of business concerns, and for ultimate consumers. The first two are marketing functions; the third is not.

Buyers and Purchasing Agents. The various types of stores buy for resale. If there is a special individual who buys for the store or for a department, he is known as the *buyer*. Many buyers are responsible for selling what they buy. Those individuals who are in close touch with the needs and desires of their customers are more able to select goods that will readily sell than are those who do not have such contacts.

Those who buy items that will be used up by a manufacturing concern in the course of its operations usually are called *purchasing agents*. Sometimes they are on the payroll of the company they serve; sometimes they are independent businessmen working for the company on commission. Purchasing agents do not just buy what they think their employers or principals might need; they usually buy to rather exacting specifications furnished by engineers, production managers, or other officials.

Purchasing agents must read trade papers, listen to salesmen, peruse catalogs, and keep in touch with production problems in the plant. Often they can suggest alternate or substitute products that might yield better results at less cost.

Purchasing Department. The purchasing department receives many types of requests from members of the organization. These must be turned into purchase orders. Often it is necessary to request bids from several competing suppliers. And frequently contracts must be prepared and executed.

Requisitions with less exacting specifications must be converted into purchase orders that can be understood by the suppliers. If the materials have been used previously, the department's files should yield the precise information required. Otherwise, suppliers' catalogs must be studied, telephone calls must be made, and perhaps salesmen may be asked to call.

Often the date of delivery is important and, where it is, the schedule of shipments must be clearly understood.

Sometimes considerable judgment must be exercised in placing orders. If a long-time, reliable supplier charges a little more than a relatively unknown firm, should the new firm be tried? Some buyers might split the order under such circumstances. Others would stay with the old supplier. Should there be a question of impending scarcity of supplies, it might be smart to pay a little more and be sure of a reliable source. On the other hand, a steady supply might be assured by splitting all orders among several firms, even though the cost would be greater per order.

Buying ethics is often troublesome. *Personal preference* of buyers should not influence them in placing orders. Salesmen often send expensive gifts to buyers and purchasing agents: watches, mink stoles, weekends at expensive vacation spots, theater tickets, and so on. Most companies require that such gifts be returned. But how about a cigar or a drink? Should a dinner invitation be accepted? Relatively small favors generally are accepted.

Most firms give favorable consideration to purchasing from those who buy the firm's products.

Upon delivery of the goods, the receiving department notifies the appropriate testing department. If the goods pass, the purchasing department is so informed. If there is a discrepancy of some kind, the purchasing department is expected to contact the vendor and decide whether to reject the shipment, accept it with a price concession, or negotiate other arrangements.

Orders are placed, of course, in the expectation that the goods will be delivered on time. If they do not arrive when needed or if unforeseen circumstances arise in the plant of the purchaser, the order may be canceled. Often the conditions under which cancellations are permitted are spelled out in the contract. However, even when the contract is silent in this respect, cancellations are frequent. Nearly always the vendor accepts the loss and does not object. If he brings suit, it is certain that he will never get another order from the customer. If he does nothing, he might get another order and make up his loss.

Size of Order. The *size* of an order depends on several factors. The buyer or the purchasing agent must exercise his best judgment in quantifying each of these factors. If business might fall off in the near future because of style changes or other reasons, it might be advisable to follow a *hand-to-mouth* buying policy, i.e., placing smaller orders at more frequent intervals. But if larger quantities of a firm's product are being sold, if prices are rising, or if scarcities are expected, it would be wise to *stockpile* inventories. Purchasing continuously used products in such a way as to take advantage of price rises and minimize the effects of price drops is *speculative buying*. It is risky to buy heavily in expectation of profits on price increases. Insurance charges rise, rent or floor space charges rise, and there are hazards of fire, spoilage, and inability to sell the finished products rapidly. There is even the possibility that rising prices may reverse themselves and drop.

When conditions are relatively normal, the *most economical quantities* of materials that are continuously used can be found by adding all costs for varying order sizes. These costs can be classified into those that *rise* as order sizes rise and those that *decrease* as order sizes rise. As order sizes rise, expenses that rise are insurance, storage costs, taxes, and interest on capital invested in inventories. As order sizes rise, the cost per unit of the product usually decreases, cost of preparing orders decreases, transportation charges per unit tend to drop, and possibly packing charges will be lower.

Of course, minimum quantities of the product must be kept on hand between the time an order is placed and the time it is received plus an amount to allow for possible delays. It is easy to approximate the most economical order quantity by using an empirical approach similar to the following example:

Assume the following factors:

A given material is used continuously at the rate of 1,000,-000 pounds a year.

Carrying charges (storage, insurance, taxes, interest, and handling) are 15 percent per year of the inventory value.

The cost of placing an order is $25.

The minimum safety quantity always carried in stock is 10,000 pounds.

In less-than-carload lots (less than 30,000 pounds) the delivered price is 10 cents per pound.

In carload lots (over 30,000 pounds) the delivered price is 8 cents.

To solve the problem empirically the procedure involves assuming orders of various sizes somewhat as follows:

If one order a year is placed, the *average* inventory will be 10,000 plus one-half of 1,000,000, or 510,000 pounds. Its value is $40,800, and carrying charges are $40,800 × 0.15, or $6,120. (This assumes that the storage space can be used for other purposes as the materials are used up.) Total charges (for purposes of illustration and greatly simplified) for 1 order per year:

Carrying charges	$6,120
Cost of ordering	25
Total	$6,145

If 10 orders are placed per year the picture changes somewhat. Inventory fluctuates between 10,000 pounds (minimum stock) and 100,000 pounds (one-tenth of 1,000,000), for an average of 60,000 pounds. Carload rates still apply, so the value is 60,000 × 0.08, or $4,800, and the carrying charges are 15 per cent of $4,800, or $720.

Carrying charges	$720
Cost of ordering	250
Total	$970

If 20 orders are placed per year the average inventory is 35,000 pounds, and the carrying charges are 35,000 × 0.08 × 0.15 = $420.

Carrying charges	$420
Cost of ordering	500
Total	$920

If 30 orders are placed per year the average inventory is 26,667 pounds and the carrying charges are 26,667 × 0.08 × 0.15 = $320.

Carrying charges	$320
Cost of ordering	750
Total	$1,070

If 40 orders are placed per year the average inventory is 22,500 and the carrying charges are 22,500 × 0.10 (less-than-carload price) × 0.15 = $338.

Carrying charges	$ 338
Cost of ordering	1,000
Total	$1,338

To recapitulate:

Size of order (pounds)	Carrying charges	Cost of order	Total cost
1,000,000	$6,120	$ 25	$6,145
100,000	720	250	970
50,000	420	500	920
33,000	320	750	1,070
25,000	338	1,000	1,338

It is now obvious that for the simple conditions assumed and for the five different sizes of orders for which calculations were made, the most economical quantity to order at one time is 50,000 pounds.

Consumer Buying. *Ultimate consumers* have buying characteristics not shown by the other two types. They spend most of their time pursuing other activities, whereas buyers and purchasing agents spend most or all their time buying, and are expert at it.

Those who buy for the family often buy on impulse. Frequently they buy for reasons of pride rather than utility. Although many ultimate consumers shop extensively and buy shrewdly, most cannot hope to make the necessary tests, check available prices, and make all the necessary calculations so as to find the best buy in each of the hundreds of items required by the average family.

As the shopper scans the shelves he or she sees brands made familiar through advertising. These items usually are purchased with little effort made to decide whether one 14-oz. can for 63¢ is a better buy than two 16-oz. cans for $1.60.

Two private rating agencies have been available to consumers for many years: Consumers' Research and Consumers Union. Monthly reports and yearly handbooks are sent to subscribers in which many items are listed, with preferences indicated. Tests are made on items purchased in stores throughout the country. It is obvious that only branded items can be used as otherwise consumers would be unable to identify the goods rated, and it is also obvious that such a task, even when only a very small percentage of all available products is tested, is a Herculean one. Nevertheless, the relatively small percentage of consumers who subscribe to these services find them exceedingly helpful.

The U.S. Agricultural Marketing Administration issues pamphlets full of information on agricultural products. But, again, relatively few consumers are interested enough to obtain them. The Agricultural Marketing Administration also makes available to producers an official inspection service for canned fruits and vegetables, meat, and eggs. Those who avail themselves of this service can use the proper standard grades on their labels. Many large food producers do not use the service. They prefer to advertise their own grades and they claim that the standard grades do not take into account superior flavor and other qualities that must be judged subjectively.

QUESTIONS FOR DISCUSSION

1. What is the difference between a buyer and a purchasing agent?
2. Would you say that the purchasing department is merely a "rubber stamp" department? Explain your answer.
3. Where should members of the purchasing department draw the line when offered gifts by salesmen?
4. How much consideration should the purchasing department give to reciprocity?
5. When should a hand-to-mouth buying policy be followed?
6. Is it ever wise to engage in speculative buying? Explain your answer in some detail.

7. What items of cost rise and what fall as order sizes rise?
8. In general, how is the most economical order size calculated?
9. Why are most consumers not as clever at buying as are store buyers and industrial purchasing agents?
10. Name a few informational agencies available to consumers.

SELECTED REFERENCES

England, Wilbur B., *Modern Procurement Management*, 5th ed., Richard D. Irwin, Homewood, Ill., 1970.

Heinritz, Stuart F., and Paul V. Farrell, *Purchasing: Principles and Applications*, 5th ed., Prentice-Hall, Englewood Cliffs, N. J., 1971.

Westing, J. H., I. V. Fine, and Gary Joseph Zenz, *Purchasing Management*, 3rd ed., John Wiley & Sons, New York, 1969.

Wingate, John W., and Joseph Friedlander, *The Management of Retail Buying*, Prentice-Hall, Englewood Cliffs, N. J., 1963.

CHAPTER 21

SELLING AND ADVERTISING

An important part of marketing is the promotion of sales. This activity is divided into personal selling and advertising.

SELLING

In the broad sense, selling includes all activities contributing to the creation of demand for a specific product. In the narrow and more familiar sense *selling* means personal salesmanship. A paid sales appeal placed with any of the advertising media is an *advertisement*. News stories involving the company, its officers, and/or the product, involving no cost to the company, is a form of advertising called *publicity*. It is the purpose of this chapter to discuss both selling and advertising, with some material on publicity and a broader activity called *public relations*.

The Importance of the Selling Function. As the efficiency of industry has increased and as producers have expanded out of local marketing areas into neighboring territories, competition for customers has become increasingly sharp. Not only has competition between producers of similar products been heightened, but there has been an increasing struggle among the producers of widely differing products for a share of the consumer's dollar. There are, of course, periods of acute shortage in goods of all kinds, but over the years there has developed a feeling of dependence upon those who by promoting demand for the company's products are directly responsible for keeping the wheels turning. Of course, the salesman's work would go for naught if the production department ceased to function, if those unsung heroes, the maintenance people, failed at their job, and if any one of dozens of other departments did not do a good job. But there is a dramatic quality in coming back from the field with a briefcase loaded with fat orders that is not found in repairing the motor which drives the machinery which fills those orders. Except in periods of labor and materials shortage, there is a feeling that any ranking of the functions of business in order of importance should place selling near the top.

Market Research and Product Analysis. The basis of all business lies in the reaction of the customer to the product or service. If he is favorably impressed he may buy. Usually he will not buy if he does not need the product or service, or if he has no money. Salesmen can sell products and services to those who do not need them, but to do so tends to create ill will. Likewise, sales can be made to those who have no money. Again, to do so means future collection troubles, ill will on the part of the customer, and financial loss to the company. Therefore selling begins with a study of the products or services of the concern with relation to specific market areas. Such studies can be extremely involved. They include such matters as income levels, buying motives and habits, what products consumers want or are likely to accept, how products should be packaged, whether they should be made cheaply with frequent style changes or expensively for durability, etc. Often the question of price is difficult to determine. It is not always true that demand will be stimulated by price cutting. There is a widespread mistrust of goods priced below the accepted level. Salesmen who offer such price concessions inevitably are asked, "What is wrong with the goods?" It may be better to compete on the basis of service rather than price.

After such detailed studies the sales department determines sales potentials for various areas and assigns specific quotas to salesmen covering those areas.

The Sales Department. The sales department is responsible for inducing customers to use its products. The activities involved in achieving this objective are classified into planning, field work, and personal selling. The *sales manager* is responsible for coordinating this work.

Planning includes price studies, market research, the determination of sales territories, the assignment of salesmen to territories, the study of cycles of demand and arranging for sales conventions in off seasons, selecting and training salesmen and service employees, and many other activities. *Field work* is an adjunct to personal selling and involves demonstrations, setting up special displays, settling misunderstandings, servicing the product, and so on. *Personal selling* is, of course, getting the order.

The sales manager must be a leader. He may or may not be a good salesman, but he must be able to inspire and motivate the sales force.

There are at least three types of sales organization: by territories, by product lines, and by customers. *Territorial* organization divides the country into major areas, each in charge of a *divisional sales manager*. Smaller territories are then given to individual *salespersons*, who methodically search for customers and follow up inquiries.

It is important to divide sales territories in such a way that all have approximately equal sales potential. In this connection, the Federal Bureau of the Census has figures that might help. The company must research the connection between its product or products and available statistics. A fairly simple illustration is that of a product used by motorists. It can safely be assumed that sales territories can be drawn on the basis of car registrations. If the product is useful to all persons, distribution of the general population can form the basis of sales territories. Usually a combination of indices will be used. Other such figures are income tax returns, bank deposits, magazine circulation, and retail stores.

The sales force can be organized, also, by *product lines*. This is done where the firm makes several products, variations of one product, or one that can be used by distinctly differing customer groups. Glass is an example. Window glass for private homes can be sold to hardware stores, plate glass can be sold as needed to replace store-front windows and in new construction, and glass can be sold to manufacturers for use in the products they produce. In the same geographical area a different salesman very likely would be used for each type of user.

A third form of organization of the sales force is by *customers*. The product may be the same, but the sales approach differs from one class to another. For instance: one salesperson may call on stores, one on manufacturers, and another on governmental agencies.

A very important duty of the sales manager is that of *selecting* qualified individuals for his sales force. The criterion of success in sales work usually is the volume of sales per year. By studying the personal qualities of men and women who have top sales records and comparing them with individuals with poor records the sales manager (or a testing psychologist on his staff) often can determine what qualities to seek in an applicant and what qualities to avoid. Of course, the presence of favorable qualities does not guarantee top performance, but such qualities in a new employee greatly increase the chances that he or she will make good.

Before a person can be *trained*, the job must be analyzed. With knowledge of what the job requires, both the salesperson and the coach can work toward developing and strengthening the needed personal qualities. Training is accomplished through observation of actual or demonstration sales performances and correction by a coach of practice and actual selling experiences, reading assignments, listening to demonstration records and tapes, conferences, panel discussions, and lectures.

Personal Selling. Whether the customer comes to the store or whether the salesman seeks out his prospects in their own homes or offices the basic principles are the same, and a salesman's success depends to a large degree upon the extent to which such principles can be followed. There are various stages in a sale; some writers group them into four, some more. Before the sale begins, however, it is assumed that the salesman knows (1) how to sell, (2) the importance of dressing conservatively and without too much jewelry, (3) the importance of cleanliness and neatness, (4) the importance of knowing as much as possible about the product or service he is selling, (5) what objections he will meet and what information will overcome such objections, and (6) all policies of the company regarding prices, discounts, shipping dates, returns, credit terms, etc. It is assumed, also, that the salesman sincerely believes in the product or service he is selling. Such belief gives the sales talk a depth of sincerity and an infectious quality of restrained enthusiasm which cannot otherwise be attained.

The first stage of a specific sale might be called the *preapproach*. During this stage the salesman learns about the prospect. If the sale is important enough the salesman may seek out the answers to many questions concerning likes and dislikes, peculiarities, hobbies, marital status, names and ages of children if any, clubs, college, military service, etc., before he calls on his prospect. This information is invaluable in avoiding embarrassing and awkward statements as well as in finding a common ground for conversation and mutual interests which tend to promote friendship. The salesclerk in a store who cannot expect to make a very large sale and who has no opportunity to do research on his prospects merely sizes them up as they enter the store or the sales area.

The *approach* is the first contact with the prospect. A natural greeting, one that is neither brash nor timid, neither too noisy nor too quiet, is best. The salesman should look at the prospect and should allow the prospect to take the initiative with respect to shaking hands. A simple statement as to who is calling and the purpose of the call completes this phase. The retail clerk behind a counter should walk to the point nearest to the customer and show genuine pleasure at the opportunity of serving him. This phase is badly mismanaged by many retail salespeople, who do not realize or care what a bad impression they make by (1) ignoring customers, (2) making customers wait while they finish private conversations with other salespeople, (3) acting annoyed, (4) showing impatience by tapping nervously on the counter or pointedly looking at the clock, (5) saying "yeah?" while finishing something that could wait, and so on. The proper approach sets the stage for a pleasant negotiation of the sale.

The next stage is that of *attracting attention*. The prospect's attention is concentrated first on the salesman. The purpose of this stage is to transfer attention to the product. This is done most effectively by handing the product to the prospect and then by picking up something else so the prospect cannot hand it back. If it is a machine, making it work will attract attention. If it is something to be read, the salesman should keep still long enough to let the prospect concentrate on the meaning of the words. If it is a car, let the prospect drive it. He might even like to see the motor, though the salesman must be alert to change his tactics if it is apparent that what is being done to attract attention is not having the desired effect.

The next stage involves *arousing interest*. This is done by allowing the prospect to hold, or watch, or drive the product while the salesman points out novel features, how it works, or what it can do. Questions are encouraged, objections are anticipated, and testimonials are cleverly woven into the conversation.

The stage of *desire* emerges imperceptibly and the salesman encourages the process by picturing the advantages of ownership. If the prospect is an industrial user the arguments at this point are chiefly rational in nature: how much money can be saved, how much better the quality of work will be, etc. If the prospect is an ultimate consumer often an emotional appeal will have the desired effect: "Can't you just imagine how popular you will be with this yellow convertible?" But the rational appeal should not be neglected when dealing with consumers, and the emotional appeal has been known to work with hard-headed businessmen.

The *close* is the crucial stage. If the salesman has judged his prospect's reaction correctly, the customer will respond by signing on the dotted line when the fountain pen is put into his hand. But if the salesman moves too swiftly he may lose the sale. Often, however, it is enough to lay the pen down and pick up the sale again in the interest stage, then try to intensify the desire. The second effort to close may be successful. The retail salesperson may have trouble getting the prospect to decide upon the exact item. Desire is present but freedom of choice is blocked by the presence of too many patterns and colors. The tactic at this point is to narrow choice. Eliminate the items where desire is weakest, always keeping an odd number of items before the prospect. It is easier for a customer to decide from among five or three than from among four or two.

The last stage is the *getaway*. It involves a quick cleanup of samples, absence of voluble let-down conversation, a figurative assuring pat on the back, and a graceful withdrawal from the presence of a satisfied customer.

Individuals who sell are *motivated* in various ways. Money is one. But every person wants certain job satisfactions, and if the work does not come up to his expectations, unhappiness prevails in spite of good pay. Sales managers know that every person is motivated differently, but that the following factors move most to greater interest and effort: recognition, the esteem of others, treatment that builds self-respect, congenial associates and surroundings, chance of promotion, and adequate pay.

Most salespersons work on *straight salary*. Although the incentive value of this method is thought to be low, still an employee on straight salary has a feeling of security. Freed from financial worries induced by widely fluctuating sales, such persons usually consistently do their best for purposes of recognition, possible promotion, and higher salaries. Nearly always, *missionary* salesmen, those introducing a new product or service and those doing nonselling work, are paid by this method.

Many salespersons are paid on a *commission* basis. Such individuals are paid by results, not by time. Those who are top producers and who want to be independent prefer this method. The firm finds it advantageous not to pay when few or no sales are made, but it is often a disadvantage to be unable to direct an employee working on a commission basis to do nonselling work.

A popular method of reimbursing salespersons is by combining *salary and commission* plans. The salary provides security and the commission provides added income for the more energetic salespersons.

Various types of *bonuses* are given to salaried salespersons. They are computed on the basis of sales over quotas, this year over last year, a proportion of company profits, and so on.

Many firms motivate their sales force by means of *annual conventions*. The social atmosphere, inspirational speeches, awards and recognition of outstanding performance, dinners, and entertainment, all tend to raise morale and charge the employees with ambition to work harder.

Most individuals respond favorably to *fair treatment* from the company. Adjustments of complaints and avoidance of harsh conditions are appreciated. Most of all, however, the salesperson wants an occasional promotion; not just a pay raise, but a shift to a better territory and a chance someday to be district sales manager and possibly sales manager. Nothing kills incentive more than bringing in outsiders to fill vacancies.

ADVERTISING AND PUBLICITY

The various types of advertising campaigns are designed to accomplish one or more of such aims as informing and educating prospective users, stimulating inquiries, influencing changes in consumer demand, creating positive desire for ownership, building up favorable attitudes toward the product and the firm, familiarizing consumers with brand names, and making good salesmen want to work for a company which lends support to the men in the field. Some concerns put the entire responsibility for selling their products upon advertising, but more often advertising is used to pave the way for the personal contact which closes the sale and to give the person who has already purchased the product assurance that he acted wisely.

Advertising Media. The problem of choosing the proper medium or media of advertising is resolved by determining how the potential customer is reached most effectively. In practice this often is difficult, for there are factors other than the media employed which influence the results of advertising. Nevertheless, by keeping as many factors as possible constant and by varying the media it is possible to determine with a fair degree of accuracy which of a number of media costs the least per customer or per unit of sales.

The most common forms of media are newspapers, magazines, billboards, radio, television, and mail. Customarily advertisers turn over to *advertising agencies* most of the work of writing copy, preparing the art work, and placing the advertisements. These agencies are paid by the owners of the media, usually at the rate of a 15 percent allowance off net space or time charges. An advertiser would pay his agent, for instance, $100 plus art work expense, cost of plates, and other direct expenses. The agent then would pay the expense items, with or without a small discount, and he would pay the owner of the medium $85. Often a 1 percent or 2 percent cash discount is also allowed. Actually the services of the agent cost the advertiser nothing, for had he placed the advertisement directly, the charges to him would have been the same.

The Effectiveness of the Advertisement. Often the effects of advertising are delayed or cumulative in nature. A magazine advertisement may produce sales many months after the magazine is issued, or a direct-mail circular may be laid aside and read later. A new product or a new brand may be advertised without immediate results, but as the name is repeated in successive advertisements, the public may gradually begin to buy the product. Confidence in a product and belief in the advertiser's claims tend to mount with time. Advertisers are not discouraged if first advertisements do not pull.

In an effort to get clues as to the pulling power of different advertisements, a device known as *keying* is used. An immediate response is requested and that response is channeled into forms that will be recognized. A radio or TV announcement will be followed by a free offer. To obtain the free article the listener is asked to write within 24 hours "in care of the station to which you are listening." This pinpoints the response. Or, the listener is asked to write to "Department 99" which identifies the letter as a response from advertisement No. 99. If the same advertisement appears in *Redbook* and *Ladies' Home Journal*, the key in the first could be R99 and in the second, L99. Thus the effectiveness of the media could be studied in combination with an apprasial of the advertisement.

Large advertisers often test a given advertisement or campaign by running it in two similar cities. The procedure varies greatly but could be somewhat as follows:

Inventory counts are made in the retail outlet stores in each of two cities A and B. After the standard time has elapsed, inventory counts are again made in both cities. Opening inventories plus additions to stock less closing inventories equals the amount of sales. The same procedure is followed later, with the advertisement or campaign being tested in city A. Care must be taken that the conditions are approximately equivalent in both cities during the test. There cannot, for instance, be a fair or convention in one city and not in the other, a blizzard or a flood in one city and not in the other, etc. Sales are again determined for the test period. Then for a period afterward sales are again recorded. The results might be shown in tabular form as follows:

	Four weeks preadvertising test	*Four weeks advertising test*	*Four weeks postadvertising test*
Sales in city A (test city)	$ 50,000	$ 60,000	$ 55,000
Sales in city B (control city)	100,000	110,000	105,000

There are many pitfalls in a study of this nature, but the supposition is that sales in city A would have picked up $5,000 even had the advertising not been done, for sales picked up 10 percent in the control city where no advertising was done during the three 4-week periods. The inference, then, is that the campaign was responsible for an additional $5,000 sales in city A during the second period. Likewise, with sales in the third period 10 percent above those in the first period in city A, it can be assumed that the campaign accounted for one-half the increase, for the control city shows only a 5 percent increase in the third period over the first period. This is, however, a crude and inexact way of measuring the effects of advertising, and in addition, the method is expensive.

Advertising agencies frequently make recognition tests to determine the effectiveness of advertising campaigns. Series of advertisements are shown to large numbers of buyers and potential buyers. In each of the advertisements, however, the brand names and names of the producer are obliterated. The respondents are then asked to identify the products. The degree to which identification is successfully made is supposed to indicate the degree of effectiveness of the advertisements.

Advertising Ethics. Most advertisers are careful to make true statements and just claims for their products. Most media owners attempt to maintain high standards of advertising ethics. But there always are some people who will lie, cheat, and take unfair advantage of consumers and competitors. To deal with such individuals, trade associations have established codes of ethics and have tried to persuade their more shady colleagues to discontinue their unfair practices. Trade practice agreements have been set up under the aegis of the Federal Trade Commission. These agreements forbid false advertising, among other things.

Better business bureaus, well known as champions of consumers against the fraudulent schemes of dishonest businessmen, were originally founded by honest businessmen to protect themselves.

Nearly all the states have passed *Printers' Ink* statutes. These are patterned after a model statute proposed in 1911 by *Printers' Ink* magazine (now *Marketing Communications*) for the purpose of dealing with dishonest and misleading advertising. The effectiveness of these statutes is doubtful. They do not apply to products and services sold in interstate commerce and they are not effectively enforced for intrastate products.

Perhaps most advertising is honest and factual; some is delightful to read or listen to. Too much of it, however, insults the intelligence of a ten-year-old, is blatantly false and misleading, or is in poor taste and objectionable. Many advertisements repeat *ad nauseam* the claim that the product is better than that of the three leading competitors. Perhaps most listeners or readers do not even hear or see the word "leading." Others get the distinct impression that the advertised product actually is better than three competing products but that the advertiser is covering up the fact that it is inferior to all the others.

There seems to be no way to curb the loud, rapid-fire, breathless TV presentation, the announcer who keeps the claims technically correct but who soft pedals disadvantages and plays up advantages, or the bad timing that intrudes offensive material at dinnertime (stopped only by turning off the set). This sort of objectionable advertising continues to be used because it gets results. Advertising psychologists have proved by many tests that listeners, viewers, and readers of objectionable advertisements tend, over time, to remember the names of the products or services but to forget the details of the presentations.

Publicity and Public Relations. News stories about the firm and its products for which the company does not pay are known as *publicity*. The *public relations* officers of the firm, or independent public relations agents, constantly are alert to the news value of happenings involving the company and its products and services. These are written up and distributed (usually with pictures) to the news media. Editors are glad to use such material if it meets the following criteria: it is well written, it is about specific and provable facts, it does not include obvious sales promotion, and pictures are sharp, glossy prints that will make good cuts.

Public relations attempts to create a favorable image among employees, customers, and the general public. While publicity usually is restricted to news stories, public relations covers a broader range of activities. It begins with sincere good will on the part of the officers of the company and its forms can be divided into fundamental and remedial.

Fundamental public relations involves all sorts of activities designed to build a feeling of friendliness and good will toward the company. Fair dealing with everyone having any type of relations with the company is basic. The girls who answer the telephone have an importance in this respect not generally realized. A cold, indifferent tone of voice hurts; a warm and friendly tone helps. All employees who have dealings with the public should be trained to exhibit friendliness and helpfulness. Waiters and waitresses often are trained to treat customers as though they were guests in their own homes. Job applicants are rejected in a courteous and regretful manner. Department heads exhibit friendly leadership and do not perform as petty czars.

A popular form of training is *role playing*. Many companies organize regular conferences for their employees in which individuals are assigned roles. Situations then are acted out, after which good and bad elements are discussed. This approach usually gets better results than lectures and reading assignments.

The managers of some companies keep in the public eye by making frequent speeches and writing journal articles.

After a crisis of some kind the company usually engages in *remedial public relations* action. If the product has to be recalled because of a serious defect, an attempt usually is made to overcome the ill effects by explanations and in other ways. A good public relations department can do much, also, to overcome the bad image created by strikes, mischievous rumors, accidents, and so on. In stressing the favorable and redeeming factors, care must be taken to tell the truth and not gloss over or misrepresent what actually happened.

QUESTIONS FOR DISCUSSION

1. Define selling, advertising, and publicity.
2. What is the purpose of market research and how is it conducted?
3. What three ways are sales departments organized?
4. What are the seven parts of a sale?
5. If you were in sales work what do you think would motivate you the most to do a good job? List several motivating factors in order of their importance.
6. What is meant by an advertising medium?
7. Name three agencies that combat false advertising.
8. Describe an advertisement that attracted you, and one that repelled you.
9. Distinguish between publicity and public relations.
10. Name two kinds of public relations activities and tell what they seek to accomplish.

SELECTED REFERENCES

Davis, Kenneth R., and Frederick E. Webster, Jr., *Sales Force Management*, Ronald Press Co., New York, 1968.

Dunn, S. Watson, and Arnold M. Barban, *Advertising*, 3rd ed., Holt, Rinehart & Winston, New York, 1973.

Ferber, Robert, Donald F. Blankertz, and Sidney Hollander, Jr., *Marketing Research*, Ronald Press Co., New York, 1964.

Frey, Albert Wesley, and Jean C. Halterman, *Advertising*, 4th ed., Ronald Press Co., New York, 1970.

Gaw, Walter A., *An Outline of Advertising*, Littlefield, Adams & Co., Totowa, N. J., 1966.

Huttig, Jack, *Psycho-Sales Analysis: The New Art of Self-Taught Sales Success*, Littlefield, Adams & Co., Totowa, N. J., 1973.

Kleppner, Otto, *Advertising Procedure*, 6th ed., Prentice-Hall, Englewood Cliffs, N. J., 1973.

Marsh, V. Grant, *Salesmanship: Modern Principles and Practices*, Prentice-Hall, Englewood Cliffs, N. J., 1972.

Marsten, John, *The Nature of Public Relations*, McGraw-Hill, New York, 1963.

CHAPTER 22

TRANSPORTATION AND STORAGE

In the language of the economist, production gives form utility to goods, transportation gives place utility, and storage gives time utility. Goods are of little value unless they are made available where and when they can be used. This chapter is concerned with making goods available at the right places and the right times. The physical distribution system consists of two subsystems: transportation and warehousing.

TRANSPORTATION

The subsystem of transportation has two divisions: carriers and agencies.

The *carriers* operate railways, waterways, truck lines, pipelines, and airlines. From a legal standpoint, carriers are classified into common carriers, contract carriers, and private carriers. Although the following material applies to *common carriers*, those companies that extend their services to all comers, it should be mentioned that some producing companies move their products by the use of *contract carriers*, where many customs and laws do not apply as they do to common carriers. Rates, schedules, routes, and other details are arranged between the shipper and the contract carrier. Some producing companies use *private carriers*, that is, transportation means that are owned and operated by the company that uses them.

The services of transportation *agencies* are available to the general public. They operate between shippers and all types of carriers. They are the United States Parcel Post, the Railway Express Agency, the United Parcel Service, and freight forwarding companies. They collect, consolidate, ship, and deliver packages. The services of the first three of these agencies are well known to the public. Packages usually are taken to their offices for shipment, although they do pick up packages under some conditions, usually for large shippers.

Freight forwarding companies are less well known. They pick up relatively small quantities of freight and charge l.c.l. (less-than-carload) rates. Then they consolidate this freight and ship it at c.l. (carload) rates, which are lower, claiming the difference as their compensation. It is common practice for shippers to several customers to send the orders at c.l. rates as far as possible, then to have agents split the carload and ship at l.c.l. rates the relatively short distances remaining to the individual customers.

Railroad Rates. There are three zones within the United States for rate-setting purposes: *Eastern* (also called *Official*), *Southern*, and *Western*. Goods are classified for rate purposes into eight to ten groups and *blanket rates* are set for each group within each zone and from each zone to each of the other two zones. If a new product does not fit into any of the classifications, a request is made to the Interstate Commerce Commission, which must approve all rates. There are many such exceptions to the blanket zone rates. These are called *commodity rates*.

The theory underlying all railroad rates is that they are set as high as the traffic will bear and in such a way as to give maximum benefit to the carriers. If a community is discriminated against, the I.C.C. gives the matter study and may grant the desired relief. It is obvious, however, that all such requests cannot be approved. Under the federal law that created the Interstate Commerce Commission (1887), charges for short hauls may not be greater than for long hauls of the same product moving in the same direction over the same line, the shorter being included within the longer. This provision, known as the *long-and-short haul clause*, dealt with the previous practice of railroads of charging low competitive rates between two cities served by two or more rival lines, but raising rates to and from intermediate points served by only one of the lines. Although total charges for short hauls cannot exceed those for long hauls, the rates per mile can. Lower charges per mile for long hauls are called *through rates* and the higher charges for short hauls are *local rates*.

Special Services. The railroads have recognized that processing companies located along their lines between large cities would be discriminated against if they had to receive goods and reship them at local rates. They have, therefore, set up *transit rates* under which a shipper can have his goods processed at an intermediate point, then reship at a rate that makes the total equivalent to the through rate. A small fee must, however, be paid for this privilege.

It is not unusual, particularly among agricultural producers, for a shipper to send a carload or more of his product to a distant point, then wish it had been sent somewhere else. Sudden changes in weather patterns cause changes in demand for a great variety of products: a cold snap may create a sudden demand for warmer clothing, skis, ice skates, and sleds: heavy rain may call for raincoats, umbrellas, rubbers, and boots; a tornado for emergency equipment and building materials; hot weather for electric fans, air-conditioning equipment, soft drinks, and lemons for lemonade. A carload of material can be consigned to one point and, while it is on the way without being unloaded, be *reconsigned* to a new destination farther along without a rate change, but with a small additional fee. Likewise, carload lots of agricultural products can be shipped to certain *diversion* points, where they can be inspected, graded, and reshipped for the same rate plus a relatively small fee.

There are other special services offered by railroads calling for charges between c.l. and l.c.l. rates. If a car is sent regularly between two points, lower than l.c.l. rates are charged on it. If a carload of merchandise is sent to more than one consignee on the line, c.l. rates are charged on the entire shipment to the first consignee's location and l.c.l. rates are charged on the distance remaining to each of the remaining destinations. If a car is made up of mixed merchandise sent to several consignees at the same destination, the charge for the carload will be the c.l. rate applicable on the commodity carrying the highest rate.

When a car is set on the siding at its destination, one to two days is allowed for unloading. If more time than the specified limit is taken, the company must pay a small daily charge called *demurrage*.

The Traffic Department. The traffic manager and his department are concerned with all aspects of receiving and shipping goods. He specifies carriers and routes on incoming shipments. He supervises unloading, checking, and storing activities. He checks transportation charges and approves payments to the carriers.

If the company's customers do not specify carriers and routes, the traffic department checks rates and schedules, and selects the most efficient means of shipping the goods. Usually, this department supervises packing and marking packages and crates. It arranges for boxcars, barges, trucks, and transportation to airports. If the company uses its own trucks, this department is responsible for maintaining the equipment and for specifying what should be purchased. Claims and insurance are also handled, and bills of lading are prepared. If rush procedures are called for, or if shipments go astray, expediters from the traffic department get things moving.

Bills of Lading. Each shipment of freight must be accompanied by a bill of lading identifying the merchandise. *Straight* bills of lading are nonnegotiable and are made out to the consignee. When signed by a representative of the railroad, a bill of lading constitutes a receipt for the merchandise. Terms of the contract of transportation·are printed on it. Although a copy of a straight bill of lading is sent to the consignee, he can obtain the goods on arrival simply by claiming them.

Order bills of lading are negotiable and must be signed by the consignee and given to the carrier before the goods will be surrendered. Banks will lend money using order bills of lading as collateral. The shipper can collect the value of the shipment from his banker, who can send the bill of lading to the consignee's bank which collects from the consignee before the goods are released. Agricultural products often are consigned to a commission house or a broker under an order bill of lading which later can be endorsed over to a customer found while the products are enroute. If the customer is in a different area the